# SuperWrite

## ALPHABETIC WRITING SYSTEM

### COMPREHENSIVE COURSE VOLUME 1

A. JAMES LEMASTER, Ed.D.
**Professor of Business Education**
**Rider College**
**Lawrenceville, New Jersey**

ELLEN G. HANKIN, Ph.D.
**Educational Consultant**
**Cooperstown, New York**

KB02AA/KB02AAU
PUBLISHED BY
**SOUTH-WESTERN PUBLISHING CO.**
CINCINNATI, OH          DALLAS, TX          LIVERMORE, CA

**Credits:**
**Acquisitions Editors:** Karen Schmohe
Benjamin H. Willard Jr.
**Senior Developmental Editor:** Richard E. Adams
**Production Editor:** Rebecca R. Roby
**Associate Editor:** Thomas W. Bailey
**Designer:** J. E. Lagenaur
**Production Artist:** Richard Moore
**Script Artist:** Anna Durham
**Marketing Manager:** Al S. Roane

ISBN: 0-538-60800-5 (KBO2AA)
0-538-70510-8 (KBO2AAU)

Library of Congress Catalog Card Number: 90-60319


2 3 4 5 6 7 8 9 0 D 9 8 7 6 5 4 3 2 1

Printed in the United States of America

# PREFACE

*SuperWrite* is an abbreviated writing system based primarily on long-hand and secondarily on phonetics. It is a quick, easy-to-learn writing system that is easy to write and read. *Webster's Ninth New Collegiate Dictionary* was the reference source for pronunciations.

*SuperWrite* does not require memorizing a new alphabet or changing one's normal writing style. There are no special symbols. To make learning easy, all 26 longhand letters are used.

*SuperWrite* is not designed for extremely high writing speeds. However, students should be able to increase their writing speed significantly. Many will be able to double their writing speed, and others will be able to do even better.

## PURPOSES

*SuperWrite* is designed for three purposes:

1.  To assist business executives and students to increase their speed in making legible notes at a faster speed.

2.  To supply a fast and legible note-taking system that can be learned quickly for use in the office by information processing personnel.

3.  To give the entering, prospective, or returning secretary the ability to take notes from dictation and transcribe them in usable form.

## VOLUME ONE

*SuperWrite, Volume One* is designed to be used at the secondary, college, and adult levels. It begins with simple abbreviating principles and builds lesson by lesson to more advanced principles. The text presents the principles in the easiest form possible.

*SuperWrite, Volume One* contains 40 lessons. Part 1, Lessons 1 through 20, covers Principles of Construction. Part 2, Lessons 21 through 40, covers Beginning Transcription. A lesson may be presented in one class period, or it may be divided and presented in two lessons. For classes which meet for several hours once or twice per week, two or three lessons may be taught in one extended class period. Students should spend a comparable amount of time out of class reading and writing the lesson.

# PART 1

## PRINCIPLES OF CONSTRUCTION

A typical lesson in Part 1 of *Volume One* contains several abbreviating principles and a number of words for which there are special abbreviations. Abbreviating principles are introduced through a "read, spell, write" exercise in which a word is shown first in type, then as it is spelled in *SuperWrite,* and finally as it is written in *SuperWrite.* The students are then asked to copy the words in *SuperWrite* in their own notebooks. Words for which there are special abbreviations are shown in type and then in *SuperWrite.* The students are asked to copy the *SuperWrite* for each word in their own notebooks.

Each lesson in Part 1 contains an Application section consisting of sentences, letters, or memorandums that apply the principles. The Application is followed by a key to give the student immediate reinforcement. The students are asked to read and copy the Application of each lesson.

Beginning with Lesson 6, each lesson contains a supplemental document entitled "A Word to the Wise." These documents may be used for individual reading in or out of class, for extra writing practice, or for testing.

# PART 2

## BEGINNING TRANSCRIPTION

Part 2 of *Volume One* is designed to teach beginning transcription skills as well as continue speed development. Various lessons contain exercises on keyboarding style, punctuation, spelling, and vocabulary development.

Each lesson in Part 2 begins with a *SuperWrite* review. Abbreviations, word beginnings, word endings, and various other principles are covered. The students are asked to read the review words, referring to the key if necessary. They are then asked to copy the words in their own notebook.

Keyboarding style exercises begin with Lesson 21. There are 14 lessons containing these exercises. They include such items as letters, memorandums, and report formats as well as the correct form to type dates, times of day, and amounts of money. The Application emphasizes the keyboarding style element introduced in the current lesson.

Punctuation rules begin in Lesson 21 and are included in 10 lessons. Some of the rules include the use of commas in compound sentences, with items in a series, and with introductory elements. The Application emphasizes the punctuation rule covered in the current lesson.

Beginning with Lesson 22, spelling words are included in each lesson. Many commonly used but often misspelled words are included, 10 in each lesson. The Application consists of business documents that contain the spelling words from the lesson.

Vocabulary development begins with Lesson 26, where 5 vocabulary words are presented. Each lesson thereafter has 5 additional vocabulary words for the students to learn. The vocabulary words are included in the Application.

The Application section of Lessons 21-35 includes four business documents. These documents contain illustrations of the *SuperWrite* principles, the punctuation rules, the spelling words, and the vocabulary terms. Document 1 is a Timed Reading. The students may time their individual reading rate and compare the rate with a suggested goal. Document 2 is a Speed Builder. The teacher may dictate the document on a speed-building plan. Document 4 is a Punctuation Check designed to check student ability to use the punctuation marks taught to that point in the text.

The punctuation marks are included in the first three *SuperWrite* documents in each lesson. Internal punctuation marks are not included in the fourth document, the Punctuation Check. The key to the four documents follows the *SuperWrite*. (The fourth key includes the punctuation marks that were omitted from the *SuperWrite* documents; the reasons for using the punctuation marks are also noted.) The students are asked to read and copy all four documents and insert the necessary punctuation in the last document before typing it in the correct format.

Business letters make up the content of the Application of Lessons 21-30. Memorandums are introduced and included along with business letters in Lessons 31-35. Extended business reports make up the content of the Applications of Lessons 36-40.

## WORD COUNTS

The words in the Application exercises are counted in groups of 20. In the sets of sentences in Lessons 1 and 2, the words are quite short, and actual word counts are used. In everyday writing, however, an average word is somewhat longer and contains more than one syllable. Over the years, the 1.4-syllable word has been accepted in business education. Beginning with Lesson 3, the 1.4-syllable count is used. Beginning with Lesson 4, names are included; and salutations are introduced in Lesson 5. Word counts always begin with the first paragraph rather than with the name or salutation.

## THE SYSTEM

*SuperWrite* follows the principle of abbreviating from the longhand spelling. Long vowels are written to aid in legibility. Short vowels within words are not written. Initial and final vowels are written. If a letter or letters is pronounced as an unrelated sound, the phonetic letter is written. For example, <u>phone</u> is written **f-o-n** and <u>few</u> is written **f-u.**

There are 75 special abbreviations standing for 98 words in *SuperWrite.* These are short and highly suggestive forms for frequently used words. For example, the abbreviation for the word <u>for</u> is **f.**

There are 14 word beginnings and 9 word endings. For example, the word beginning **be-** is written **b,** and the word ending **-ment** is written **m.**

## SUPPLEMENTAL MATERIALS

A comprehensive teacher's manual is available for use with *SuperWrite, Volume One.* The manual contains suggested teaching procedures, supplemental dictation documents, tests, and a complete key.

A complete workbook is available for purchase for use with *SuperWrite, Volume One.* The workbook lessons may be completed in class, or they may be part of the homework assignment. The key to the workbook is included in the teacher's manual.

Two sets of tapes containing material from *Volume One* and the Teacher's Manual are available for additional writing and transcription practice.

A dictionary containing over 5,000 words written in *SuperWrite* is also available.

## ACKNOWLEDGMENT

The authors wish to thank the following teachers who used *SuperWrite* in their classes and made many useful suggestions:

Dr. Barbara Apel, West Clermont Career Center, Cincinnati, Ohio
Dr. Melba Benson, The University of Texas at Arlington, Arlington, Texas
Ms. Michele N. Boston, Marshwood High School, Eliot, Maine

## A FINAL WORD

*SuperWrite* is designed to give the secretary, the student, and the executive a way to write quickly with a minimum of learning time. It should be quite beneficial to every person who studies it.

# THE AUTHORS

**Dr. A. James Lemaster.** Dr. Lemaster is a professor of business education and office administration at Rider College in Lawrenceville, New Jersey. He is the co-author of 13 Gregg shorthand textbooks, numerous teaching aids, and journal articles. He has served as a speaker and business education consultant throughout the world.

Dr. Lemaster has taught at every secondary and postsecondary level from junior high school through graduate school. His teaching experience includes work in the Odessa, Texas, public schools and at the University of Houston. He served as director of business education at Baruch College of the City University of New York.

**Dr. Ellen Gladys Hankin.** Dr. Hankin's teaching and business careers span a period of 50 years. She has taught in high schools, postsecondary schools, colleges, and universities in various parts of the country. She has been active in local, regional, and national professional organizations and served as president of the Florida Business Education Association. She was the recipient of the "Outstanding Business Teacher" award from the Administrative Management Society in Miami, Florida. Over these years, she also has worked with business in several capacities, including coordinator, consultant, in-service instructor, and seminar speaker.

# CONTENTS

## APPENDIX

# PART 1

## PRINCIPLES OF CONSTRUCTION

# *LESSON 1*

## *PRINCIPLES OF CONSTRUCTION*

### *Silent Letters*

● In order to write faster, in *SuperWrite* you will not write silent letters.

In the following words, what letters are silent?

| | | |
|---|---|---|
| day | see | aid |
| save | dough | easy |

In the word <u>day</u>, the **y** is silent.

In <u>see</u>, one **e** is silent.

In <u>aid</u>, the **i** is silent.

In <u>save</u>, the **e** is silent.

In <u>dough</u>, the **u**, the **g**, and the **h** are silent.

In <u>easy</u>, the **a** is silent.

The letters that should be written are:

| | | |
|---|---|---|
| day, **d-a** | see, **s-e** | aid, **a-d** |
| save, **s-a-v** | dough, **d-o** | easy, **e-s-y** |

Read, spell, and then write in your own notebook the following words, omitting any silent letters. Do not use capital letters; capitals will be used later.

| **Read** | **Spell** | *SuperWrite* |
|---|---|---|
| fee | **f-e** | *fe* |
| say | **s-a** | *sa* |

(continued)

| Read | Spell | SuperWrite |
|------|-------|------------|
| feed | f-e-d | *fed* |
| pay | p-a | *pa* |
| prize | p-r-i-z | *priz* |
| rice | r-i-c | *ric* |
| daisy | d-a-s-y | *dasy* |
| phone | f-o-n | *fon* |

Notice that in <u>phone</u>, **ph** has the sound of **f** and is written **f.**

## Punctuation

●    Marks of punctuation are the same as those in longhand.

## Abbreviations

There are a number of words in the English language for which there are special abbreviations. In *SuperWrite* you will also use a number of special abbreviations. They are marked with an **A** in the lists. Here is your first group. Practice writing them in your own notebook until you can do so without hesitation.

| Words | Abbreviations |
|-------|---------------|
| you, your (A) | *u* |
| will (A) | *l* |
| as, is (A) | *s* |

## APPLICATION

A number of sentences follow using the principles you have learned. Practice the exercises in the following way.

1.  Spell and read each sentence in Set 1. If you have trouble with any word, refer to the key immediately.

2.  Write each sentence in Set 1 in your own notebook.

3.  Continue the above steps for the remaining sets.

1. u fe s lo. 2. l u pa u fe? 3. u fe s
zero. 4. s u no, my fe s zero. 5. u
gam s esy.

1. s u fac pal? 2. my fac s pal. 3. he
s fin. 4. l u se me? 5. s u no, he s
lazy.

1. s u sa, u pa s lo. 2. sav u pa. 3. l
u sav u pa? 4. he l sav u pa. 5. s
my nam esy? 6. u nam s esy.

## Set 1-1

(Counted in Actual Words)

**1.** /Your fee is low.    **2.** Will you pay your fee?    **3.** Your fee is zero.    **4.** As you know, my fee is zero./    **5.** Your game is easy. (24)

## Set 1-2

**1.** /Is your face pale?    **2.** My face is pale.    **3.** He is fine.    **4.** Will you see me?    **5.** As you know, he is/lazy. (21)

## Set 1-3

**1.** /As you say, your pay is low.    **2.** Save your pay.    **3.** Will you save your pay?    **4.** He will save your pay./    **5.** Is my name easy?    **6.** Your name is easy. (28)

# LESSON 2

## PRINCIPLES OF CONSTRUCTION

### The Letter T

● In order to speed your writing, do not cross **t's**.

t  ⟋          **tea**  *le*          **eat**  *el*

| Read | Spell | *SuperWrite* |
|------|-------|--------------|
| tea | **t-e** | *le* |
| eat | **e-t** | *el* |
| feet | **f-e-t** | *fel* |
| treat | **t-r-e-t** | *lrel* |
| try | **t-r-y** | *lry* |

### Long Vowels

● In *SuperWrite* we will consider a long vowel one that is pronounced in a word similar to how it is pronounced alone. For example:

**a** as in <u>ate</u>        **e** as in <u>eat</u> and <u>near</u>     **i** as in <u>light</u>

**o** as in <u>vote</u>       **u** as in <u>hue</u>

In addition, we will consider the **u** in <u>rule</u>, the **y** in <u>try</u>, and the **y** in <u>easy</u> to be long.

| ate | near | light | easy |
|-----|------|-------|------|
| vote | hue | try | |

● Write long vowel sounds.

Read, spell, and then write the following words in your own notebook.

| Read | Spell | *SuperWrite* |
|------|-------|--------------|
| date | d-a-t | *dat* |
| feed | f-e-d | *fed* |
| here | h-e-r | *her* |
| die | d-i | *di* |
| roll | r-o-l | *rol* |
| true | t-r-u | *tru* |
| fly | f-l-y | *fly* |
| lazy | l-a-z-y | *lazy* |

## Abbreviations

Here is the next set of abbreviations. Write them in your own notebook.

| Words | Abbreviations |
|-------|---------------|
| are, or, our (A) *hour* | *r* |
| can (A) | *c* |
| for (A) | *f* |

## APPLICATION

Here are several more sets of sentences. Practice as you did in Lesson 1. Read the sentences, referring to the key if you have trouble. Then copy the *SuperWrite* in your notebook.

## Set 2-1

1. s I told u, r tir s lo. 2. c u gag r tir? 3. l u try? 4. I c gag u tir f u, r u c gag u on tir. 5. r u ril? 6. u r lazy.

## Set 2-2

1. I c pla r nic tun f u. 2. r tun s esy. 3. l u sta, r l u go? 4. I mit fly hom. 5. my ag s 21; r u 21? 6. s I told u, he s 22.

## Set 2-3

1. r u fin? I fel fin. 2. c u sta f le, r l u lev? 3. I mit lev. 4. s u no, I c sta. 5. r le s ic cold. 6. s u le ic cold? 7. c u pla my esy gam? 8. I c try.

## Set 2-4

1. r u her f r pla? 2. c u sta, r l u lev? 3. I c sta f u pla; I c sta s lat s u c 4. u rol a nic pla. 5. my pla s esy.

## Set 2-1

**1.** /As I told you, our tire is low.    **2.** Can you gauge our tire?    **3.** Will you try?    **4.** I can gauge your/tire for you, or you can gauge your own tire.    **5.** Are you right?    **6.** You are lazy. (36)

## Set 2-2

**1.** /I can play our nice tune for you.    **2.** Our tune is easy.    **3.** Will you stay, or will you go?    **4.** I/might fly home.    **5.** My age is 21; are you 21?    **6.** As I told you, he is 22. (37)

## Set 2-3

**1.** /Are you fine? I feel fine.    **2.** Can you stay for tea, or will you leave?    **3.** I might leave.    **4.** As you/know, I can stay.    **5.** Our tea is ice cold.    **6.** Is your tea ice cold?    **7.** Can you play my easy game?/    **8.** I can try. (43)

## Set 2-4

**1.** /Are you here for our play?    **2.** Can you stay, or will you leave?    **3.** I can stay for your play; I/can stay as late as you can.    **4.** You wrote a nice play.    **5.** My play is easy. (36)

# LESSON 3

## PRINCIPLES OF CONSTRUCTION

### Different Long Vowel

● When a letter or letters is pronounced as a different long vowel, write that long vowel. For example, in the word <u>freight</u>, the **e-i** combination is pronounced **a;** therefore, we will write **f-r-a-t.**

Read, spell, and then write the following words.

| Read | Spell | SuperWrite |
|------|-------|------------|
| freight | f-r-a-t | *fral* |
| pool | p-u-l | *pul* |
| move | m-u-v | *muv* |
| few | f-u | *fu* |

### Short Vowels
### Short Vowel in the Body of a Word

We will consider most other vowel sounds to be short.

● Do not write short vowels in the body of a word.

For example, in the word <u>even</u>, we would write **e-v-n,** omitting the **e** in the body of the word. Read, spell, and then write the following words.

| Read | Spell | SuperWrite |
|------|-------|------------|
| even | e-v-n | *evn* |
| lesson | l-s-n | *lsn* |

(continued)

| Read | Spell | SuperWrite |
|------|-------|------------|
| center | c-n-t-r | *cntr* |
| softball | s-f-t-b-l | *sftbl* |
| correct | c-r-c-t | *crct* |
| written | r-t-n | *rtn* |
| cough | c-f | *cf* |

## Initial Short Vowel

● Write the vowel if the word begins with a short vowel sound.
For example, in the word <u>add</u>, the beginning short vowel **a** is written.
Read, spell, and then write the following words.

| Read | Spell | SuperWrite |
|------|-------|------------|
| add | a-d | *ad* |
| earn | e-r-n | *ern* |
| if | i-f | *if* |
| object | o-b-j-c-t | *objct* |
| ought | o-t | *ot* |
| us | u-s | *us* |
| oven | o-v-n | *ovn* |
| honor | o-n-r | *onr* |

## Final Short Vowel

● Write the vowel if a word ends in a short vowel sound.
For example, in the word <u>data</u>, the final short vowel **a** is written.

Read, spell, and then write the following words.

| Read | Spell | SuperWrite |
|------|-------|------------|
| data | d-a-t-a | *dala* |
| era | e-r-a | *era* |
| saw | s-a | *sa* |
| law | l-a | *la* |

## Abbreviations

Here is the next set of abbreviations. Write them in your notebook.

| Words | Abbreviations |
|-------|---------------|
| at, it, to (A) | *l* |
| has, have (A) | *h* |
| very (A) | *v* |
| do (A) | *d* |

## APPLICATION

Read the following sets, referring immediately to the key if you have any trouble. Then write them in your own notebook.

h u gn l vol ryt? he h gn. s u no, he l vol l r ofc. if u r l lest 18, u c vol. u ag s 18; u ol l vol. d u wnt me l driv u l vol, r d u wnt l driv? u vol s ncsry. l s v lal, bl u c stl vol. l u vol f me?

d u pln l atnd clg? u ol l h a pln mad. my pln s mad.

he h a pln f clg. he l atnd cls l r locl clg. he l stdy la. s u no, l s v gd l stdy la.

u idea s ril. if u r gd l la, u c ern gd pa. he l ern v gd pa.

I c lev r ofc l 5, bl I mil sla ll 6 r 7.

l s v lal. r u rdy l lev u ofc? I sa hm l hs la ofc. he s rdy l lev f hom. he l lry l mel us lalr.

d u wnl l h dnr l 7 r l 8? s u no, I pln l h dnr l 8.

l u clcl dala f my srva? I l oblan dala f u if l s ncsry. I c clcl dala l r ofc, r u c clcl l.

d u h enf dala l d u jb? no, bl he h enf dala l d l. he l cl u l u hom l 7 lnil.

s I told u, he h dn a v gd jb.

## Set 3-1

(Counted in Words of 1.4 Syllables)

/Have you gone to vote yet? He has gone. As you know, he will vote at our office. If you are at least 18, you can/vote. Your age is 18; you ought to vote. Do you want me to drive you to vote, or do you want to drive? Your vote is/necessary. It is very late, but you can still vote. Will you vote for me? (54)

## Set 3-2

/Do you plan to attend college? You ought to have a plan made. My plan is made.

He has a plan for college. He will/attend class at our local college. He will study law. As you know, it is very good to study law.

Your/idea is right. If you are good at law, you can earn good pay. He will earn very good pay. (56)

## Set 3-3

/I can leave our office at five, but I might stay till six or seven.

It is very late. Are you ready to leave/your office? I saw him at his law office. He is ready to leave for home. He will try to meet us later.

Do/you want to have dinner at seven or at eight? As you know, I plan to have dinner at eight. (56)

## Set 3-4

/Will you collect data for my survey?

I will obtain data for you if it is necessary. I can/collect data at our office, or you can collect it.

Do you have enough data to do your job?

No, but he/has enough data to do it. He will call you at your home at seven tonight.

As I told you, he has done a/very good job. (62)

# LESSON 4

## PRINCIPLES OF CONSTRUCTION

### Sh

● The sound of **sh** is spelled many ways in longhand. In *SuperWrite* it is written capital **S.**

Read, spell, and then write the following words.

| Read | Spell | *SuperWrite* |
|------|-------|--------------|
| shoe | **sh-u** | *Su* |
| issue | **i-sh-u** | *iSu* |
| sugar | **sh-g-r** | *Sgr* |
| cash | **c-sh** | *cS* |
| official | **o-f-sh-l** | *ofSl* |
| special | **s-p-sh-l** | *spSl* |

### Ch

● **Ch** as in chief is written capital **C.**

Read, spell, and then write the following words.

| Read | Spell | *SuperWrite* |
|------|-------|--------------|
| chief | **ch-e-f** | *Cef* |
| reach | **r-e-ch** | *reC* |
| teacher | **t-e-ch-r** | *leCr* |
| bleacher | **b-l-e-ch-r** | *bleCr* |

## Word Ending -Ing

● The word ending **-ing** as in <u>growing</u> is written as a <u>disjoined</u> **g**.

grow  *gro*          growing  *gro g*

Read, spell, and then write the following words.

| Read | Spell | SuperWrite |
|------|-------|------------|
| growing | **g-r-o- g** | *gro g* |
| keeping | **k-e-p- g** | *kep g* |
| writing | **r-i-t- g** | *ril g* |
| agreeing | **a-g-r-e- g** | *agre g* |
| knowing | **n-o- g** | *no g* |

## Adding S to a Word

● To add **s** to a word, write **s**.

For example, <u>plays</u> is written **p-l-a-s**; <u>feels</u>, **f-e-l-s**; <u>laws</u>, **l-a-s**.
Write the following words in *SuperWrite*, including the final **s**.

| Word | Add *s* | SuperWrite |
|------|---------|------------|
| play | plays | *plas* |
| fee | fees | *fes* |
| price | prices | *prics* |
| feel | feels | *fels* |
| drama | dramas | *drmas* |
| law | laws | *las* |

## Abbreviations

Write the abbreviations for the following words.

| Words | Abbreviations |
|-------|---------------|
| we (A) | *e* |
| which (A) | *C* |
| soon (A) | *sn* |

## Personal Titles

● Personal titles such as Mr. or Mrs. are written in *SuperWrite* the same as they are in longhand, but the period is omitted.

Write the personal titles in your notebook.

| Title | SuperWrite |
|-------|------------|
| Mr. | *Mr* |
| Mrs. | *Mrs* |
| Miss | *Miss* |
| Ms. | *Ms* |
| Dr. | *Dr* |

## Names

● A name is written in full in longhand the first time it is used. Only the first letter is written when the name occurs again in the same document.

**Mr. Jones spoke to our club.**

*Mr Jones spok l r clb.*

**Did you meet Mr. Jones?**

*dd u mel Mr J?*

## APPLICATION

Read the following documents and then write them in your notebook.

Mr Davis:

wn I wnt Spg, I sa a v nic Cr C s slg f a lo pric. l s on spsl sal f a da r so l r locl ofc sply stor.

d u fel prCsg a nu Cr f r ofcs s a gd pln, Mr D? if u r Sr e Sd d l, l u go l se l wn u h a Cnc?

I h an idea prCsg l sn l sav us mny.

Bill Jones

Mrs Dalton:

s u no, Miss Mary Green, r dstrcl Cef, vsld r Sp f a fu das. durg hr vsl Se rol sm nols, C I l alC, cncrng r Sp.

Miss G fels e r opralg v wl, bl e mil d an evn blr jb if e lry. Se h mny ideas C r v gd. I fel Sr e c us hr ideas. c e lk l u ofc sn?

Carl Lee

Dr Carter:

I jsl lkd l an old frnd, Ms Sara Cates, hu h sm lnd C I fel e Sd prCs f r nu stor.

hr ask g pric s hi, bl I h an idea Se s lg l accpl a lll ls mny. d u fel e Sd mak hr an ofSl ofr f hr lnd? I hop u l cl me l my ofc sn.

Ken Gray

Ms Clay:

s u no, e Sd sn Cus nu crpl g f r ofcs. f r man ofc, e msl lry l gl a v strng crpl C l sta clen. f r Sp g rum, e Sd Cus an evn strngr crpl. l h l stnd up l v hvy us.

l u go Sp g f nu crpl sn, r d u wnl me l d r Sp g?

Ann Morris

## DOCUMENT 4-1

Mr. Davis:

/When I went shopping, I saw a very nice chair which is selling for a low price. It is on special sale for a/day or so at our local office supply store.

Do you feel purchasing a new chair for our offices is a good/plan, Mr. Davis? If you are sure we should do it, will you go to see it when you have a chance?

I have an/idea purchasing it soon will save us money. Bill Jones (71)

## DOCUMENT 4-2

Mrs. Dalton:

/As you know, Miss Mary Green, our district chief, visited our shop for a few days. During her visit she wrote some/notes, which I will attach, concerning our shop.

Miss Green feels we are operating very well, but we might do an/even better job if we try. She has many ideas which are very good. I feel sure we can use her/ideas. Can we talk at your office soon? Carl Lee (69)

## DOCUMENT 4-3

Dr. Carter:

/I just talked to an old friend, Ms. Sara Cates, who has some land which I feel we should purchase for our new store.

Her/asking price is high, but I have an idea she is willing to accept a little less money. Do you feel/we should make her an official offer for her land? I hope you will call me at my office soon. Ken Gray (59)

## DOCUMENT 4-4

Ms. Clay:

/As you know, we should soon choose new carpeting for our offices. For our main office, we must try to get a/very strong carpet which will stay clean. For our shipping room, we should choose an even stronger carpet. It has to stand/up to very heavy use.

Will you go shopping for new carpet soon, or do you want me to do our shopping? Ann/ Morris (61)

# LESSON 5

## PRINCIPLES OF CONSTRUCTION

### Th

● **Th** as in <u>these</u> is written as a <u>crossed</u> **t**.

| Read | Spell | SuperWrite |
|------|-------|------------|
| these | **th-e-s** | *tes* |
| them | **th-m** | *tm* |
| both | **b-o-th** | *bot* |
| bathe | **b-a-th** | *bat* |
| bother | **b-th-r** | *btr* |
| tooth | **t-u-th** | *lut* |

### Abbreviations

| Words | Abbreviations |
|-------|---------------|
| the (A) | *t* |
| and, in (A) | *n* |

## Salutations and Closings

● Write the first letter or abbreviation in lower case for salutations and closings.

| Words | SuperWrite |
|---|---|
| Dear | *d* |
| Ladies and Gentlemen | *l n g* |
| Yours truly | *u l* |
| Very sincerely yours | *v s u* |

## Geographic Names

● The names of cities are written in full in longhand the first time they are used. Only the first letter is written if the word occurs again in the same document.

● The names of states should be abbreviated using the United States Postal Service abbreviations shown on page 431.

*he plas f t Cincinnati tem n C, OH.*

**He plays for the Cincinnati team in Cincinnati, Ohio.**

## APPLICATION

Read the following documents and then write them in your own notebook.

## DOCUMENT 5-1

*Miss Janet James    d Miss J:*
*wn I vstd Mr n Mrs Lane n tr*
*hom n Portland, OR, a da r so ago, I*
*lkd l tr dtr, Ann. Se told me tl Se*

wrld l vsl u n u hom sn.

s u no, A s 18 n h jsl fnÅd hi scul. evn to Åe dd v wl n hi scul n P, Å h an idea tl Åe neds sm hlp n Cus g t ril clg.

d u fel u c gv hr t hlp Åe neds, Miss J? if u d, l u cl hr l hr hom?

v s

l n g:

e r v hpy l ll u tl Miss Mary Key l hd r nu slor n Chicago, ÅL. e r v sry tl Åe s lev g r man slor, bl e no Åe l d s wl l t nu slor s Åe h dn her. Åe s t ril prsn f t jb.

e r hop g f gd sals n r nu C slor n wÅ M t v bsl n hr nu jb.

Carl Bates

Dr William Shaw  d Dr S:

 Miss Lane vsld me n my hom
ts mrng, n e lkd a wil. l s gd tl
Se s plng f t futr.

 Se hops l vsl bot locl clgs n
Reno, NV, sn l se C 1 Se liks btr.

 Se l ril u n a da r so s sn s
Se h mad up hr mind cncrng hr
plns.      u l

Mr n Mrs R L Key  d Mr n Mrs K:

 s u no, I spok l u sn n my hom
a da r 2 ago. e r v hpy tl he vsld
r clg her n Milwaukee, WI, evn to
e lkd f jsl a fu mnls. I l mal hm
t paprs he ma ned n a da r so.

 l s a gd idea f hm l vsl otr
sculs. wn he h hd a Cnc l se bot
area clgs, e hop tl he l Cus rs.
       v c u

# DOCUMENT 5-1

Miss Janet James
Dear Miss James:

/When I visited Mr. and Mrs. Lane in their home in Portland, Oregon, a day or so ago, I talked/to their daughter, Ann. She told me that she wanted to visit you in your home soon.

As you know, Ann is 18 and/has just finished high school. Even though she did very well in high school in Portland, I have an idea that she/needs some help in choosing the right college.

Do you feel you can give her the help she needs, Miss James? If you do, will you/call her at her home? Very sincerely yours, (88)

# DOCUMENT 5-2

Ladies and Gentlemen:

/We are very happy to tell you that Miss Mary Key will head our new store in Chicago, Illinois. We are/very sorry that she is leaving our main store, but we know she will do as well at the new store as she has done/here. She is the right person for the job.

We are hoping for good sales in our new Chicago store and wish/Mary the very best in her new job. Carl Bates (69)

# DOCUMENT 5-3

Dr. William Shaw
Dear Dr. Shaw:

/Miss Lane visited me in my home this morning, and we talked a while. It is good that she is planning for the/future.

She hopes to visit both local colleges in Reno, Nevada, soon to see which one she likes/better.

She will write you in a day or so as soon as she has made up her mind concerning her plans. Yours truly, (58)

# DOCUMENT 5-4

Mr. and Mrs. R. L. Key
Dear Mr. and Mrs. Key:

/As you know, I spoke to your son in my home a day or two ago. We are very happy that he visited/our college here in Milwaukee, Wisconsin, even though we talked for just a few minutes. I will mail him the/papers he may need in a day or so.

It is a good idea for him to visit other schools. When he has had/a chance to see both area colleges, we hope that he will choose ours. Very cordially yours, (77)

# LESSON 6

## PRINCIPLES OF CONSTRUCTION

### Abbreviations

| Words | Abbreviations |
|-------|---------------|
| am, more (A) | *m* |
| be, been, by (A) | *b* |
| month (A) | *mo* |

### Word Beginning Be-

● The word beginning **be-** as in <u>became</u> is written **b**.

| Read | Spell | SuperWrite |
|------|-------|------------|
| became | b-c-a-m | *bcam* |
| believe | b-l-e-v | *blev* |
| begin | b-g-n | *bgn* |
| because | b-c-s | *bcs* |
| beyond | b-y-n-d | *bynd* |

### Word Beginnings In-, En-

● The word beginnings **in-** as in <u>inside</u> and **en-** as in <u>endanger</u> are written **n,** before a consonant.

| Read | Spell | SuperWrite |
|------|-------|------------|
| **in-** | | |
| inside | **n-s-i-d** | *nsid* |
| invite | **n-v-i-t** | *nvit* |
| indeed | **n-d-e-d** | *nded* |
| instead | **n-s-t-d** | *nstd* |
| **en-** | | |
| endanger | **n-d-a-n-g-r** | *ndangr* |
| encourage | **n-c-r-g** | *ncrg* |
| endeavor | **n-d-v-r** | *ndvr* |
| entire | **n-t-i-r** | *ntir* |

## Word Beginning Re-

● The word beginning **re-** as in <u>repair</u> is written **r.**

| Read | Spell | SuperWrite |
|------|-------|------------|
| repair | **r-p-r** | *rpr* |
| receipt | **r-c-e-t** | *rcet* |
| reply | **r-p-l-y** | *rply* |
| result | **r-s-l-t** | *rslt* |
| retire | **r-t-i-r** | *rtir* |
| regroup | **r-g-r-u-p** | *rgrup* |

## Word Beginning De-

● The word beginning **de-** as in <u>decide</u> is written **d.**

| Read | Spell | SuperWrite |
|------|-------|------------|
| decide | d-c-i-d | *dcid* |
| delay | d-l-a | *dla* |
| delight | d-l-i-t | *dlit* |
| depend | d-p-n-d | *dpnd* |
| defuse | d-f-u-s | *dfus* |

## APPLICATION

Read and write the following documents.

## DOCUMENT 6-1

*Mr Keith Case:        d Mr C:*

*I m sry nded l ll u tl Mrs Smith n I l nl b l t dnr C u h plnd l onr Ann Sanders wn Se rlirs.*

*e l nl alnd bcs e r nl plng l rtrn l Dallas b t dal u h plnd t dnr. s u no, e h b n Vail, CO, f an nlir mo.*

*if t dnr c b dlad a da r so, e l b m tn hpy l b tr.*

*u r s*

Mr n Mrs Ben C Smith    d Mr n Mrs S:

I m v sry u l nl b bk n Dallas, TX, b t dal e pln l h t dnr l onr Ms Sanders.

e h b pln g t dnr f m tn 3 mos. l msl nl b dlad bcs e h nvild m tn 20 gsls, n eC h accpld.

ma I ncrg u l lak Ms S l lnC wn u rlrn l D.

u c

l n g:

I m v hpy l ll u tl Mr James Blake l b rlrn g l t ofc sn. s u no, Mr B h b il f m tn 3 mos. f t psl mo, he h b rsl g l hs sn's hom n Phoenix, AZ.

evn to Mr B fels wl, Dr Gray blevs he Sd nl sla n t ofc v lng eC da ll he rgans hs hlt.

(continued)

b slag l t ofc a Srl wil eC da,
he c rsum mny dules. l s nded
ncrg g l no tl Mr B l b rlrn g sn,
n e l b dlild l h hm bk.

A B Tate

Miles Jenkins:

I m dlild l ll u tl dur g t psl
6 mos sals n eC rgn h b go g up
wil csls h nl ncresd. sals n t
Los Angeles, CA, rgn n t Santa Fe,
NM, rgn h ncresd m tn 20%.

e r Sr tl ts l b v ncrg g nus
f u n u slf, M.

I blev tl b ncres g r sals bgl
jsl a lll, e c ncres r ncm evn m
n t mos ahd. d u agre?

A C Moore

# DOCUMENT 6-1

Mr. Keith Case
Dear Mr. Case:

/I am sorry indeed to tell you that Mrs. Smith and I will not be at the dinner which you have planned to/honor Ann Sanders when she retires.

We will not attend because we are not planning to return to Dallas by the/date you have planned the dinner. As you know, we have been in Vail, Colorado, for an entire month.

If the dinner/can be delayed a day or so, we will be more than happy to be there. Yours very sincerely, (77)

# DOCUMENT 6-2

Mr. and Mrs. Ben C. Smith
Dear Mr. and Mrs. Smith:

/I am very sorry you will not be back in Dallas, Texas, by the date we plan to have the dinner to/honor Ms. Sanders.

We have been planning the dinner for more than three months. It must not be delayed because we have/invited more than 20 guests, and each has accepted.

May I encourage you to take Ms. Sanders to lunch when/you return to Dallas. Yours cordially, (67)

# DOCUMENT 6-3

Ladies and Gentlemen:

/I am very happy to tell you that Mr. James Blake will be returning to the office soon. As you know,/Mr. Blake has been ill for more than three months. For the past month, he has been resting at his son's home in Phoenix, Arizona./

Even though Mr. Blake feels well, Dr. Gray believes he should not stay in the office very long each/day till he regains his health.

By staying at the office a short while each day, he can resume many duties. It/is indeed encouraging to know that Mr. Blake will be returning soon, and we will be delighted to have/him back. A. B. Tate (104)

# DOCUMENT 6-4

Miles Jenkins:

/I am delighted to tell you that during the past six months sales in each region have been going up while costs have/not increased. Sales in the Los Angeles, California, region and the Santa Fe, New Mexico, region have/increased more than 20 percent.

We are sure that this will be very encouraging news for you and your staff, Miles./

I believe that by increasing our sales budget just a little, we can increase our income even more in the/months ahead. Do you agree? A. C. Moore (87)

# SUPPLEMENTARY ACTIVITY

## A Word to the Wise

Beginning with Lesson 6, a supplementary activity is included in each lesson. The documents are entitled "A Word to the Wise," and they appear in type. Using the type as a guide, write the documents in *SuperWrite* in your own notebook, or follow any special instructions given by your teacher.

Self-Confidence

/If you have been discouraged by failures in the past, here are some ideas to increase your self-confidence.

If/you believe you are going to fail, the battle is lost at the beginning. If you believe you can do a job,/the battle is half won.

Say the words "I am going to do this job very well" and the job will be easy.

When/you have finished, review what you have done. You may well find that you have done much more than you had planned. This will delight/and encourage you.

Set goals that you can meet. Then you must strive to finish each job. Day by day, month by month, you will increase/your self-confidence. (104)

# LESSON 7

## PRINCIPLES OF CONSTRUCTION

### Word Ending -Tion

● The word ending **-tion** is spelled many ways in longhand. In *SuperWrite* it is written <u>capital **S.**</u>

| Read | Spell | *SuperWrite* |
|------|-------|------------|
| location | **l-o-c-a-shun** | *locaS* |
| relation | **r-l-a-shun** | *rlaS* |
| vocation | **v-o-c-a-shun** | *vocaS* |
| suspension | **s-s-p-n-shun** | *sspnS* |
| sufficient | **s-f-shun-t** | *sfSt* |
| efficiency | **e-f-shun-c-y** | *efScy* |
| physician | **f-s-shun** | *fsS* |

### Ou, Ow

● The sound of **ou** as in <u>house</u> is written in full, **ou.**

| Read | Spell | *SuperWrite* |
|------|-------|------------|
| **ou** | | |
| house | **h-o-u-s** | *hous* |
| proud | **p-r-o-u-d** | *proud* |
| ounce | **o-u-n-c** | *ounc* |

● The sound of **ow** as in <u>now</u> is written in full, **o-w**.

| Read | Spell | SuperWrite |
|------|-------|------------|
| **ow** | | |
| now | **n-o-w** | *now* |
| flower | **f-l-o-w-r** | *flowr* |
| brown | **b-r-o-w-n** | *brown* |

## *Word Ending -Ly*

● The word ending **-ly** as in <u>lately</u> is written **l**.

| Read | Spell | SuperWrite |
|------|-------|------------|
| lately | **l-a-t-l** | *latl* |
| briefly | **b-r-e-f-l** | *brefl* |
| highly | **h-i-l** | *hil* |
| only | **o-n-l** | *onl* |
| nationally | **n-shun-l-l** | *nShll* |
| annually | **a-n-u-l-l** | *anull* |
| family | **f-m-l** | *fml* |
| steadily | **s-t-d-l** | *stdl* |
| easily | **e-s-l** | *esl* |

## *Abbreviations*

| Words | Abbreviations |
|-------|---------------|
| from (A) | *fm* |
| of (A) | *o* |

| Words | Abbreviations |
|-------|---------------|
| year (A) | *yr* |
| let (A) | *le* |

## APPLICATION

## DOCUMENT 7-1

Mrs Chay:

sals n most o r rtal stors h b ncres g slol bt stdl dur g t pst 3 yrs. e r v proud o ts, bt r csts h ncresd s wl.

n fct, fm t frst o t yr tru t end o lst mo, e actull lst mny n r 2 loca$s n Atlanta, GA. alto sals r up still, nt ncm s down.

t bord o drctrs rcntl votd t le tes stors rman n opra$ f a fu m mos t se if sals c b ncresd n csts hld down.

(continued)

I m Sr, Mrs C, tt u l d u bst t
hlp tes stors ncres tr efScy l rman
n opraS. e l mak a finl dcS b t
end o t yr.

                                    RC Key


## DOCUMENT 7-2

Miss Jane Hall          d Miss H:
smr s jsl around t crnr, n u l
likt bgn makg u vacaS plns sn.
makg gnrl vacaS plns s usull fn,
bt actull makg rsrvaSs n prCsg
tkts c b v tirg.
ts yr, wy nt le r trvl agncy hndl
t dtals f u? e h b hndlg vacaS dtals
f trvlrs sC s u f m tn 20 yrs. e c
pln a vacaS f u t NY, CA, r FL.
jsl nam t plac u wnt t go, n e l d
t rst.

e c mak u hotl rsrvaSs. e c prCs
u plan tkts. e c evn arang l lak u
fm u hous l t ar trmnl.

tes r onl a fu o t mny dtals e c
hndl esl n efStl f u. e ncrg u l cl
us now l ll us wr u wnt l go n won
u wS l lev. e l lak l fm tr.

v s u

Dr Sam Chase          d Dr C:

r u spnd g m tn u Sd l kep u
hous cul n t smr mos? if u ar
cndSr s m tn 10 yrs old, u ma actull
b wast g powr s wl s mny.

dpnd g on t locaS o u hous, a nu
ar cndSr c esl cl u powr csts merl n
hf.

cl us now, n le 1 o t slf fm r man
ofc stp b u hom l gv u an estml o t

(continued)

csl o rplac g u old sslm. l l lak onl a fu mnls. tr l nl b a Crg, n u l h no oblga$.

u l

Mr Carlos Lopez          d Mr L:

I m dlild l anounc tl fm now ll t end o t yr, e l h a sp$l sal on mny ilms f u hous n u fml.

ilms C usull sl l mC hir prics l b on sp$l sal f t lsl 2 mos o t yr onl. u c slcl ilms fm r sp$l clc$ f onl a frc$ o t pric u wd nrmll pa.

d nl wal; b t end o t yr, r slk l h b dpleld. cm n now n le us $o u r fin slc$. e l b walg f u.

v l u

## DOCUMENT 7-1

Mrs. Chay:

/Sales in most of our retail stores have been increasing slowly but steadily during the past three years. We are/very proud of this, but our costs have increased as well.

In fact, from the first of the year through the end of last month, we/actually lost money in our two locations in Atlanta, Georgia. Although sales are up slightly, net income/is down.

The board of directors recently voted to let these stores remain in operation for a few more/months to see if sales can be increased and costs held down.

I am sure, Mrs. Chay, that you will do your best to help these/stores increase their efficiency to remain in operation. We will make a final decision by the end/of the year. R. C. Key (124)

## DOCUMENT 7-2

Miss Jane Hall
Dear Miss Hall:

/Summer is just around the corner, and you will likely begin making your vacation plans soon.

Making general/vacation plans is usually fun, but actually making reservations and purchasing tickets/can be very tiring.

This year, why not let our travel agency handle the details for you? We have been/handling vacation details for travelers such as you for more than twenty years. We can plan a vacation for you/to New York, California, or Florida. Just name the place you want to go, and we will do the rest.

We/can make your hotel reservations. We can purchase your plane tickets. We can even arrange to take you from your/house to the air terminal.

These are only a few of the many details we can handle easily and/efficiently for you. We encourage you to call us now to tell us where you want to go and when you wish to leave./We will take it from there. Very sincerely yours, (169)

## DOCUMENT 7-3

Dr. Sam Chase
Dear Dr. Chase:

/Are you spending more than you should to keep your house cool in the summer months? If your air conditioner is more than/ten years old, you may actually be wasting power as well as money.

Depending on the location of/your house, a new air conditioner can easily cut your power costs nearly in half.

(continued)

Call us now, and let one/of the staff from our main office stop by your home to give you an estimate of the cost of replacing your old/system. It will take only a few minutes. There will not be a charge, and you will have no obligation. Yours/truly, (101)

## DOCUMENT 7-4

Mr. Carlos Lopez
Dear Mr. Lopez:

/I am delighted to announce that from now till the end of the year, we will have a special sale on many/items for your house and your family.

Items which usually sell at much higher prices will be on special/sale for the last two months of the year only. You can select items from our special collection for only a/fraction of the price you would normally pay.

Do not wait; by the end of the year, our stock will have been depleted./Come in now and let us show you our fine selection. We will be waiting for you. Very truly yours, (98)

## SUPPLEMENTARY ACTIVITY

### A Word to the Wise

Using a Dictionary

/It never pays to let a word go if you have a doubt concerning its spelling.

Why? A person reading your/paper could actually be misled. Or worse still, the reader may concentrate on the error and pay no attention/to your main ideas. The person may even look down on you for not checking your paper.

It is a good/idea to have a small dictionary in your briefcase. It will always be handy, and there will be no/reason for not using it.

Don't take a chance concerning the spelling of a word; it is not worth the risk. Let this be/the year you resolve: "I will use a dictionary regularly from now on."

A good dictionary can be/your best friend. (122)

# LESSON 8

## PRINCIPLES OF CONSTRUCTION

### Word Ending -Ment

● The word ending **-ment** as in <u>payment</u> is written **m**.

| Read | Spell | *SuperWrite* |
|------|-------|------------|
| payment | **p-a-m** | *pam* |
| treatment | **t-r-e-t-m** | *tretm* |
| engagement | **n-g-a-g-m** | *ngagm* |
| settlement | **s-t-l-m** | *stlm* |
| attachments | **a-t-ch-m-s** | *atCms* |
| elementary | **e-l-m-r-y** | *elmry* |

### Word Ending -Ble

● The word ending **-ble** as in <u>capable</u> is written **b**.

| Read | Spell | *SuperWrite* |
|------|-------|------------|
| **-ble** | | |
| capable | **c-a-p-b** | *capb* |
| trouble | **t-r-b** | *trb* |
| possible | **p-s-b** | *psb* |
| able | **a-b** | *ab* |
| table | **t-a-b** | *tab* |

## Abbreviations

| Words | Abbreviations |
|---|---|
| after (A) | *afl* |
| business (A) | *bus* |
| company (A) | *co* |
| responsible (A) | *rsp* |

## Quantities

The quantity hundred is written **h**; thousand is written as a <u>crossed</u> **t.**

hundred *h*          thousand *t*

| Quantity | SuperWrite |
|---|---|
| 300 | *3 h* |
| $500 | *$5 h* |
| $2,000 | *$2 t* |
| $300,000 | *$3 h t* |

## APPLICATION

### DOCUMENT 8-1

*Mr C R Brown          d Mr B:*

*f m tn a yr, u h b prLs g gds fm r co l sl n u rtal bus eslbl$m n Wichita, KS. u orgnll agred l pa f t*

ilms C u prCsd on a mol bass, n u
pam rcrd hd b v gd f nerl a yr.

bl afl 90 das, u h nl snl us u
pams f t lsl 2 Spms. u l rcl tl u bl
$2 t wrt o gds fm us 3 mos ago n $5 h
wrt o gds fm r co 2 mos ago.

l frsl e tl t bls hd slpd u mind.
bl bcs u h nl rspndd l r rmindrs,
e now blev tl l s psb u bus s h g
fnnSl lrbs.

e c mak arangms l gv u an adSl
mo r so l mak u pams, bl u msl
lak rsp acS now b le g us no wl
t lrb s won'l u cl us lda. u crdl
ral g cd psbl b dmgd if u d nl.
                                    u l

l n g:

r rvisd co bgl f t cm g yr s

(continued)

alCd. s u c esl se, e r now plng
f an ncres n bus.

afl onl 3 yrs n bus, e blev e c
aclull aCev gros sals o $8 h t r $9 h t
nxl yr.

s u no, u aCevms h gvn us a
gral del o ncrgm, n I m v proud
o u rcrd. eC o u h b prsnll rsp
f an ncres n sals o m tn $10 t
dur g t psl yr.

l u le me h u ideas on t bgl s
sn s psb. I hop l fnS r rvu b t
end o t mo.

Ann Wright

Dr M W Casey        d Dr C:

    u nol ask g f a rfrnc f Mr Slade arivd lda. Mr S hd b on t slf o r co nerl 3 yrs wn he lfl. he srvd n t acounls pab dvS f 1 yr n n t Cef acounlnl's ofc nerl 2 yrs. he ernd a bgn g slry o $20 t, n he gl a ras o $2 h a mo afl onl 1 yr. he lfl r co afl bg her nerl 3 yrs l opn hs on bus n Des Moines, IA.

    Mr S s a dpndb prsn hu h v gd jgm. he hndls hs bus n a capb n rsp wa, n he h my hisl rcmndaS.

                              v s u

Miss Kim Lacy:

l l b psb f u l mak arangms l acl s my rplacm l t bus cnvnS n Charlotte, NC, nxl mo?

I m rsp f co labr rlaSs, n I l b awa on co bus n VA, wr e r hg labr lrbs. if e d nl reC an erl sllm, l s psb I l nl b rlrn g ll afl t frsl o t yr.

e now eslmal tr l b 9h r prhps l t l t cnvnS, n I blev r co Sd dfnll h a prsn tr. l u le me h u ansr sn.

Lee Downs

## DOCUMENT 8-1

Mr. C. R. Brown
Dear Mr. Brown:

/For more than a year, you have been purchasing goods from our company to sell in your retail business establishment/in Wichita, Kansas. You originally agreed to pay for the items which you purchased on a/monthly basis, and your payment record had been very good for nearly a year.

But after ninety days, you have not/sent us your payments for the last two shipments. You will recall that you bought $2,000 worth of goods from us/three months ago and $500 worth of goods from our company two months ago.

At first we thought the bills/had slipped your mind. But because you have not responded to our reminders, we now believe that it is possible/your business is having financial troubles.

We can make arrangements to give you an additional month or so/to make your payments, but you must take responsible action now by letting us know what the trouble is. Won't you/call us today. Your credit rating could possibly be damaged if you do not. Yours truly, (176)

## DOCUMENT 8-2

Ladies and Gentlemen:

/Our revised company budget for the coming year is attached. As you can easily see, we are now planning/for an increase in business.

After only three years in business, we believe we can actually achieve gross/sales of $800,000 or $900,000 next year.

As you know, your achievements have/given us a great deal of encouragement, and I am very proud of your record. Each of you has been personally/responsible for an increase in sales of more than $10,000 during the past year.

Will you let me/have your ideas on the budget as soon as possible. I hope to finish our review by the end of the/month. Ann Wright (122)

## DOCUMENT 8-3

Dr. M. W. Casey
Dear Dr. Casey:

/Your note asking for a reference for Mr. Slade arrived today. Mr. Slade had been on the staff of our/company nearly three years when he left. He served in the accounts payable division for one year and in the chief/accountant's office nearly two years. He earned a beginning salary of $20,000 and he got/a raise of $200 a month after only one year. He left our company after being here/nearly three years to open his own business in Des Moines, Iowa.

Mr. Slade is a dependable person/who has very good judgment. He handles his business in a capable and responsible way, and he has my/highest recommendation. Very sincerely yours, (129)

## DOCUMENT 8-4

Miss Kim Lacy:

/Will it be possible for you to make arrangements to act as my replacement at the business convention in/Charlotte, North Carolina, next month?

I am responsible for company labor relations, and I will be/away on company business in Virginia, where we are having labor troubles. If we do not reach an/early settlement, it is possible I will not be returning till after the first of the year.

We now estimate/there will be 900 or perhaps 1,000 at the convention, and I believe our company should/definitely have a person there. Will you let me have your answer soon. Lee Downs (114)

## SUPPLEMENTARY ACTIVITY

### A Word to the Wise

Planning—the Road to Success

/Would you start on a company business trip of 500 or 1,000 miles and have no road map? No/responsible person would.

But many students begin each school year and have no real plan. If you have no plan, after a/while you will realize you do not know where you are going or when you should get there.

If you plan well, it is/possible that you will accomplish a great deal. If you do not make good plans, your accomplishments will be small indeed. In/addition, you will waste energy and lose months or even years. You may even arrive at a destination/where you did not intend to go!

There is no substitute for good planning. Plan your school year and the rest of your life/ as well. (121)

# *LESSON 9*

### *Oi, Oy*

● The sound of **oi** as <u>oil</u> is written in full, **o-i**.

| Read | Spell | *SuperWrite* |
|------|-------|-------------|
| **oi** | | |
| oil | **o-i-l** | *oil* |
| toil | **t-o-i-l** | *toil* |
| choice | **ch-o-i-c** | *Coic* |
| poise | **p-o-i-s** | *pois* |

● The sound of **oy** as in <u>boy</u> is written in full, **o-y**.

| Read | Spell | *SuperWrite* |
|------|-------|-------------|
| **oy** | | |
| boy | **b-o-y** | *boy* |
| destroy | **d-s-t-r-o-y** | *dstroy* |
| royal | **r-o-y-l** | *royl* |

### *Word Beginnings Im-, Em-*

● The word beginnings **im-** as in <u>impress</u> and **em-** as in <u>emphasize</u> are written **m**.

| Read | Spell | *SuperWrite* |
|------|-------|-------------|
| **im-** | | |
| impress | **m-p-r-s** | *mprs* |

(continued)

| Read | Spell | SuperWrite |
|------|-------|------------|
| impossible | m-p-s-b | *mpsb* |
| import | m-p-o-r-t | *mport* |

**em-**

| | | |
|------|-------|------------|
| emphasize | m-f-s-i-z | *mfsiz* |
| emphasis | m-f-s-s | *mfss* |
| embassy | m-b-s-y | *mbsy* |

## Quantities

● The quantity million is written **m**; billion is written **b**.

million    *m*          billion    *b*

| Quantity | SuperWrite |
|----------|------------|
| 5 million | *5 m* |
| 8 billion | *8 b* |

## Abbreviations

| Words | Abbreviations |
|-------|---------------|
| was, were, with (A) | *w* |
| importance, important (A) | *imp* |
| department (A) | *dept* |
| week, work (A) | *wk* |
| employ (A) | *mpl* |

## Capitalization

● When a word is to be capitalized and it is not written in full, write two short lines under the first letter. Note: If the word to be capitalized begins a sentence, do not write cap marks under the word.

National     *n͇Sl*

If several words in a series are to be capitalized, write the cap marks under the first word only.

National Oil Company     *n͇Sl oil co*

| Terms | SuperWrite |
|---|---|
| the West | *t w͇sl* |
| the East Coast | *t e͇sl cosl* |
| Southern Supply Company | *s͇trn sply co* |
| Central Gas Company is closed. | *c͇ntrl gs co s closd.* |

## APPLICATION

## DOCUMENT 9-1

*Mrs Rodriguez:*

    *c u psbl join us f a v imp bus mel g o depl hds o t s͇trn co n r LA ofc t frsl o nxl mo? s u no, t mel g w orgnll scduld ts mo. l w Cangd l ncres alndnc.*

    *I msl mfsiz t imp o ts mel g; e l b wkg on an imp co pln C dels w t*

(continued)

Coic o nvstm frms n C e l plac blwen
$9 h m n $1 b fm t mple rlirm fnd.
bcs u w hd o t bgt cmle lsl yr, u
npl l b nvlub l us.

e ned u ansr sn. if l s mpsb f
u l b w us, le Mr Miller no afl t frsl
o t wk.

May White

l depl hds:

l s w plSr tl I mak an anouncm
o gral imp l eC mple. lsl wk t onrs
o r co w ab l reC an agrem l prCs
cnlrol g slk n t nSl oil co o Ogden,
UT. t slk C w prCsd s wrt m tn
$5 h m n l brng r loll nvslm n t
oil ndslry l nerl $3 b.

I wnl l mfsiz tl t mrgr l rsll n
no rdcS o wk slf n l aclull brng
mpruvd bnfls l mples o bot cos.

m dlals cncrn g ts imp prLs l
b mald l eC wkr n a wk r so.

       *Bill Meadows*

*Miss Simms:*

  t speC C u gav lsl wk l t bus
mel g o t depl hds o r co w v
mprsv. u mfss on lng-lrm nvslms
hd a gral mpcl. n fcl, u w rsp f r
b g ab l mak l lesl 1 v imp dcS
cncrn g r mple bnfl fnd.

  afl u lk, e dcidd l nvsl $1 b w t
eslrn co o Philadelphia, PA. e l likl
plac t rman g $20 m w 3 r 4 otr cos
nxl yr.

  u plad a rol o gral imp n hlp g
us Cus gd nvslm cos, Miss S. s a rsll
o u gd wk, I m Sr e w ab l mak
sound Coics.

       *L C Trent*

l t slf:

lsl wk w 1 o majr imp l t Essex co.
dur g t wk r nvoics w m tn $6 m,
C w $1 h t hir tn dur g t sam wk
lsl yr. 8 o r 10 depts aclull sl nu
1-wk sals rcrds.

r loyl mples w drcll rsp f ts
mprsv rcrd. I m v proud o eC wkr
n r co. I wS l w psb f me l tk w
eC o u prsnll, bt l s nt psb f me
l d so. l s v imp to, tl eC o u no
e vlu u loylly n ddcaS.

w u cntnud hrd wk, e l sl evn
hir rcrds n t yrs ahd.

R D Babb

## DOCUMENT 9-1

Mrs. Rodriguez:

/Can you possibly join us for a very important business meeting of department heads of the Southern/Company in our Louisiana office the first of next month? As you know, the meeting was originally/scheduled this month. It was changed to increase attendance.

I must emphasize the importance of this meeting; we will/be working on an important company plan which deals with the choice of investment firms in which we will place/ between $900 million and $1 billion from the employee retirement fund. Because you were head/of the budget committee last year, your input will be invaluable to us.

We need your answer soon. If/it is impossible for you to be with us, let Mr. Miller know after the first of the week. May White (139)

## DOCUMENT 9-2

To Department Heads:

/It is with pleasure that I make an announcement of great importance to each employee. Last week the owners of/our company were able to reach an agreement to purchase controlling stock in the National Oil Company/of Ogden, Utah. The stock which was purchased is worth more than $500 million and will bring our/total investment in the oil industry to nearly $3 billion.

I want to emphasize that the merger/will result in no reduction of work staff and will actually bring improved benefits to employees of/both companies.

More details concerning this important purchase will be mailed to each worker in a week or so./Bill Meadows (122)

## DOCUMENT 9-3

Miss Simms:

/The speech which you gave last week at the business meeting of the department heads of our company was very/impressive. Your emphasis on long-term investments had a great impact. In fact, you were responsible for our/being able to make at least one very important decision concerning our employee benefit fund./

After your talk, we decided to invest $1 billion with the Eastern Company of Philadelphia,/ Pennsylvania. We will likely place the remaining $20 million with three or four other companies/next year.

You played a role of great importance in helping us choose good investment companies, Miss Simms. As a/result of your good work, I am sure we were able to make sound choices. L. C. Trent (134)

To the Staff:

/Last week was one of major importance to the Essex Company. During the week our invoices were more than/ $6 million, which was $100,000 higher than during the same week last year. Eight of our ten/departments actually set new one-week sales records.

Our loyal employees were directly responsible/for this impressive record. I am very proud of each worker in our company. I wish it were possible/for me to talk with each of you personally, but it is not possible for me to do so. It is very/important, though, that each of you knows we value your loyalty and dedication.

With your continued hard work,/we will set even higher records in the years ahead. R. D. Babb (132)

## SUPPLEMENTARY ACTIVITY

### A Word to the Wise

Loyalty to Your Employer

/As a worker, you must be loyal to your employer. It is impossible to emphasize this enough./Whether your employer grosses $100,000, $1 million, or even $1 billion a/year, loyalty is necessary. It was important in the past, and it will be of great importance in the/ future.

An employee who wishes to remain with a company must be loyal. A disloyal employee/ will soon be looking for a job with a different company. If you were able to take back a disloyal/remark, you would likely do so. But once a remark is made, it is impossible to retract. You can avoid/a great deal of trouble by thinking first and speaking later.

Whether you are a weekly worker or a monthly/worker—whether you work in the sales department or the finance department—whether you work in the front office/or the back, company loyalty is essential. (169)

# LESSON 10

## PRINCIPLES OF CONSTRUCTION

### Qu

● **Qu** as in <u>quite</u> is written **q**.

| Read | Spell | SuperWrite |
|------|-------|------------|
| quite | **q-i-t** | *qil* |
| quail | **q-a-l** | *qal* |
| quit | **q-t** | *ql* |
| request | **r-q-s-t** | *rqsl* |

### Word Ending -Ity

● The word ending **-ity** as in <u>locality</u> is written as a <u>disjoined</u> **t**.

| Read | Spell | SuperWrite |
|------|-------|------------|
| locality | **l-o-c-l- t** | *locl l* |
| quality | **q-l- t** | *ql l* |
| charity | **ch-r- t** | *Cr l* |
| sincerity | **s-n-c-r- t** | *sncr l* |
| quantities | **q-n-t- ts** | *qnl ls* |

## Abbreviations

| Words | Abbreviations |
|---|---|
| how (A) | *hw* |
| out (A) | *ot* |
| require (A) | *rqr* |
| they (A) | *ty* |

## APPLICATION

### DOCUMENT 10-1

Mrs Jane Ford          d Mrs F:

if u r cncrnd w t qll o lif n r locl l, u l ws l gv u sport l t wk b g dn b a grup o loyl clzns. s u ma no, t clzns w apoinld l t cmle b <u>mar</u> Carson.

ts wk e r mak g an imp srva l dlrmn hw t rsdnls o t area fel cncrn g nvirnml iSus n if ty wnl a la psd l mpruv t qll o t wlr n ar n r vcn l.

if sC a la s psd, l l, qil nlrll, afcl mny mplrs bot n n ol o t cly.

ty mil b rqrd l adpl nu, strngnt
opral g plns l mel t nu rqrms.

e wnt l no hw u fel, s an mplr,
cncrn g ts iSu, C l b o sC gral imp
l t m tn 2 m clzns hu l lv n wk
n ts area n t yrs ahd.

ma I ncrg u l fl ol n rlrn t
alCd srva l r pblc rlaSs depl sn
le me mfsiz tl u rspns l b kpl
cnfdnSl.

cu

Miss Abbott:

l u accpl t rspl o hd g a cmle l
wk on a nu rcrds rlnS sslm f t
nSl co?

r filg sslm w dsind m tn 20 yrs
ago, n e no tl l s now qil ol o
dal. e blev e ma h b kep g mny
paprs tl r lu old l b o vlu, n n

(continued)

al liklhd ty ßd b dstroyd. bl if e
w l tro ol paprs e r rqrd b la
l rtan, l wd b qil bd.

e msl apoinl a prsn o atr l l wk
w t mples n eC depl. tl prsn msl no
al t legl rqrms n hw ty afcl buss
sC s rs, so tl e d nl tro ol imp
dcums.

ma l mfsiz t imp o ts psß. u h
t capbl l hndl t jb v wl, Miss A.
if u c accpl ts apoinlm, le me no afl
t frsl o t wk un n hw u wd lik
l mplm u plns.

RG Baird

Mr Charles Trent        d Mr T:
    l s a plßr l srv s a rfrnc f Mr
Tom Carr, hu wkd f me l my co, t
Yates oil co o Denver, CO, a fu yrs ago.

t prsnl rfrnc Sel C u askd me l fl ol s alCd.

I m hpy l ll u hw I fel cncrn g Mr C n hs abl s a wkr. Mr C h b a frnd o my fml f m tn 10 yrs. he w an mple o my co f nerl 5 yrs. he gls alng wl w otrs, n ty lik hm prsnll.

Mr C s a prsn o nlgr l n rlib l. he s loyl l hs mplr, n he ds hs wk qkl. he s dpndb n ds nl rqr clos suprvS. I blev he cd hndl a psS o atr l n rspl w u co, if he w gvn l.

ts Sd gv u an idea o hw wl Mr C dd wn he w mpld b my co n hw mprsd e w w hm. I l b hpy l fl ol adSl paprs f Mr C if ty r rqrd.

v s u

l t slf:

s u no, t Warren co h wkd sldl f
t psl 2 yrs on t plns f an ad$ o
majr imp l r cmun l. ty r now
nerl fn$d, n ty l b rlesd l t prs
wn e h wkd ol t lsl fu imp dlals.
e w ab l prlcs t rqrd lnd, C s a
Coic pll ajoing t cnlry clb jsl ol o
t cly lmls.

e blev u l agre w us tl t flo q
fgurs r qil mprsv. wn t cnlr s
finll fn$d, l l ncmps 10 t acrs n
l h rqrd an nvslm o nerl $1 b. l
l h 2 t houss, an ofc bld q, n a
qll $p q ml. t ml, C l h m tn 1 m
sqr fel o flor spac, l h 4 lrg depl
slors n 1 h otr $ps.

if u wd njoy se q jsl hw t cnlr
l lk n hw wl l cmplms t cmun l,
drp b t co ofcs. t scal mdl, C w

*[handwritten shorthand text]*

dsind f pblcl prpss, l b on dspla
f r mples fm now ll t end o t
wk.

*A E Cain*

## DOCUMENT 10-1

Mrs. Jane Ford
Dear Mrs. Ford:

/If you are concerned with the quality of life in our locality, you will wish to give your support to the/work being done by a group of loyal citizens. As you may know, the citizens were appointed to the committee by Mayor Carson.

This week we are/making an important survey to determine how the residents of the area feel concerning/environmental issues and if they want a law passed to improve the quality of the water and air in our/vicinity.

If such a law is passed, it will, quite naturally, affect many employers both in and out of/ the city. They might be required to adopt new, stringent operating plans to meet the new requirements.

We want/to know how you feel, as an employer, concerning this issue, which will be of such great importance to the more/than 2 million citizens who will live and work in this area in the years ahead.

May I encourage you/to fill out and return the attached survey to our public relations department soon. Let me emphasize that/your response will be kept confidential. Cordially yours, (190)

## DOCUMENT 10-2

Miss Abbott:

/Will you accept the responsibility of heading a committee to work on a new records retention/system for the National Company?

Our filing system was designed more than twenty years ago, and we know/that it is now quite out of date. We believe we may have been keeping many papers that are too old to be of/value, and in all likelihood they should be destroyed. But if we were to throw out papers we are required by law/to retain, it would be quite bad.

We must appoint a person of authority to work with the employees in/each department. That person must know all the legal requirements and how they affect businesses such as ours, so/that we do not throw out important documents.

(continued)

May I emphasize the importance of this position. You have/the capability to handle the job very well, Miss Abbott. If you can accept this appointment, let me/know after the first of the week when and how you would like to implement your plans. R. G. Baird (176)

## DOCUMENT 10-3

Mr. Charles Trent
Dear Mr. Trent:

/It is a pleasure to serve as a reference for Mr. Tom Carr, who worked for me at my company, the Yates/Oil Company of Denver, Colorado, a few years ago. The personnel reference sheet which you asked me/to fill out is attached.

I am happy to tell you how I feel concerning Mr. Carr and his ability/as a worker. Mr. Carr has been a friend of my family for more than ten years. He was an employee of/my company for nearly five years. He gets along well with others, and they like him personally.

Mr. Carr/is a person of integrity and reliability. He is loyal to his employer, and he does/ his work quickly. He is dependable and does not require close supervision. I believe he could handle a/position of authority and responsibility with your company, if he were given one.

This should/give you an idea of how well Mr. Carr did when he was employed by my company and how impressed we/were with him. I will be happy to fill out additional papers for Mr. Carr if they are required. Very/sincerely yours, (202)

## DOCUMENT 10-4

To the Staff:

/As you know, the Warren Company has worked steadily for the past two years on the plans for an addition of/major importance to our community. They are now nearly finished, and they will be released to the press when/we have worked out the last few important details. We were able to purchase the required land, which is a choice plot/adjoining the country club just out of the city limits.

We believe you will agree with us that the following/figures are quite impressive. When the center is finally finished, it will encompass 10,000 acres/and will have required an investment of nearly $1 billion. It will have 2,000 houses, an office/building, and a quality shopping mall. The mall, which will have more than 1 million square feet of floor space, will have four/large department stores and 100 other shops.

If you would enjoy seeing just how the center will look and how/well it compliments the community, drop by the company offices. The scale model, which was designed for/ publicity purposes, will be on display for our employees from now till the end of the week. A. E. Cain/(200)

# SUPPLEMENTARY ACTIVITY

## A Word to the Wise

### Setting Priorities

/How do some persons get important things done quite easily, while others seem to be busy but never get/important jobs finished?

The secret is in setting priorities. To be sure that you get the most important things/ done, make a list of all the things you are required to do. They should then be ranked by priority. The most important/item should be at the top, and the least important item should be at the bottom.

Then begin working at/the top of the list. As you finish one job, check it off and move down to the next.

At the end of the day, you will/be delighted to see what you have accomplished. The secret is that the most important jobs get done first. If a/few jobs are left out at the bottom of the list, don't worry; they were the least important ones.

Set priorities/to get your important work done. (146)

# LESSON 11

## PRINCIPLES OF CONSTRUCTION

### Word Beginnings For-, Fore-, Fur-

● The word beginnings **for-** as in <u>forget</u>, **fore-** as in <u>foremost</u>, and **fur-** as in <u>further</u> are written **f.**

| Read | Spell | SuperWrite |
|------|-------|------------|
| **for-** | | |
| forget | **f-g-t** | *fgt* |
| forgive | **f-g-v** | *fgv* |
| form | **f-m** | *fm* |
| formerly | **f-m-r-l** | *fmrl* |
| **fore-** | | |
| foremost | **f-m-o-s-t** | *fmost* |
| forecast | **f-c-s-t** | *fcst* |
| forego | **f-go** | *fgo* |
| **fur-** | | |
| further | **f-th-r** | *ftr* |
| furnace | **f-n-c** | *fnc* |
| furniture | **f-n-t-r** | *fntr* |

## Abbreviations

| Words | Abbreviations |
|---|---|
| appreciate (A) | *ap* |
| please (A) | *pl* |
| enclose (A) | *enc* |
| thank (A) | *tk* |
| provide (A) | *pvd* |

## APPLICATION

## DOCUMENT 11-1

d frnd:

   e r dlild l anounc tl t cntrl fnlr co, 1 o t fmosl fnlr cos n ts area, l b opn g a nu slor n St Louis afl t frsl o t yr. s u ma no, e h pvdd fin fnlr l lo prics l t rsdnls o MO snc 1940.

   pl lak a fu moms now l lk l t encd cllg. e no u l ap t hi qll o al r fnlr fm r fml lv g rum sls l r nfml dn fnlr.

(continued)

tks l vlum sals, e c pvd u w ql l fnlr l qil rsnb prics. hw c u lak advnlg o r gral vlus? jsl wC t mal f u spSl nvlaS l t grnd opn g. l l cnlan ftr dlals C cd b o gral imp l u. n adS, a $25 gfl crlfcl l b encd f us w u frsl prCs o $1 h r m. u ma Cus 1 ilm ol o m tn 1 t n r lvl nu slor n ddcl $25 fm t pric. ts s r wa o sa g tk u n Sog r sncer apS l r loyl cslmrs hu h bl tr fnlr fm us tru t yrs.

e no u l b pld w r nu slor; e lk fwrd l se g u sn.

u s

Ms Ann Daniels    d Ms D:

s u ma rcl, lsl yr u rcmndd Mr Alan Davis f an imp ps∫ n r co, estrn fntr stors. he h b a v gd mple f us, n e sncerl ap u rcmnda∫. tks f u hlp.

onc agn, e ned hlp tt u c pvd, Ms D. a fmr mple o u co, Mr J D Duncan, h rtn l us cncrn g an imp ps∫ s a fmn n t dlvry depl o r fntr co. he lls us tt he w mpld b u co nerl 2 yrs, n tt he wkd n t ∫p g depl. if e mpl hm s a fmn, he l b rsp f suprvis g l lesl 10 wkrs n r dlvry depl.

l u pl pvd us w sm fcls cncrn g Mr D? if u l also fl ot t encd fm, e l sncerl ap t. pl tl us hw u fel cncrn g Mr D's

(continued)

abl l d t wk rqrd n a lrg
co lik rs. n ads, e wd lik l
no if u w hpy w bot t qll
n qnll o hs wk n if u wd mpl
hm agn.

    tk u f u cms; ty r sncerl apd.

                  v c u

---

**DOCUMENT 11-3**

Dr M W Brent      d Dr B:

    l w v nic vsl g u n r ofc n
Tulsa, OK, lsl wk; I njoyd r lk.
tk u f askg me l rdsin t sals
depl o Simms n co. I ap u bus. s
e agred, I l pvd t ncsry plns
f a fe o $4 t. n ads, I l rcmnd
fnSgs f t depl.

    I m encg 2 cpes o t inSl plns.
le me mfsiz, to, tl ty r n drfl
fm. I fel tr r a fu mpruvms tl

ma wl b rgrd. ty r dlald n
t encd nol.

I l ap l if u l lk l t plns n
poinl ol adSl dlals C I ma h
fgln. if u fse otr lrbs, pl le me
no b t frsl o t mo. I l fgo
lak g ftr acS ll I her fm u.

tks agn, Dr B, f pvdg me
t oprlun l l b o srvc l u.

u l

Mr Warren Kent      d Mr K:

tk u f u nqiry cncrn g t
psbl o u join g t nSl co s Cef
fmn. tks also f u nic cms cncrng
r bus; e ap tm.

u sem l b a rsp prsn hu s
v wl qlfid f ts imp psS. u
crdnSls r mprsv nded.

(continued)

encd s r slndrd mplm fm.
pl fl l ol n s mC dlal s psb
n t spac pvdd n rlrn l l us.
n ad$, e wd ap l if u wd ask
2 o u fmr mplrs l fn$ us w
rfrncs. e rgr tl ty b mald
drcl l r hom ofc.

pl le us no hw sn u cd bgn
wk g, pvdd u r hird. e lk
fwrd l mel g u prsnll n t ner
fulr.

v s u

## DOCUMENT 11-1

Dear Friend:

/We are delighted to announce that the Central Furniture Company, one of the foremost furniture companies/in this area, will be opening a new store in St. Louis after the first of the year. As you may/know, we have provided fine furniture at low prices to the residents of Missouri since 1940./

Please take a few moments now to look at the enclosed catalog. We know you will appreciate the high quality/of all our furniture from our formal living room sets to our informal den furniture.

Thanks to volume/sales, we can provide you with quality furniture at quite reasonable prices. How can you take advantage/of our great values? Just watch the mail for your special invitation to the grand opening. It will contain/further details which could be of great importance to you. In addition, a $25 gift certificate/will be enclosed for use with your first purchase of $100 or more. You may choose one item out of/more than 1,000 in our lovely new store and deduct $25 from the price. This is our way of saying/thank you and showing our sincere appreciation to our loyal customers who have bought their furniture/from us through the years.

We know you will be pleased with our new store; we look forward to seeing you soon. Yours sincerely,/(240)

## DOCUMENT 11-2

Ms. Ann Daniels
Dear Ms. Daniels:

/As you may recall, last year you recommended Mr. Alan Davis for an important position in our/company, Eastern Furniture Stores. He has been a very good employee for us, and we sincerely/appreciate your recommendation. Thanks for your help.

Once again, we need help that you can provide, Ms. Daniels. A former/employee of your company, Mr. J. D. Duncan, has written to us concerning an important/position as a foreman in the delivery department of our furniture company. He tells us that/he was employed by your company nearly two years and that he worked in the shipping department. If we employ/him as a foreman, he will be responsible for supervising at least ten workers in our delivery/department.

Will you please provide us with some facts concerning Mr. Duncan? If you will also fill out the/enclosed form, we will sincerely appreciate it. Please tell us how you feel concerning Mr. Duncan's ability/to do the work required in a large company like ours. In addition, we would like to know if you were happy/with both the quality and quantity of his work and if you would employ him again.

Thank you for your comments;/they are sincerely appreciated. Very cordially yours, (232)

Dr. M. W. Brent
Dear Dr. Brent:

/It was very nice visiting you in our office in Tulsa, Oklahoma, last week; I enjoyed our talk. Thank/you for asking me to redesign the sales department of Simms and Company. I appreciate your business./As we agreed, I will provide the necessary plans for a fee of $4,000. In addition, I/will recommend furnishings for the department.

I am enclosing two copies of the initial plans. Let me/emphasize, though, that they are in draft form. I feel there are a few improvements that may well be required. They are/ detailed in the enclosed note.

I will appreciate it if you will look at the plans and point out additional/details which I may have forgotten. If you foresee other troubles, please let me know by the first of the month. I will/forego taking further action till I hear from you.

Thanks again, Dr. Brent, for providing me the opportunity/to be of service to you. Yours truly, (167)

Mr. Warren Kent
Dear Mr. Kent:

/Thank you for your inquiry concerning the possibility of your joining the National Company as/chief foreman. Thanks also for your nice comments concerning our business; we appreciate them.

You seem to be a/responsible person who is very well qualified for this important position. Your credentials are/impressive indeed.

Enclosed is our standard employment form. Please fill it out in as much detail as possible in/the space provided and return it to us. In addition, we would appreciate it if you would ask two of/your former employers to furnish us with references. We require that they be mailed direct to our home/office.

Please let us know how soon you could begin working, provided you are hired. We look forward to meeting you/personally in the near future. Very sincerely yours, (151)

# SUPPLEMENTARY ACTIVITY

## A Word to the Wise

Sufficient Fuel

/Would you start out to school or to work in a car with only enough fuel to get you half way there? You likely would/not, but you might start out in the morning with little or no food. If so, you are not providing your body with/the fuel it needs to get you through the morning.

If you could take with you a small package with a little magic/enclosed that would furnish the energy you need, you might very well do so. That magic could be enclosed/in a package of cereal, a piece of fruit, and a slice of toast.

You must furnish your body with sufficient/fuel. Do not forget; before you leave in the morning, take a few minutes to provide your body with the right fuel./You will be pleased with the results, and you will appreciate the feeling of good health that comes with the right nutrition./Your body will say thanks. (145)

# LESSON 12

## PRINCIPLES OF CONSTRUCTION

### Word Ending -Ful

● The word ending **-ful** as in <u>grateful</u> is written **f.**

| Read | Spell | SuperWrite |
|------|-------|------------|
| grateful | **g-r-a-t-f** | *gratf* |
| helpful | **h-l-p-f** | *hlpf* |
| careful | **c-r-f** | *crf* |
| wonderful | **w-n-d-r-f** | *wndrf* |

### Word Beginnings Inter-, Enter-

● The word beginning **inter-** as in <u>interview</u> is written capital **N.**

| Read | Spell | SuperWrite |
|------|-------|------------|
| **inter-** | | |
| interview | **inter-v-u** | *Nvu* |
| interfere | **inter-f-e-r** | *Nfer* |
| interpret | **inter-p-r-t** | *Nprt* |

The word beginning **enter-** as in <u>enterprise</u> and the word <u>enter</u> are also written <u>capital</u> **N.**

| Read | Spell | SuperWrite |
|------|-------|------------|
| **enter-** | | |
| enter | **enter** | *n* |
| enterprise | **enter-p-r-i-s** | *npris* |
| entertain | **enter-t-a-n** | *nlan* |
| entertainment | **enter-t-a-n-m** | *nlanm* |

## Abbreviations

| Words | Abbreviations |
|-------|---------------|
| ever, every (A) | *ev* |
| about (A) | *abt* |
| complete (A) | *cmp* |
| interest (A) | *inl* |

## Compound Words

● The *SuperWrite* for each word is retained when words are combined to form a compound word.

Words extended from abbreviations are marked **A+** in the lists.

| Read | SuperWrite |
|------|------------|
| can (A) | *c* |
| not | *nt* |
| cannot (A+) | *cnt* |
| how (A) | *hw* |
| ever (A) | *ev* |
| however (A+) | *hwev* |

(continued)

| Read | SuperWrite |
|------|------------|
| with (A) | *w* |
| out (A) | *ot* |
| without (A+) | *wot* |

## APPLICATION

## DOCUMENT 12-1

l n g:

  t NnSl TV co s v proud l ll
u abl an inl g n Nlan g vdeolap
nlilld _hw_ l mpruv sals fcsl g.
evvr l h b Son, ev prsn hu h
sen l h b mprsd b t cmp, acurl
cnlnl o t lap. e no u l ap l
also.

  tks l a grnl o $1 m fm t ==eslrn==
oil co, ev clg truol t area c b
pvdd w a cpy o ts mprsv,
hlpf lap fre o Crg. u c gl u cpy
o ts imp lap esl b ril g drcl l
r pblc l depl. hwev, e ncrg u l
acl qkl n l alow 6 wks f dlvry.

ev snc t lap w rlesd, inl h b qil hi, n e r nl ab l fl r rqsls s qkl s e wd lik.

pl ril now f ts dlilf lap so tl u n u sludnls ma njoy l sn. u ma N u rqsl b cmp g t encd fm n rlrn g l l r MA bus ofc.

u l

Dr Donald Frazier    d Dr F:

h u ev wSd tl u cd njoy hi- gl l TV rcpS ev da bl v ofn found tl jsl wn u wnld l se a spcfc So, u iv nl ab l d so bcs o locl Nfernc? if ts h ev hpnd l u, u ma b inld n t wndrf srvc pvdd b r cab TV co. r co s cld t DE cab Nlanm nlwk.

(continued)

f onl $15 a mo, e l fnS u w m tn 30 Cnls o inl g. Nlan g Sos ev da o t yr. tks l r cmpl nu, hi- gl l lcncl sslm, t rcpS tl s pvdd s wndrfl cler ev da. r sbscribrs r nvr lrbd b locl Nfernc, pur pclr gl l, r nois u l h prfcl pclr n sound gl l wnev u lrn on u sl.

if u wd lik l h ftr fcls abl t DE cab Nlanm nlwk, pl cmp n rlrn t encd fm l r Wilmington, DE, ofc wol dla. e l N u mam on r mal g lsl n snd u r bulf ilslrald broSr n abl 1 wk.

u r l

Ms Doris Doyle          d Ms D:

     s u no, l s o gral imp l gl t hisl rlrn on ev dlr u nvsl. t Conroe sav gs bnk pvds ls nvslrs w a hi ral o inl. wtr u r sav g f a bulf nu hous, a hom Nlanm cnlr, r psbl an mporld cr, e h a sav gs pln f u. e pa 10% inl on $10 t lfl on dpsl f 1 yr. flrm, e pa 9% inl on $5 h lfl on dpsl onl 2 yrs.

     e no u l ap t prsnl alnS r hlpf mples l gv u. fm t mom u N r bulfl apoinld lby, u l aclull fel cmpl l hom.

     tks l r efSl srvc, bnk g l t C sav gs bnk l nvr Nfer w u scdul. l l rgr onl a fu mnls l cmp u evda bnk g. trf, u l qkl b on u wa l wrev u wk laks u w almosl no NrpS n u scdul.

(continued)

l lrn m abl r bnk, pl red t
encd broSr. f m fcls abl r inl
rals, fl ol t encd fm n rlrn l
l us. e l fnS u w r updald inl
ral lab ev wk.

drp b r ofc wnev u r n t area,
n le us So u around r bnk. e r
opn ev wkda, n e lk fwrd l
se g u.

u c

l n g:

NnSl prs s hpy l anounc
cmpS o a hlpf nu bk C S m Sr
u l ap. l s nlilld wl ev rsp
prsn Sd no abl fre Npris. l w
rln b Dr Laura Moore w a fwrd
b Dr Jane Keats, bot o hum r
NnSl atr ls n t feld o fre Npris.

t bk cnlans 6 crfl rln Cplrs
abl ev aspcl o t fre Npris sslm,
w spOl mfss on ecnmcs. if u h
ev wnld a Srl, inlg bk on fre
Npris, now u c gl 1 f onl $17.
hwev, u msl acl qkl; t ofr l nl
b gd afl t frsl o t yr.

pl fl ol t encd fm wol dla
n snd l l us alng w u Ck. wn
u gl u cpy, if u d nl blev l s 1
o t mosl inlg, usf, n hlpf
bks ev rln abl fre Npris, jsl
rlrn l. e l Cerfl rfnd u mny.

ril f u cpy lda. e, her l
NnSl prs, lk fwrd l her g fm
u. e r Sr u l tk us f ll g u abl
ts fin nu bk.

c u

## DOCUMENT 12-1

Ladies and Gentlemen:

/The International TV Company is very proud to tell you about an interesting and/ entertaining videotape entitled *How to Improve Sales Forecasting.* Everywhere it has been shown, every person/who has seen it has been impressed by the complete, accurate content of the tape. We know you will appreciate it/also.

Thanks to a grant of $1 million from the Eastern Oil Company, every college throughout the/area can be provided with a copy of this impressive, helpful tape free of charge. You can get your/copy of this important tape easily by writing direct to our publicity department. However,/we encourage you to act quickly and to allow six weeks for delivery. Ever since the tape was released,/interest has been quite high, and we are not able to fill our requests as quickly as we would like.

Please write now for/this delightful tape so that you and your students may enjoy it soon. You may enter your request by completing/the enclosed form and returning it to our Massachusetts business office. Yours truly, (196)

## DOCUMENT 12-2

Dr. Donald Frazier
Dear Dr. Frazier:

/Have you ever wished that you could enjoy high-quality TV reception every day but very often found/that just when you wanted to see a specific show, you were not able to do so because of local/interference? If this has ever happened to you, you may be interested in the wonderful service provided/by our cable TV company. Our company is called the Delaware Cable Entertainment Network.

For/only $15 a month, we will furnish you with more than 30 channels of interesting, entertaining/shows every day of the year. Thanks to our completely new, high-quality technical system, the reception/that is provided is wonderfully clear every day. Our subscribers are never troubled by local/interference, poor picture quality, or noise. You will have perfect picture and sound quality whenever you turn on/your set.

If you would like to have further facts about the Delaware Cable Entertainment Network, please complete/and return the enclosed form to our Wilmington, Delaware, office without delay. We will enter your name on/our mailing list and send you our beautiful illustrated brochure in about one week. Yours very truly, (219)

Ms. Doris Doyle
Dear Ms. Doyle:

/As you know, it is of great importance to get the highest return on every dollar you invest. The Conroe/Savings Bank provides its investors with a high rate of interest. Whether you are saving for a beautiful/new house, a home entertainment center, or possibly an imported car, we have a savings plan for you. We/pay 10 percent interest on $10,000 left on deposit for one year. Furthermore, we pay 9 percent/interest on $500 left on deposit only two years.

We know you will appreciate the/personal attention our helpful employees will give you. From the moment you enter our beautifully/appointed lobby, you will actually feel completely at home.

Thanks to our efficient service, banking at the/Conroe Savings Bank will never interfere with your schedule. It will require only a few minutes to complete/your everyday banking. Therefore, you will quickly be on your way to wherever your work takes you with almost no/interruption in your schedule.

To learn more about our bank, please read the enclosed brochure. For more facts about our/interest rates, fill out the enclosed form and return it to us. We will furnish you with our updated interest/rate table every week.

Drop by our office whenever you are in the area, and let us show you around/our bank. We are open every weekday, and we look forward to seeing you. Yours cordially, (256)

Ladies and Gentlemen:

/International Press is happy to announce completion of a helpful new book which I am sure you will/appreciate. It is entitled *What Every Responsible Person Should Know About Free Enterprise.* It was/written by Dr. Laura Moore with a foreword by Dr. Jane Keats, both of whom are international authorities/in the field of free enterprise.

The book contains six carefully written chapters about every aspect of/the free enterprise system, with special emphasis on economics. If you have ever wanted a short,/interesting book on free enterprise, now you can get one for only $17. However, you must act/quickly; the offer will not be good after the first of the year.

Please fill out the enclosed form without delay and/send it to us along with your check. When you get your copy, if you do not believe it is one of the most/interesting, useful, and helpful books ever written about free enterprise, just return it. We will cheerfully/refund your money.

Write for your copy today. We, here at International Press, look forward to hearing from/ you. We are sure you will thank us for telling you about this fine new book. Cordially yours, (216)

### A Word to the Wise

Finish the Job

/It may not take a special person to start a job, but it often takes someone quite special to finish it. The/successful business person is one who not only begins a job, but also completes it.

Some who enter the/world of business are able to begin a job, but they quickly lose interest. The successful worker, however,/completes every job—often without interruption.

An employer is not interested in hearing/reasons why a job has not been finished. What the employer wants to hear is "Yes, the job is completed."

When you/begin a job, plan about how long every step should take, and then devote your very best efforts to completing the/job on schedule. (123)

# LESSON 13

## PRINCIPLES OF CONSTRUCTION

### Word Beginning Un-

● The word beginning **un-** as in <u>unless</u> is written **u.**

| Read | Spell | *SuperWrite* |
|------|-------|--------------|
| unless | **u-l-s** | *uls* |
| until | **u-t-l** | *ull* |
| unlike | **u-l-i-k** | *ulik* |

### Word Beginning Pre-

● The word beginning **pre-** as in <u>preview</u> and <u>prefer</u> is written **p-r.**

| Read | Spell | *SuperWrite* |
|------|-------|--------------|
| preview | **p-r-v-u** | *prvu* |
| prefer | **p-r-f-r** | *prfr* |
| precise | **p-r-c-i-s** | *prcis* |

### Word Beginning Pro-

● The word beginning **pro-** as in <u>profile</u> and <u>profit</u> is also written **p-r.**

| Read | Spell | *SuperWrite* |
|------|-------|--------------|
| profile | **p-r-f-i-l** | *prfil* |

(continued)

| Read | Spell | *SuperWrite* |
|------|-------|-----------|
| profit | **p-r-f-t** | *prfl* |
| produce | **p-r-d-u-c** | *prduc* |

## Abbreviations

| Words | Abbreviations |
|-------|---------------|
| include (A) | *incl* |
| information (A) | *info* |
| program (A) | *pgm* |
| consider, consideration (A) | *cns* |

## APPLICATION

## DOCUMENT 13-1

*Dr Kenneth Tyler    d Dr T:*

*tk u f u nol ask g f info abl r bus dala prcs g cnfrnc; l arivd lda. e r hpy u r cns g brng g svrl o u mples l t cnfrnc. I m Sr ty ap u cns n l find t cnfrnc l b qil hlpf n tr wk.*

uflmll, e l ml b ab l pvd al t info u rqr f abl a mo. I prfr ml l rles info ull I m Sr l s cmpl acurl.

e h prprd t prlmnry pgm, n e h nvild an mprsv grup o spekrs, inclg svrl fm ol o t cnlry. t spekrs r cnsd l b NnSl atrls n t feld o dala prcsg. hwev, e l ml no C o tm l b ab l b w us ull ty snd tr fml accplncs, C l prbbl b n abl 3 r 4 wks.

wn t pgm s sl, I l fmS al t info u ned, inclg a cmp prsnl dala Sel f ev spekr. tk u f u inl n cns, Dr T. e aSr u e l h a hi-qll pgm tl l b bot inlg n Nlang.

vcu

Mrs Ellen Leith      d Mrs L:

tk u f u r tlf nol. tks also f t info tl I h b slcld l hd t pgm cmle f r NnSl bus cnfrnc. I cns ts an onr, n I ap l. I h gvn ts apoinlm crf cns n h dcidd tl I cnl accpl t rspl.

I wd nl b ab l prpr t pgm prprl bcs I l b wk g on a prjcl o gral imp n r Atlanta, GA, ofc. I l b levg s sn s I cmp wk on t depl lrvl n Nlanm bgl, C Sd b abl t frsl o t mo. I l prbbl b ol o lown ull sprng. uflnll, ts l incl t wk o t cnfrnc. l l also incl t nlir mo bf t cnfrnc. I cd nl hndl t prpraSs jsl bf t cnfrnc, nr cd I aclull alnd t cnfrnc. trf, I d nl cns l n r bsl inl f me l accpl ts imp apoinlm.

hwev, I l d evtng psb l hlp
ol w t prlmnry wk. if t cmle
wnls me l pvd asslnc now, pl le
me no.

pl gv ts info l t cmle, n ll tm
I ap tr cns. I no ty l find a
prsn hu l hndl t jb prprl.

v s u

Ms Sue Bell:

encd s a nol fm Dr Gray tk g
us f r nvlaS, bl dclin g r ofr
l leC r co cmpulr pgm g cors
ts sprng. uf?nll, Se h alrdy accpld
a leCg apoinlm n NH n l b wk g
nerl ev da ull smr. r cors wd
Nfer w hr scdul. trf, Se l b uab
l leC r cors uls e poslpon l. I m,
o cors, qil uhpy abl ts.

(continued)

e cd cns wal g ull Dr G cmps
hr asinm; hwev, e mil prfr l h
a dfrnl leCr. pl gv ts mlr crf
cns.

n t psl e h nl gvn cns l ofr g
t cors n t smr bcs ts incls t
mos mny o r mples r on vaca$.
ty r, trf, nl inld n alnd g a
co cors.

pl pvd ts info l Maria
Martinez, hd o t info prcs g
depl, n le me no if u blev e $d
cns ofr g t cors n t smr r if u
prfr a dfrnl leCr.

                              Ann Stern

Dr Alice Thurmond      d Dr T:

lsl wk I alndd t NnSl info prcsg cnfrnc spnsrd b t bus depl l wstrn clg. I wnl l mfsiz hw mC I njoyd ts mprsv pgm. I h alndd mny pgms o ts lyp n ts area durg t psl 3 yrs; hwev, I cns ts t bsl I h ev alndd. fm t mom I Nd on t frsl mrng ull I lfl on t lsl aflnun, eC spekr pvdd hlpf, prclcl ideas on info prcsg. al spekrs hd prprd tr lks prprl w crf alnS l ev dlal. fm t bgn g ull t end, ev speC w inlg s wl s Nlang.

I blev e Sd qv sm cns l prprg sC a pgm l Mason clg her n Jackson, MS. I no e cd alrcl l lesl 1 t, inclg abl 5 h leCrs n sludnls.

(continued)

*[handwritten shorthand text]*

wd u cns incl g sc a pgm n r scdul f nxt yr, Dr T? if u blev e sd gv ts mtr cns, pl le me no s sn s psb; I lk fwrd t u rply.
s u

## DOCUMENT 13-1

Dr. Kenneth Tyler
Dear Dr. Tyler:

/Thank you for your note asking for information about our business data processing conference; it arrived/today. We are happy you are considering bringing several of your employees to the conference. I/am sure they appreciate your consideration and will find the conference to be quite helpful in their work./

Unfortunately, we will not be able to provide all the information you require for about a/month. I prefer not to release information until I am sure it is completely accurate.

We have prepared/the preliminary program, and we have invited an impressive group of speakers, including several/from out of the country. The speakers are considered to be international authorities in the field/of data processing. However, we will not know which of them will be able to be with us until they send/their formal acceptances, which will probably be in about three or four weeks.

When the program is set, I will/furnish all the information you need, including a complete personal data sheet for every speaker./Thank you for your interest and consideration, Dr. Tyler. We assure you we will have a high-quality/program that will be both interesting and entertaining. Very cordially yours, (235)

Mrs. Ellen Leith
Dear Mrs. Leith:

/Thank you for your very thoughtful note. Thanks also for the information that I have been selected to head the/program committee for our international business conference. I consider this an honor, and I/appreciate it. I have given this appointment careful consideration and have decided that I cannot/accept the responsibility.

I would not be able to prepare the program properly because I will/be working on a project of great importance in our Atlanta, Georgia, office. I will be leaving as soon/as I complete work on the department travel and entertainment budget, which should be about the first of the/month. I will probably be out of town until spring. Unfortunately, this will include the week of the conference./It will also include the entire month before the conference. I could not handle the preparations just/before the conference, nor could I actually attend the conference. Therefore, I do not consider it/in our best interest for me to accept this important appointment.

However, I will do everything/possible to help out with the preliminary work. If the committee wants me to provide assistance now, please/let me know.

Please give this information to the committee, and tell them I appreciate their consideration./I know they will find a person who will handle the job properly. Very sincerely yours, (257)

Ms. Sue Bell:

/Enclosed is a note from Dr. Gray thanking us for our invitation, but declining our offer to teach our/company computer programming course this spring. Unfortunately, she has already accepted a teaching/appointment in New Hampshire and will be working nearly every day until summer. Our course would interfere with/her schedule. Therefore, she will be unable to teach our course unless we postpone it. I am, of course, quite unhappy/about this.

We could consider waiting until Dr. Gray completes her assignment; however, we might/ prefer to have a different teacher. Please give this matter careful consideration.

In the past we have not/given consideration to offering the course in the summer because this includes the months many of our/employees are on vacation. They are, therefore, not interested in attending a company course.

Please provide/this information to Maria Martinez, head of the information processing department, and let me/know if you believe we should consider offering the course in the summer or if you prefer a different/teacher. Ann Stern (203)

Dr. Alice Thurmond
Dear Dr. Thurmond:

/Last week I attended the international information processing conference sponsored by the Business/Department at Western College. I want to emphasize how much I enjoyed this impressive program. I have/attended many programs of this type in this area during the past three years; however, I consider this/the best I have ever attended. From the moment I entered on the first morning until I left on the last/afternoon, each speaker provided helpful, practical ideas on information processing. All speakers/had prepared their talks properly with careful attention to every detail. From the beginning until the end,/every speech was interesting as well as entertaining.

I believe we should give some consideration to/preparing such a program at Mason College here in Jackson, Mississippi. I know we could attract at least/1,000, including about 500 teachers and students.

Would you consider including such a program/in our schedule for next year, Dr. Thurmond? If you believe we should give this matter consideration, please let/me know as soon as possible; I look forward to your reply. Sincerely yours, (214)

## SUPPLEMENTARY ACTIVITY

### A Word to the Wise

Procrastination—the Enemy of Success

/"I'm not prepared to start. I cannot start until I have more information. I'll do it to-morrow."

Have you/ever said something like this to yourself? If so, it is quite probable that you are programming yourself to fail.

It/is common to have trouble starting a job, and this includes most of us. Often just getting started is the/hardest part of a project. But consider this: A job cannot be finished until it is started. Here is something/else that merits your consideration: Things that are put off until tomorrow never get done.

To be successful,/decide what you must accomplish, and then tackle the most difficult jobs first. The little jobs will fall in line./

Procrastination is the enemy of success. (129)

# LESSON 14

## PRINCIPLES OF CONSTRUCTION

### Word Beginning Ex-

● The word beginning **ex-** as in <u>extra</u> is written **x.**

| Read | Spell | *SuperWrite* |
|------|-------|------------|
| extra | **x-t-r-a** | *xtra* |
| expert | **x-p-r-t** | *xprt* |
| expire | **x-p-i-r** | *xpir* |
| explain | **x-p-l-a-n** | *xplan* |

### Abbreviations

| Words | Abbreviations |
|-------|---------------|
| any (A) | *ny* |
| executive (A) | *exec* |
| insurance (A) | *ins* |
| hour (A) | *hr* |
| present (A) | *pr* |
| time (A) | *tm* |

Miss Janet Field          d Miss F:

ull rcntl, r co w n t lif ins bus xclusvl. hwevr, a fu mos ago e bgn pvdg hom ins. t encd bro&r prs al t info abl r nu plces, inclg r lo rals.

if t plcy on u hom l xpir ts yr, le l o r execs prpr a prsnl hom ins prposl f u. l l incl cmp info abl hw l o r xclnl plces c sav u mny. l l lak ls tn an hr o u tm. if u mel r rgrms, u c njoy cnsb sav gs. n fcl, l s psb e c sav u fm 10% l 20% r prhps evn m on t csl o u pr hom ins.

if u r intd n obtan g m info abl r nu ins pgms r if e ma

b o srvc l u n ny otr wa, pl
cl r exec ofcs n Birmingham,
AL. cl nytm blwen t hrs o 9 n
t mrn g n 5 n t aftnun. e l b
v gld l her fm u.

s u

Mr Frank Garner          d Mr G:
   2 mos ago e rol u tl t pam
f t hlt ins f u n u fml w psl
du. lsl mo e rol u tl u plcy wd
xpir n 30 das. alto u pr plcy h
lcncll xpird l ts lm, e l cns
xlnd g u plcy f an xlra mo w
no Nrps if e her fm u sn.
       if u r hg fnnsl prblms n r
nl prprd l pa l t pr lm, pl cl
n lk w l o r acounl execs abl u

(continued)

ins pgm. if u prfr, jst stp b l
se us. r ofcs r opn 10 hrs ev da.
an exec l b tr l tk w u abt u
ins plcy blwen t hrs o 8 n 6
ev wkda.

ma I mfsiz tt l s o gral imp
tt e her fm u sn. e l gv u ev cns,
n e l cns d g nytng psb l hlp,
incl g ajst g u plcy n lor g u rats.
bt l s mpsb f us l d nytng ull
e gt t ncsry info fm u.

s u

---

Ms K C Kelley          d Ms K:
    d u h sfSt lif ins f u fml n
cas o u dt? alto most sccsf bus
execs frml blev ty h enf ins, mny
h onl a sml porS o t totl actull
nedd f tr pr rqrms. no l nos

---

xcll wl xtra xpnss l pln f; no 1
c prdcl t futr. hwev, evon Sd
lak t rspl o mak g sm prpras
f ufsen prblms.

her r 2 imp points C I m Sr
mrl u cns.

1. u fml Sd h sfSt ncm l cnlnu
tr crnl slyl o lif wol NrpS n
futr yrs if u wl di.

2. u Cldrn Sd nl h l lev tr pr
sculs if u w nl tr l pvd f tm.

tes r 2 xclnl rsns u Sd rvu u
ins pgm now. cm b r ofcs ny
wkda, n le us xmn u nlir ins
pgm. 1 o r execs l b tr l gv u
cmp info. e r opn 9 hrs ev da,
incl g t nun hr. slp b nyltm
afl 9 n t mrn g. e r opn ull 6 n
t aflnun, n e lk fwrd l seg u.

v c u

Mrs BA White        d Mrs W:

u l rcl tl rcntl u rol f an exec
ins plcy w r co n tl lsl wk u
lk t rqrd fscl xmnaS.

I m dlild l ll u tl u psd t
xmnaS esl. u r prl n xclnl fscl
cndS, n u h b apruvd f t fl $2 h t
exec ins plcy.

a cpy o t plcy C e prprd f u
s encd. pl lak sm lm now l
rvu crfl al t prvSs incld n t
plcy. l l lak ls tn an hr, n l l
b lm wl spnl. if u wd lik l nqir
abl my o t prvSs r if u ned my
otr info abl u ins pgm, u ma
cl r ofcs nylm afl t hr o 9 n
bf t hr o 6 ny wkda.

u pr qrlrl pam s $3 h. if u
pa anull, hwev, u pam l b onl

#1 t, C s a cnsb savgs l u. a rlrn nvlop s encd f u frsl pam. tks f u bus; e sncerl ap l, Mrs W.

v c u

## DOCUMENT 14-1

Miss Janet Field
Dear Miss Field:

/Until recently, our company was in the life insurance business exclusively. However, a few months/ago we began providing home insurance. The enclosed brochure presents all the information about our/new policies, including our low rates.

If the policy on your home will expire this year, let one of our/executives prepare a personal home insurance proposal for you. It will include complete information/about how one of our excellent policies can save you money. It will take less than an hour of your time. If/you meet our requirements, you can enjoy considerable savings. In fact, it is possible we can save you from/10 percent to 20 percent or perhaps even more on the cost of your present home insurance.

If you are/interested in obtaining more information about our new insurance programs or if we may be of/service to you in any other way, please call our executive offices in Birmingham, Alabama./Call anytime between the hours of nine in the morning and five in the afternoon. We will be very glad to/hear from you. Sincerely yours, (205)

Mr. Frank Garner
Dear Mr. Garner:

/Two months ago we wrote you that the payment for the health insurance for you and your family was past due. Last/month we wrote you that your policy would expire in 30 days. Although your present policy has technically/expired at this time, we will consider extending your policy for an extra month with no interruption/if we hear from you soon.

If you are having financial problems and are not prepared to pay at the/present time, please call and talk with one of our account executives about your insurance program. If you prefer,/just stop by to see us. Our offices are open ten hours every day. An executive will be there to/talk with you about your insurance policy between the hours of eight and six every weekday.

May I emphasize/that it is of great importance that we hear from you soon. We will give you every consideration, and we/will consider doing anything possible to help, including adjusting your policy and lowering/your rates. But it is impossible for us to do anything until we get the necessary information/from you. Sincerely yours, (205)

Ms. K. C. Kelley
Dear Ms. Kelley:

/Do you have sufficient life insurance for your family in case of your death? Although most successful business/executives firmly believe they have enough insurance, many have only a small portion of the total/actually needed for their present requirements. No one knows exactly what extra expenses to plan for;/no one can predict the future. However, everyone should take the responsibility of making some/preparations for unforeseen problems.

Here are two important points which I am sure merit your consideration./
1. Your family should have sufficient income to continue their current style of life without interruption in/future years if you were to die.
2. Your children should not have to leave their present schools if you were not there to provide/for them.

These are two excellent reasons you should review your insurance program now. Come by our offices/any weekday, and let us examine your entire insurance program. One of our executives will be there to/give you complete information. We are open nine hours every day, including the noon hour. Stop by anytime/after nine in the morning. We are open until six in the afternoon, and we look forward to seeing you./Very cordially yours, (224)

# DOCUMENT 14-4

Mrs. B. A. White
Dear Mrs. White:

/You will recall that recently you wrote for an executive insurance policy with our company and/that last week you took the required physical examination.

I am delighted to tell you that you passed the/examination easily. You are presently in excellent physical condition, and you have been/approved for the full $200,000 executive insurance policy.

A copy of the policy/which we prepared for you is enclosed. Please take some time now to review carefully all the provisions included/in the policy. It will take less than an hour, and it will be time well spent. If you would like to inquire/about any of the provisions or if you need any other information about your insurance program,/you may call our offices anytime after the hour of nine and before the hour of six any weekday.

Your/present quarterly payment is $300. If you pay annually, however, your payment will be/only $1,000, which is a considerable savings to you. A return envelope is enclosed/ for your first payment.

Thanks for your business; we sincerely appreciate it, Mrs. White. Very cordially yours,/ (220)

## SUPPLEMENTARY ACTIVITY

### A Word to the Wise

Time for Study

/Any business executive knows that he or she must have time to think, to read, and to prepare for the next day's/work.

The same is true for a student. Whether you are preparing a presentation or studying for an/examination, time must be spent every day getting ready for tomorrow.

Find a quiet area where you/can study, and reserve an hour or so for each subject. Do not listen to music or try to watch TV. This/will only distract you, and you will expend extra effort.

For a reading subject like history, set aside/an hour of uninterrupted time. For a skill subject like typing, plan to practice in several short segments/of about 15 minutes each. Leave some time open so that you may extend your study if extra time should be/needed.

There is no better insurance for a student than proper study. Nothing is as disconcerting to/a student as going to class unprepared. Nothing gives a student more confidence than going to class knowing/that he or she can handle the subject well. (188)

# *LESSON 15*

## *PRINCIPLES OF CONSTRUCTION*

### *Abbreviations*

| Words | Abbreviations |
|-------|---------------|
| suggest, suggestion (A) | *sg* |
| manager (A) | *mgr* |
| management (A) | *mgl* |
| report (A) | *rpt* |

### *Word Beginning Over-*

● The word beginning **over-** as in <u>overdue</u> and the word <u>over</u> are written <u>capital</u> **O.**

| Read | Spell | *SuperWrite* |
|------|-------|-------------|
| over | **over** | *O* |
| overdue | **over-d-u** | *Odu* |
| overtime (A+) | **over-time** | *Otm* |
| overturn | **over-t-r-n** | *Otrn* |

### *Word Beginning Trans-*

● The word beginning **trans-** as in <u>translate</u> is written <u>capital</u> **T.**

| Read | Spell | SuperWrite |
|------|-------|------------|
| translate | trans-l-a-t | *Tlat* |
| transmit | trans-m-t | *Tmt* |
| transfer | trans-f-r | *Tfr* |
| transportation | trans-p-r-t-a-tion | *Tprtas* |

## APPLICATION

## DOCUMENT 15-1

l t exec cmte:

s u no, t gnrl mgr askd t
bgt cmte l wk Otm ev da lst
wk l fnS t rpt on t bgt f t
cm g yr. e ap t sgs n npt C u
pvdd l tl lm.

t frst drft o t bgt s encd. I
mst mfsiz, hwev, tl l s r frst
lry, n rvSs l b ncsry. t bgt s
abt t sam s l w lst yr. t Cangs
tl h b sgd b mgt r pointd ot n
t drft. ty incl a $2 h t ncres n t
*Tprtas* bgt, a $1 h t ncres n t sals
mgt bgt, n a $10 t ncres n t Nlanm

(continued)

bgt. tr l aclull b a dcres o abl
$2 t n t ins bgt. ts wd brng r
bus xpnss l wl O $3 m.

ma I rqsl tl u lak an hr r so
now l lk l O crfl. tr ma b sm
imp dlals C e h Olkd r prblms
C e ma nt h fsen. if u h ny
ftr sgs f r cns, I sg tl u jt
tm down n Iml u cmpd rpl l
me bf t end o t wk. ts Sd gv
us tm l cns u sgs bf e pr t
finl bgt l t exec mgr erl nxl
wk.

tk u f u hlp.        S C Boyle

Mrs Hale:

s I rpld l u bf, I h a nol fm
Al Morris, 1 o r mgt tranes, ask g
f an Ndept Ifr. he h sgd tl he

b Ifrd fm t ins depl l t Iprla$ depl. t mgr o t ins depl n t mgr o t Iprla$ depl ml f an hr yslrda. ty lkd O t sg crfl n apruvd t Ifr.

Mr M h b a loyl mple o r co, n e h alwas b qil pld w hs wk. he s a rsp prsn, n he h dn a v gd jb n t ins depl O t psl yr. ftrm, I m Sr he l also d an xclnl jb n t Iprla$ depl.

t man rsn f ask g f t Ifr l t pr lm s l pvd Mr M lm l gan an Ovru o t wk o mgl n a dfrnl area o r co. I sg t Ifr b mad efclv l ts lm.

l u pl Iml ts info l t exec mgl cmle w t sg tl ty apruv t Ifr wol dla. I wd ap gl g a rpl on my ac$ ty lak.                 Ann Case

Ms Reid:

rcntl Bill Hogan, exec mgr o r
NnSl ofc, rol l me ask g f a spnS
HaS o r rpl, ins mgl. he sgd
tl l b incld s a txl n a wkSp
C l b rqrd f nu mgrs n r
Mexico City ofc ts fl.

I blev ts s a gd sg, n e c d t
jb esl. hwev, B neds t HaS o
ins mgl b t end o smr. I prdcl
e l nt h lm l d t jb prprl wol
nvlv g abl l h hrs o mple Olm
xpns.

l u pl lk O t rpl sn n le me
no if u blev e Sd prced w t
HaS l t pr lm evn to l nvlvs
Olm xpns. if u fel e Sd, I sg tl u
ril drcl l B, n snd a cpy o u nol

l me. if e cnl d t wk l ts lm, c
u mak ny sgs tl mil hlp B?

R A Doyle

Mr Taylor:

lsl mo Dr Mike Black, exec mgr
o t B ins co n Baltimore, MD,
adrsd t bus mgl clb her l r clg
on mgl n t ins bus. s I rpld, t
pgm incld info f fulr mgrs tl
w bot prclcl n Nlan g. n hs spec
he mad svrl inl g prdcss abl t
fulr o t ins bus.

u l rcl tl e mad a rcrd g o t
spec f t locl orl hslry librry.
ts mrng I hd a cl fm Ann Carter,
drclr o t clcs. Se askd if e cd pvd
a Tcrpl o t lk. O t psl fu yrs, l h

(continued)

b r prdc l fnS Icrpls o lks wn
tr s a ned f tm, n I blev e Sd d
so agn ts lm. l Sd b a qk jb. t
man rsn I sg e d ts s f gdl, evn
wn l nvlvs svrl hrs o Olm
Icrib g rpns. t imp o manlan g
gdl cnl b Omfsizd.

    I l ap l if u l lak t rspl o
Ose g ts prjcl, Mr I. I sg tl u mpl
a prfSl lypsl hu s prfSl n wrd
prcs g l Icrib t lap. an allrnlv
sg s l ask / o r pr sludnls l d t
wk. if u cnl flo etr o tes sqs,
pl prced w t wk nywa, bl lry
l kep t rpns s lo s psb.

    I wd ap l if u wd rpl l me on
wl u dcid l d. tks f u hlp.

            R A Reilley

## DOCUMENT 15-1

To the Executive Committee:

/As you know, the general manager asked the budget committee to work overtime every day last week to/finish the report on the budget for the coming year. We appreciate the suggestions and input which you/provided at that time.

The first draft of the budget is enclosed. I must emphasize, however, that it is our/first try, and revisions will be necessary. The budget is about the same as it was last year. The changes/that have been suggested by management are pointed out in the draft. They include a $200,000/increase in the transportation budget, a $100,000 increase in the sales manage-ment budget,/and a $10,000 increase in the entertainment budget. There will actually be a decrease of/about $2,000 in the insurance budget. This would bring our business expenses to well over/ $3 million.

May I request that you take an hour or so now to look it over carefully. There may be some/important details which we have overlooked or problems which we may not have foreseen. If you have any further/suggestions for our consideration, I suggest that you jot them down and transmit your completed report to/me before the end of the week. This should give us time to consider your suggestions before we present the final/budget to the executive manager early next week.

Thank you for your help. S. C. Boyle (257)

## DOCUMENT 15-2

Mrs. Hale:

/As I reported to you before, I have a note from Al Morris, one of our management trainees, asking for/an interdepartmental transfer. He has suggested that he be transferred from the insurance department to/the transportation department. The manager of the in-surance department and the manager of the/transportation department met for an hour yesterday. They looked over the suggestion carefully and approved the/transfer.

Mr. Morris has been a loyal employee of our company, and we have always been quite pleased with/his work. He is a responsible person, and he has done a very good job in the insurance department/over the past year. Furthermore, I am sure he will also do an excellent job in the transportation/department.

The main reason for asking for the transfer at the present time is to provide Mr. Morris time/to gain an overview of the work of management in a different area of our company. I suggest/the transfer be made effective at this time.

Will you please transmit this information to the executive/management committee with the suggestion that they approve the transfer without delay. I would appreciate getting/a report on any action they take. Ann Case (229)

## DOCUMENT 15-3

Ms. Reid:

/Recently Bill Hogan, executive manager of our international office, wrote to me asking for/a Spanish translation of our report, *Insurance Management.* He suggested that it be included as a/text in a workshop which will be required for new managers in our Mexico City office this fall.

I/believe this is a good suggestion, and we can do the job easily. However, Bill needs the translation of/*Insurance Management* by the end of summer. I predict we will not have time to do the job properly without/involving about 100 hours of employee overtime expense.

Will you please look over the report soon/and let me know if you believe we should proceed with the translation at the present time even though it involves/overtime expense. If you feel we should, I suggest that you write direct to Bill, and send a copy of your/note to me. If we cannot do the work at this time, can you make any suggestions that might help Bill? R. A. Doyle/(180)

## DOCUMENT 15-4

Mr. Taylor:

/Last month Dr. Mike Black, executive manager of the Black Insurance Company in Baltimore, Maryland,/addressed the business management club here at our college on management in the insurance business. As I/reported, the program included information for future managers that was both practical and/entertaining. In his speech he made several interesting predictions about the future of the insurance/business.

You will recall that we made a recording of the speech for the local oral history library. This/morning I had a call from Ann Carter, director of the collection. She asked if we could provide a transcript/of the talk. Over the past few years, it has been our practice to furnish transcripts of talks when there is a need for/them, and I believe we should do so again this time. It should be a quick job. The main reason I suggest we do/this is for goodwill, even when it involves several hours of overtime transcribing expense. The importance/of maintaining goodwill cannot be overemphasized.

I will appreciate it if you will take the/responsibility of overseeing this project, Mr. Taylor. I suggest that you employ a professional/typist who is proficient in word processing to transcribe the tape. An alternative suggestion is to ask/one of our present students to do the work. If you cannot follow either of these suggestions, please proceed with/the work anyway, but try to keep the expense as low as possible.

I would appreciate it if you would/report to me on what you decide to do. Thanks for your help. R. A. Reilley (294)

# SUPPLEMENTARY ACTIVITY

## A Word to the Wise

Financial Security

/"Earn $5, spend $4, and you will live happily ever after. Earn $4, spend $5, and/you are on the road to disaster." This old saying seems a bit childish, but it is basically true. Everyone/ must learn to budget to achieve financial security.

You must budget wisely from the day you get your/first paycheck until the day you get your last. Management of your finances is up to you. There is really no/one to report to and no one to depend on.

Here are a few suggestions that could help.

When you get your check, "pay"/yourself first. Save at least 5 percent of your income, and keep an emergency fund. You will find it a source of/comfort when that rainy day arrives.

Start planning for retirement with your first paycheck. Even though retirement may/seem far away, the best time to plan for the future is now.

Budget first for necessities, including housing,/transportation, and food. After necessities have been planned, you may add discretionary items such as/entertainment.

Never borrow for daily expenses. Economists suggest credit be used only for major/ purchases such as houses and cars.

Be a good financial manager, and stay within your budget. Good management/leads to financial security; overspending leads to disaster. (233)

# *LESSON 16*

## *PRINCIPLES OF CONSTRUCTION*

### *Abbreviations*

| Words | Abbreviations |
|---|---|
| order (A) | *od* |
| amount (A) | *aml* |
| state, street (A) | *sl* |
| receive (A) | *rec* |
| number (A) | *no* |
| letter (A) | *lr* |

### *Word Beginning Under-*

● The word beginning **under-** as in <u>understand</u> and the word <u>under</u> are written <u>capital</u> **U.**

| Read | Spell | *SuperWrite* |
|---|---|---|
| under | **under** | *U* |
| understand | **under-s-t-n-d** | *Uslnd* |
| undertake | **under-t-a-k** | *Ulak* |
| underwrite | **under-r-i-t** | *Uril* |
| undersign | **under-s-i-n** | *Usin* |

118

Mrs Moore:

    encd s a cpy o a lr I recd fm
Ray Gwinn, r prdcs mgr, rpl g
tl r co h recd an imp od f O
4 t mSen Fcrib g unls fm t Carter
ins grup. ts s a v lrg no o
Fcrib g unls, n Mr G s qil nlrll
cncrnd abl l. he sls tl he s gld
l h t od, o cors. hwev, he mfsizs
tl l l b mpsb f hs pr slf l hndl
ts aml o wk U t pr cndss. I
Uslnd hs cncrn, n I m nclind l
agre w hm.

    n hs lr, Mr G sls tl hs man
gol s l avoid rqr g a lrg aml o
Olm wk o r fl-lm slf. if e Ulak
t prdcs o sC a sizb od, Mr G sgs
tl e mpl 20 r 30 xlra wkrs, O t
nxl 6 mos, l r Main sl plnl. ts

(continued)

wd enab us l mel r prdcS ddlin
wol Nrpl g r rgulr scdul n wol
rqr g r fl-lm slf l wk Olm.

pl le me no if u blev r exec
mgl wd cns pvd g ts no o hrl
wkrs l r M sl plnl f sC a Srl lm.

tks f u cns n ts mlr. I l ap
rec g ny sgs u h on hw l mng
ts aml o wk.                    Jane Yates

Miss Woods:

ts wk I recd a lr fm Dr J B
Chang, mgr o t NnSl lm mgl co,
sl g tl hs lalsl fnlr od hd b
mprprl fld. he mad t sg tl I lk
nl t mlr.

he odd 20 Crs f hs nu ofc l 210
Oak sl. a cpy o hs od no 8201 s
encd. uflnll, onl 18 Crs w Spd l
hm, n ty w snl l hs old ofc l

401 Elm st. n ad$, t aml on t bl w ncrcll sld s $3 t nsld o t crcl aml, $2 t.

lda I snl 20 Crs l hs O sl ofc alng w a crcl bl n t aml o $2 t n a lr o aplgy. he $d rec hs od n a da r so.

I c Uslnd hw e cd h dlvrd t Crs l t rng adrs; he Ifrd hs ofcs onl rcnll. e cd h esl Olkd hs Cang o adrs rqsl. hwev, I cnl Uslnd hw e cd h $pd t rng no o Crs r hw e cd h mad sC a lrg err n t aml o hs bl.

l u pl gl t ncsry info fm t od n blg depls. I sg tl afl u h gtrd al t fcls u rit a lr o xplna$ l Dr C. I l also ap rec g a cpy o t rpl u prpr, slg wl u w ab l find ol.                    R T Rodriguez

Ms Margaret Como    d Ms C:

tk u f u lr w u lxlbk od no 3308; e recd l lda.

e r hpy l rpl tl 1t cpes o r bk, Uslnd g mgl, r b g Spd l t mgr o t bkslor l Jones bus clg l 501 Main sl, n t slm l b snl drcl l u acounl g ofc l 206 Broad sl. u Sd h sfSl lm afl u rec t bks l prcs tm f sal bf t bgn g o t fl lrm. ma I sg u mprnl tm w u clg lr g on t bk. a no o Npris g clgs n t sl flo ts sg. e hop t sludnls l u clg njoy usg tes inl g bks.

t aml o t nvoic s $12 t, C incls sl n locl lxs n Fprla& Crgs. ts aml s m tn $8 h U r rgulr pric bcs o t lrg no o bks u odd.

tks onc agn, Ms C; u bus h b o gral imp l r co O t yrs.

s u

Dr Leonard Pace     d Dr P:

e recd u lr abt u rcnt od f hom fnᵟgs f rsal n u stor. I m xtreml sry tt u h hd trb qtg t crct no o itms u ned fm r co. I c esl Ustnd t cncrn voicd n u lr.

Mr Paul, mgr o r Spg dept, lkd nt t mtr, n I m hpy l rpt tt he found ot wr t trb s. u od no 181 w recd t r Oak st ofc lst mo. hwev, du t an uftnt Osit, 1 bx nvr lft r Spg dept. e r sndg t rmandr o t od b xprs t u Elm

(continued)

sl slor lda. u l h t ilms n lm f u sal.

U tes cndSs, u ma crlnl h an adSl mo l mak pam n sll rec a 2% dscounl. t aml o u nxl slm l b $1 t, C incls t sl sals lx n FprlaS Crgs. u ma ddcl a dscounl o $19 fm ts aml if u pa b t end o nxl mo.

pl fqv us, Dr P. u ods l b qvn lp prir l n t fulr, n e l mak ev efl l nSr tl ty r fld prprl.

u l

PS encd s r hlda cllg. l incls mny gfl sgs f u cslmrs. ma I sg u mal u od l r mgl ofc sn l avoid t hlda rS.

# DOCUMENT 16-1

Mrs. Moore:

/Enclosed is a copy of a letter I received from Ray Gwinn, our production manager, reporting that our/company has received an important order for over 4,000 machine transcribing units from the/Carter Insurance Group. This is a very large number of transcribing units, and Mr. Gwinn is quite naturally/concerned about it. He states that he is glad to have the order, of course. However, he emphasizes/that it will be impossible for his present staff to handle this amount of work under the present conditions./I understand his concern, and I am inclined to agree with him.

In his letter, Mr. Gwinn states that his/main goal is to avoid requiring a large amount of overtime work of our full-time staff. If we undertake/the production of such a sizable order, Mr. Gwinn suggests that we employ 20 or 30 extra/workers, over the next six months, at our Main Street plant. This would enable us to meet our production deadline without/interrupting our regular schedule and without requiring our full-time staff to work overtime.

Please let me/know if you believe our executive management would consider providing this number of hourly workers/at our Main Street plant for such a short time.

Thanks for your consideration in this matter. I will appreciate/receiving any suggestions you have on how to manage this amount of work. Jane Yates (256)

# DOCUMENT 16-2

Miss Woods:

/This week I received a letter from Dr. J. B. Chang, manager of the International Time Management/Company, stating that his latest furniture order had been improperly filled. He made the suggestion that/I look into the matter.

He ordered 20 chairs for his new office at 210 Oak Street. A copy of his/order Number 8201 is enclosed. Unfortunately, only 18 chairs were shipped to him, and they were/sent to his old office at 401 Elm Street. In addition, the amount on the bill was incorrectly/stated as $3,000 instead of the correct amount, $2,000.

Today I sent 20 chairs to/his Oak Street office along with a correct bill in the amount of $2,000 and a letter of/apology. He should receive his order in a day or so.

I can understand how we could have delivered the/chairs to the wrong address; he transferred his offices only recently. We could have easily overlooked his/change of address request. However, I cannot understand how we could have shipped the wrong number of chairs or how/we could have made such a large error in the amount of his bill.

Will you please get the necessary information/from the order and billing departments. I suggest that after you have gathered all the facts you write a/letter of explanation to Dr. Chang. I will also appreciate receiving a copy of the/report you prepare, stating what you were able to find out. R. T. Rodriguez (274)

Ms. Margaret Como
Dear Ms. Como:

/Thank you for your letter with your textbook order Number 3308; we received it today.

We are happy/to report that 1,000 copies of our book, *Understanding Management,* are being shipped to the manager/of the bookstore at Jones Business College at 501 Main Street, and the statement will be sent direct to your/accounting office at 206 Broad Street. You should have sufficient time after you receive the books to process/them for sale before the beginning of the fall term. May I suggest you imprint them with your college lettering/on the back. A number of enterprising colleges in the state follow this suggestion. We hope the students/at your college enjoy using these interesting books.

The amount of the invoice is $12,000, which/includes state and local taxes and transportation charges. This amount is more than $800 under/our regular price because of the large number of books you ordered.

Thanks once again, Ms. Como; your business has/been of great importance to our company over the years. Sincerely yours, (194)

Dr. Leonard Pace
Dear Dr. Pace:

/We received your letter about your recent order for home furnishings for resale in your store. I am extremely/sorry that you have had trouble getting the correct number of items you need from our company. I can/easily understand the concern voiced in your letter.

Mr. Paul, manager of our shipping department, looked/into the matter, and I am happy to report that he found out where the trouble is. Your order Number 181/was received at our Oak Street office last month. However, due to an unfortunate oversight, one box/never left our shipping department. We are sending the remainder of the order by express to your Elm Street store/today. You will have the items in time for your sale.

Under these conditions, you may certainly have an/additional month to make payment and still receive a 2 percent discount. The amount of your next statement will be/$1,000, which includes the state sales tax and transportation charges. You may deduct a discount of/$19 from this amount if you pay by the end of next month.

Please forgive us, Dr. Pace. Your orders will be/given top priority in the future, and we will make every effort to ensure that they are filled properly./Yours truly,

PS   Enclosed is our holiday catalog. It includes many gift suggestions for your customers./May I suggest you mail your order to our management office soon to avoid the holiday rush. (259)

*A Word to the Wise*

The Self-Starter

/The lettering on the old car, parked just off the street, said "Self-Starter." The statement implied that the car actually/started itself. This, of course, was untrue. It really meant that in order to start the car, all you had to do/was push a button rather than "crank up" the engine by turning a crank manually a number of times. This/improvement in car design eliminated a great amount of work!

Businesses have always tried to hire/self-starters—those who understand their work and who can get started without the necessity of having to be "cranked/up." When companies receive letters from prospective employees, they want to know if the person is a self-starter./

Do you have to be "cranked up" to get started on a job, or do you get going on your own? Are you a/self-starter? (141)

# LESSON 17

## PRINCIPLES OF CONSTRUCTION

### Word Endings -Ple, -Pal

● The word endings **-ple** as in <u>ample</u> and **-pal** as in <u>principal</u> are written **p.**

| Read | Spell | *SuperWrite* |
|------|-------|--------------|
| ample | **a-m-p** | *amp* |
| simple | **s-m-p** | *smp* |
| multiple | **m-l-t-p** | *mltp* |
| principal | **p-r-n-c-p** | *prncp* |

### Abbreviations

| Words | Abbreviations |
|-------|---------------|
| available (A) | *av* |
| organization, organize (A) | *org* |
| paid (A) | *pd* |
| represent, representative (A) | *rep* |

Mr BD Smith        d Mr S:

tk u f u rcnt lr; e w gld l rec l. e r v hpy tl u r pld w t srvc pvdd b r nu reps n u prl o t sl. e agre tl ty rep r org v wl, n e no tl ty l ap u cms. e r espSll gld l h gd rpls on r pep.

e wS e cd srv u org b fl g u od no 2201 f l h TV sls f u fntr stor. e Ustnd tl u ned tm f rsal l u prncp locaS on Main st n Columbia, SC. hwev, e cnl mak tes sts av l u now.

u h nl pd r org t $15 t u h od us f m tn 5 mos. ts reps a lrg fnmSl rspl, n l s mpsb f us l fl ny ftr ods ull u h pd us t aml prl du.

(continued)

if u rqr xtra tm t org u
fnncs, pl le us no sn. drp b r
exec ofc ny wkda blwen t hrs
o 9 n 5. 1 o r reps l lak amp
tm l xplan a no o pam opSs
av t u.

wn u h orgd u fnncs n h pd
us t aml du, e l b gld l fl u
ods on crdt. ull tn, e sg tt u
org cns prcs g gds fm us on
a cS bass.

u l

Ms Sarah Tatum          d Ms T:

tk u f u rcnt lr. e w gld l
rec u rqst f info abt r corss C
r av l sals mgrs n reps. O t
yrs r org h mad av l reps o al
typs o buss n ts area a no o

inl g, njoyb corss. ts yr e h orgd
4 imp nu corss, C l b ofrd l t
<u>m</u>uncp bldg on Broad sl. ts reps
t lrgsl no o corss tl r org h ev ofrd
l l lm.

ty r s flos:
1. g<u>v</u> g n flo g ods
2. <u>g</u>lg ucldd acounls pd
3. <u>Us</u>lnd g ins mgl
4. <u>lr</u>n g hw l org u wk
t corss, C r dscribd n fl n t encd
bkll, mfsiz prclcl, usf prncps.

mny bus orgs n r prl o t sl
nrol l r m o tr mples n l o r
corss ev yr. e prdcl u pep l gan
a gral del if ty lak prl n l o tes
inl g, njoyb clss.

l s smp l nrol u pep n l o
tes corss. al u ned d s fl ol t
encd nrolm fm n rlrn l l us.

(continued)

t fe f eC cors s onl $1 h pr prsn, n t fl aml Sd b pd l t frsl mel g.

if e c b o ftr srvc l u org n ny psb wa, Ms T, ma e sg tl u cl us nytm.

s u

Mrs P W Troy          d Mrs T:

tk u f u nqiry abl r bl-pa g srvc; e w gld l rec u lr. t sl nSl bnk o Cleveland maks av l bus orgs n ndvduls truol OH a smp bl v usf srvc.

u c h u mol bls pd wol t ncsl o ril g a lrg no o Cks n odl cmp t FacSs. u c h al u bls, incl g ull ls n ins, pd O t llfon.

afl u r nrold n t pgm, al u
ned d s org u bls n mak / smp
fon cl eC mo. / o r reps l mak
crf nols o C orgs u wS l pa n
hw mC ty Sd b pd. eC bl l b
pd on t xcl da u sl, n u l rec
a cmp rpl, orgd b dal, o al
Jac$s l t end o ev mo.

   ts srvc c rep a savgs n lm;
l c also rep a savgs n mny. l
s av f onl $10 a mo, C s prbbl
wl U t aml u now pa.

   t prncp rsn l c sav u mny
s tl l savs us mny. bcs mny
bus orgs h acounls w r bnk,
t Jac$s l b smp Jfrs o fnds
fm u acounl l trs.

   f m info, cl / o r reps l r Mill
sl brnC ny wkda blwen t hrs
o 9 n 3.            u c

Dr Jean Addison     d Dr A:

e recd u lr ask g f info abl r nul fmd NnSl bnk g org. tks f u nqiry.

abl 6 mos ago, 10 bnks, rep g ev prl o t sl, orgd t lrgsl bnk g grup n t rgn. eC bnk hd pd a hi ral o inl on prncp nvslms f t psl 10 yrs. n adS, ty eC hd asls amlg l l lesl $5 h m. t loll asls o t nul orgd grup rep m tn $7 b.

t org w fmd n od l srv pep truol t nlir rgn. tru r cmbind slrngt, e c mak almosl ulmld fnds av l t pep o ts area.

e Uslnd t neds o r cslmrs; e d nl cns ny lon lu lrg r lu sml. f xmp, if u ned $1 t l gl a prsnl bl pd, $1 h t f a nu hous, *r $1 m l nvsl n a bus, e c hlp u.*

*e wnl l mak r dpndb, efSl srvc av l evon. if e c ev b o hlp l u, ma e sg u cl l o r reps l r Oak sl ofc, C s n u prl o town. e r opn blwen t hrs o 9 n 3, n l o r reps l b hpy l srv u n ny wa psb.*

*c u*

---

## DOCUMENT 17-1

Mr. B. D. Smith
Dear Mr. Smith:

/Thank you for your recent letter; we were glad to receive it. We are very happy that you are pleased with the/service provided by our new representatives in your part of the state. We agree that they represent our/organization very well, and we know that they will appreciate your comments. We are especially glad to/have good reports on our people.

We wish we could serve your organization by filling your order Number/2201 for 100 TV sets for your furniture store. We understand that you need them for resale/at your principal location on Main Street in Columbia, South Carolina. However, we cannot make/these sets available to you now.

You have not paid our organization the $15,000 you have/owed us for more than five months. This represents a large financial responsibility, and it is impossible/for us to fill any further orders until you have paid us the amount presently due.

If you require/extra time to organize your finances, please let us know soon. Drop by our executive office any/weekday between the hours of nine and five. One of our representatives will take ample time to explain a number/of payment options available to you.

When you have organized your finances and have paid us the amount/due, we will be glad to fill your orders on credit. Until then, we suggest that your organization consider/ purchasing goods from us on a cash basis. Yours truly, (271)

## DOCUMENT 17-2

Ms. Sarah Tatum
Dear Ms. Tatum:

/Thank you for your recent letter. We were glad to receive your request for information about our courses which/are available to sales managers and representatives. Over the years our organization has made/available to representatives of all types of businesses in this area a number of/interesting, enjoyable courses. This year we have organized four important new courses, which will be offered at/the Municipal Building on Broad Street. This represents the largest number of courses that our organization/has ever offered at one time.

They are as follows:
1. Giving and Following Orders
2. Getting/Uncollected Accounts Paid
3. Understanding Insurance Management
4. Learning How to Organize Your Work

The/courses, which are described in full in the enclosed booklet, emphasize practical, useful principles.

Many business/organizations in our part of the state enroll one or more of their employees in one of our courses every/year. We predict your people will gain a great deal if they take part in one of these interesting, enjoyable/classes.

It is simple to enroll your people in one of these courses. All you need to do is fill out the enclosed/enrollment form and return it to us. The fee for each course is only $100 per person, and the/full amount should be paid at the first meeting.

If we can be of further service to your organization in/any possible way, Ms. Tatum, may we suggest that you call us anytime. Sincerely yours, (277)

## DOCUMENT 17-3

Mrs. P. W. Troy
Dear Mrs. Troy:

/Thank you for your inquiry about our bill-paying service; we were glad to receive your letter. The State National/Bank of Cleveland makes available to business organizations and individuals throughout Ohio/a simple but very useful service.

You can have your monthly bills paid without the necessity of writing a/large number of checks in order to complete the transactions. You can have all your bills, including utilities/ and insurance, paid over the telephone.

After you are enrolled in the program, all you need do is organize/your bills and make one simple phone call each month. One of our representatives will make careful notes of which/organizations you wish to pay and how much they should be paid. Each bill will be paid on the exact day you state, and/you will receive a complete report, organized by date, of all transactions at the end of every month.

This/service can represent a savings in time; it can also represent a savings in money. It is available/for only $10 a month, which is probably well under the amount you now pay.

The principal/reason it can save you money is that it saves us money. Because many business organizations have accounts/with our bank, the transactions will be simple transfers of funds from your account to theirs.

For more information, call/one of our representatives at our Mill Street branch any weekday between the hours of nine and three. Yours cordially,/(260)

## DOCUMENT 17-4

Dr. Jean Addison
Dear Dr. Addison:

/We received your letter asking for information about our newly formed international banking/organization. Thanks for your inquiry.

About six months ago, ten banks, representing every part of the state,/organized the largest banking group in the region. Each bank had paid a high rate of interest on principal/ investments for the past ten years. In addition, they each had assets amounting to at least $500 million./The total assets of the newly organized group represent more than $7 billion.

The/organization was formed in order to serve people throughout our entire region. Through our combined strength, we can make almost/unlimited funds available to the people of this area.

We understand the needs of our customers;/we do not consider any loan too large or too small. For example, if you need $1,000 to/get a personal bill paid, $100,000 for a new house, or $1 million to invest in/a business, we can help you.

We want to make our dependable, efficient service available to/everyone. If we can ever be of help to you, may we suggest you call one of our representatives at our Oak/Street office, which is in your part of town. We are open between the hours of nine and three, and one of our/representatives will be happy to serve you in any way possible. Cordially yours, (255)

# SUPPLEMENTARY ACTIVITY

## A Word to the Wise

Organizing Your Work Area

/Some people seem to be well organized while others suffer from a lack of organization.

To be well/organized, you should start by examining your work area. A good desk can be a great assistance in helping/you to get organized. Even a small desk can help, if you make use of every bit of space available.

Reserve certain areas in your desk for special work. For example, reserve a place for unpaid bills and other/unfinished business. Items which cannot be finished should be placed in this area. The secret to making it work, however,/is to be sure that the area is cleared once a week.

Time devoted to organizing your work area is time/well invested. The principal reason is that if your work area is well organized, your work will also/be well organized.

Your work is representative of the way you work. Does your work represent you well? Take a/close look at your work area to see if you need to improve it. (172)

# LESSON 18

## PRINCIPLES OF CONSTRUCTION

### Prefix Before a Short Vowel

● If a root word begins with a short vowel sound, the vowel is retained when a prefix is added.

| Read | Spell | *SuperWrite* |
|------|-------|--------------|
| act | a-c-t | *acl* |
| react | r-a-c-t | *racl* |
| other | o-th-r | *otr* |
| another | a-n-o-th-r | *anotr* |

### Suffix After a Short Vowel

● If a root word ends with a short vowel sound, the vowel is retained when a suffix is added.

| Read | Spell | *SuperWrite* |
|------|-------|--------------|
| law | l-a | *la* |
| lawyer | l-a-y-r | *layr* |
| draw | d-r-a | *dra* |
| drawing | d-r-a- g | *drag* |

## Abbreviations

| Words | Abbreviations |
|---|---|
| question (A) | q |
| regard (A) | rgd |
| cover (A) | cv |

## APPLICATION

### DOCUMENT 18-1

Mr Roy Lynch     d Mr L:

abt 2 yrs ago, I opnd a Sp n t muncp Sp g ml on Pine st. t tl tm I Nd nt a cntrct w t NnSl nvslm co, onrs o t ml, n pd tm a $2t scur l dpst. I h pd tm $8 h rnt ev mo snc tn.

my les w f 2 yrs; an opS w pvdd f anotr 2 yrs. I fll Sr tl t les cvd t fl 4 yrs, n I h orgd my bus on tl bass. O a mo ago, I le t mgt o t muncp Sp g ml

no tl I nlndd l rnu t les. hwev,
lsl wk I recd a lr fm tr pep
slg tl ty w nl rnu g my les.

I cnl Uslnd wy my les s nl
bg rnud f anotr 2 yrs. ftrm,
I h nl b ab l gl a rep fm t org
l ansr my qs rgd g ts prblm.
I cns tr acS ulaf, n I blev tl tr
s a smp breC o cnlrcl b t Nn&l
nvslm co.

l u pl lk O my cnlrcl, C s encd,
n gv me u racS        t flo g qs,
C r o gral imp l me:

1. s ts prblm cvd n my pr
   cnlrcl?

2. wd u sg I hir a layr l rep
   · me?

3. wl opSs r av l me l t pr
   lm?

(continued)

tk u f u cns n wlev hlp u ma b ab l gv me, Mr L. L ap u hlp; ny sgs u mak l b wlcm.

s u

## DOCUMENT 18-2

l n g:

3 mos ago r org mpld Mr D R Long s mgr o r nu rcrds mgl depl. he h wkd closl w r layrs n w reps o eC prncp depl. he h pd clos alnS l tr sgs cncrn g t rqrms o r org. he h mad a no o xclnl sgs n h b rsp f la g t groundwk f r nu pgm. e l sn bgn t aclul rorg o r co fil g ssl m. ev depl w t xcpS o t ins depl l b incld n t nu pgm.

her r ansrs l a fu imp qs rgd g r nu ssl m: gnrl fils, C

Sd b av l evon, l b rorgd n Ifrd l a cntrl fil g area. onl prsnl fils l b kpl n privl ofcs. (I msl mfsiz tt ts rul cvs mples l ev lvl.) inaclv fils l b Ifrd l t inaclv fil depl. v old paprs l b xmnd, n if ty r o no ftr vlu, ty l b dslroyd.

t prncp rsns e r lak g tes slps r l nSr tt r fil g pgm s up l dal n tt r rcrds rlnS csls r kpl s lo s psb. ts cd esl rep a savgs o O $1 h t O t nxl 10 yrs.

n od l mak t pgm wk prprl, I m rqsl g tt eC o u flo crfl t dlald ruls cvd n t encd rpl, C Mr L h prprd. if ny o u pep

(continued)

h a q w rgd l t pgm, r if ty ned ftr info tl s uoblanb n u on depl, pl ask tm l cl Mr L.

J R Dale

Mr T D Chan          d Mr C:

wl d u lk f wn u by mn's clot g? wy d u slcl 1 slor O anotr? e tnk e Uslnd t prncp rsns tl Uli u Coic.

e blev u wnl l b ab l Sp n a cmflb, wl-orgd, inl g slor tl h av al t v lalsl fSs. e blev u wnl hi ql l n gd srvc l rsnb prics. tes r xcll wl u l find l t Morgan mn's slor l frsl n Lee sls. e h av an mprsv ara o hi-ql l mn's clot g l qil rsnb prics.

e h b sccsf bcs e h pd spSl

alns l r cstmrs, hu rep almost
ev prfs. u l find on r lst o
stsfid cstmrs evon fm prfsrs
n layrs l sals reps n bus
mgrs. e r hil rgdd b al r
cstmrs; ty alwas find xcll wl
ty wnl n r stor.

r org h srvd t pep o Hartford,
CT, fm t sam locas f O 30 yrs.
e h xpndd r stor mny tms, n
r bld g prt cvs an ntir cty blk.
e r, wol q, t lrgst n bst mn's
stor n ts prt o t st. hwev, don't
lak r wrd f t. cm n sn n dscv
f uslf wl xclnt vlus e h av.

u s

PS if u h ny qs rgd g r srvc,
jst cl r tol-fre no, C s incld n
t encd brosr.

Ms Lynda Pool:

s u l rcl, lsl yr e apoinld Kathryn Moreno, l o t hil rgdd nu layrs l *Nnsl* ndslres, l a pss on r muncp advisry cmle. wil se w on t cmle, se pd alns l ev dlal rlald l muncp mgl n mad mny vlub sgs tl aclull savd r cmun l blwen $9 h t n $1 m. se w rsp f savg O $75 t n ins csls alon.

s u l rcl, hwev, K w n an alo accdnl abl 6 mos ago, n hr rcvy lk a gral aml o lm. se w, trf, uab l cmp hr fl yr on t cmle.

l s now lm l rorg r muncp advisry cmle f t cm g yr. uqbl, K dd an xclnl jb s t rep fm hr co f t frsl prl o t yr, n I Uslnd

*[shorthand handwriting]*

tl Se s now cmpl rcvd. I m, trf,
rcmndg tl Se b rapoinld l rep
hr org f anotr yr.

   if tr s ny q n u mind rgdg
ts rapoinlm, r if u h ny otr qs
rgdg t rorg, pl cl me s sn s
psb. I l b av ny da nxl wk
afl t hr o 9 n t mrng.

                   *Martin Chase*

## DOCUMENT 18-1

Mr. Roy Lynch
Dear Mr. Lynch:

/About two years ago, I opened a shop in the Municipal Shopping Mall on Pine Street. At that time I/entered into a contract with the International Investment Company, owners of the mall, and paid them a/ $2,000 security deposit. I have paid them $800 rent every month since then.

My/lease was for two years; an option was provided for another two years. I felt sure that the lease covered the full four years, and I have organized my business on that basis. Over a month ago, I let the management/of the Municipal Shopping Mall know that I intended to renew the lease. However, last week I/received a letter from their people stating that they were not renewing my lease.

I cannot understand why my lease/is not being renewed for another two years. Furthermore, I have not been able to get a representative/from the organization to answer my questions regarding this problem. I consider their action/unlawful, and I believe that there is a simple breach of contract by the International Investment Company./

(continued)

Will you please look over my contract, which is enclosed, and give me your reaction regarding the following/questions, which are of great importance to me:
1. Is this problem covered in my present contract?
2. Would you/suggest I hire a lawyer to represent me?
3. What options are available to me at the present time?

Thank you/for your consideration and whatever help you may be able to give me, Mr. Lynch. I appreciate/your help; any suggestions you make will be welcome. Sincerely yours, (291)

## DOCUMENT 18-2

Ladies and Gentlemen:

/Three months ago our organization employed Mr. D. R. Long as manager of our new records management/department. He has worked closely with our lawyers and with representatives of each principal department./He has paid close attention to their suggestions concerning the requirements of our organization. He has/made a number of excellent suggestions and has been responsible for laying the groundwork for our new/program. We will soon begin the actual reorganization of our company filing system. Every/department with the exception of the insurance department will be included in the new program.

Here are/answers to a few important questions regarding our new system: General files, which should be available to/everyone, will be reorganized and transferred to a central filing area. Only personal files will/be kept in private offices. (I must emphasize that this rule covers employees at every level.) Inactive/files will be transferred to the inactive file department. Very old papers will be examined, and if they/are of no further value, they will be destroyed.

The principal reasons we are taking these steps are to ensure/that our filing program is up to date and that our records retention costs are kept as low as possible. This/could easily represent a savings of over $100,000 over the next ten years.

In/order to make the program work properly, I am requesting that each of you follow carefully the detailed rules/covered in the enclosed report, which Mr. Long has prepared. If any of your people have a question with/regard to the program, or if they need further information that is unobtainable in your own department,/please ask them to call Mr. Long. J. R. Dale (308)

Mr. T. D. Chan
Dear Mr. Chan:

/What do you look for when you buy men's clothing? Why do you select one store over another? We think we understand/the principal reasons that underlie your choice.

We believe you want to be able to shop in a/comfortable, well-organized, interesting store that has available all the very latest fashions. We believe/you want high quality and good service at reasonable prices. These are exactly what you will find at the/Morgan Men's Store at First and Lee Streets. We have available an impressive array of high-quality men's clothing/at quite reasonable prices.

We have been successful because we have paid special attention to our customers,/who represent almost every profession. You will find on our list of satisfied customers everyone/from professors and lawyers to sales representatives and business managers. We are highly regarded by/all our customers; they always find exactly what they want in our store.

Our organization has served the/people of Hartford, Connecticut, from the same location for over thirty years. We have expanded our store/many times, and our building presently covers an entire city block. We are, without question, the largest and best/men's store in this part of the state. However, don't take our word for it. Come in soon and discover for yourself what/excellent values we have available. Yours sincerely,

PS   If you have any questions regarding our/service, just call our toll-free number, which is included in the enclosed brochure. (274)

Ms. Lynda Pool:

/As you will recall, last year we appointed Kathryn Moreno, one of the highly regarded new lawyers at International/Industries, to a position on our municipal advisory committee. While she was on the/committee, she paid attention to every detail related to municipal management and made many/valuable suggestions that actually saved our community between $900,000 and/$1 million. She was responsible for saving over $75,000 in insurance/ costs alone.

As you will recall, however, Kathryn was in an auto accident about six months ago, and her/recovery took a great amount of time. She was, therefore, unable to complete her full year on the committee./

It is now time to reorganize our municipal advisory committee for the coming year./ Unquestionably, Kathryn did an excellent job as the representative from her company for the first part/of the year, and I understand that she is now completely recovered. I am, therefore, recommending that she/be reappointed to represent her organization for another year.

If there is any question in/your mind regarding this reappointment, or if you have any other questions regarding the reorganization,/please call me as soon as possible. I will be available any day next week after the hour of/nine in the morning. Martin Chase (266)

## SUPPLEMENTARY ACTIVITY

### A Word to the Wise

Making Notes

/Making good notes will help you both in school and out. Whether you are preparing for an examination or/outlining a political speech, good notemaking skills are necessary.

When you attend a speech, listen carefully/for the main topic to be covered. Try to have a "mental conversation" with the speaker. See if you can/predict what will be said next. Listening for major and supporting ideas will help you to get the speaker's/message completely and accurately.

In an outline, the major topics covered should be indicated by/capital letters. Supporting ideas under each major heading should be indicated by numbers. If/there are minor points under these headings, they should be indicated by small letters.

You may include your reaction/to the speaker's points, but you should place your ideas in brackets so that you will not later confuse the speaker's/ideas with your own.

Your outline will help you understand the speaker better. It will help you in drawing/ conclusions about the speech and will help you organize any questions you may have regarding the talk.

Good/notemaking skills are invaluable. Work to improve your notemaking ability. (215)

# LESSON 19

## PRINCIPLES OF CONSTRUCTION

*Word Endings -Ious, -Eous, -Ous, -Us*

● The word endings **-ious** as in various, **-eous** as in courteous, **-ous** as in dangerous, and **-us** as in status are all written **u-s**.

| Read | Spell | *SuperWrite* |
|------|-------|-----------|
| **-ious** | | |
| various | **v-r-u-s** | *vrus* |
| serious | **s-e-r-u-s** | *serus* |
| **-eous** | | |
| courteous | **c-r-t-u-s** | *crtus* |
| advantageous | **a-d-v-n-t-a-g-u-s** | *advntagus* |
| **-ous** | | |
| dangerous | **d-a-n-g-r-u-s** | *dangrus* |
| famous | **f-a-m-u-s** | *famus* |
| **-us** | | |
| status | **s-t-a-t-u-s** | *status* |
| surplus | **s-r-p-l-u-s** | *srplus* |

## Mem

● The syllable **mem** as in <u>member</u> is written **m.**

| Read | Spell | SuperWrite |
|------|-------|------------|
| member | m-b-r | *mbr* |
| remember | r-m-b-r | *rmbr* |
| memory | m-r-y | *mry* |

## Abbreviations

| Words | Abbreviations |
|-------|---------------|
| avenue (A) | *ave* |
| convenience, convenient (A) | *cnv* |

## Days of the Week

● Longhand abbreviations are used for days of the week, but no periods are used.

| Day | SuperWrite |
|-----|------------|
| Sunday | *Sun* |
| Monday | *Mon* |
| Tuesday | *Tues* |
| Wednesday | *Wed* |
| Thursday | *Thurs* |
| Friday | *Fri* |
| Saturday | *Sat* |

## Months of the Year

● Longhand abbreviations are used for months of the year, but no periods are used.

| Month | SuperWrite |
|---|---|
| January | *Jan* |
| February | *Feb* |
| March | *Mar* |
| April | *Apr* |
| May | *May* |
| June | *June* |
| July | *July* |
| August | *Aug* |
| September | *Sept* |
| October | *Oct* |
| November | *Nov* |
| December | *Dec* |

## APPLICATION

Read and write the following documents.

Mr Jack Warren     d Mr W:

    u l rmbr tl on Mon, July 11, u co odd $1 t wrt o splis f u cnv stor fm r Park ave wrhous. u pd $2 h down n sind a nol sl g tl t rmandr wd b pd b Tues, Aug 23. e rol u a crlus rmindr n Sept n anotr n Oct. l s now Wed, Nov 16. anotr mo h gn b, n e h nl hrd fm u.

    e cnl Uslnd wy u h nl pd ts bl, bl e hop tl u l lak a fu mnls now l ril a Ck f $8 h l cv u bl n plac l n t mal l r exec ofcs l 201 Madison ave

    if l s nl cnv f u l pa t cmp bl l ts lm, I sg tl u le us no

now. prhps l wd b m cnv f u
l pa prl o t loll aml now n t
rsl latr. n my cas, 1 o r crtus
reps l b hpy l pvd ansrs l my
gs u ma h rqd q u bl. hwev,
dla g ny ftr l d serus dmg l u
crdl ral q.

e fel tl e h b qil gnrus, Mr W,
bt e c d ntng m. t rspl o pa q
u dts s us. e lk fwrd l her q fm
u bf t end o nxl wk. rmbr, t
slalus o u crdl dpnds on wl u
d now.

u l

l al cstmrs:

e r dlild l anounc t grnd opn g o r nu sbrbn depl stor l 4201 Yale ave. t dors l opn l 10 a m on Thurs, Apr 5. wol q, t nu stor s t lrgsl, most butf n t nlir area, n t grnd opn q l b a mrb ocaS.

n r spaSus nu stor, cnvl locald l t NscS o Main sl n Yale ave, u l b ab l find al t famus, wl-orgd depls n r prncp stor on Park ave. n adS, u l find numrus lotll nu n xcil g depls wr u c find evtng fm mporld alo prls l hi-gl l hndmad fnlr n fm flor cv gs l dlSus ckes n cndes.

e no u l ap r bulf nu stor,
C l mak Spg m smp n cnv tn
ev f u. hwev, e no tl on vrus
ocaSs u l njoy t cnv o Spg l
bot r downtown n r sbrbn locaSs.
f u cnv, u ma us u Crg crd l bot
stors. s usul, t inl l b onl 1% o t
upd blnc eC mo. rgdls o C locaS
u Cus, u l rec r crlus, efSl srvc.

    s a spSl bonus, av onl l r pr
Crg cstmrs, u l rec a $10 gfl crlfcl
l r grnd opn g. smpl pr ts lr l
ny mbr o r crlus sals slf, n t
$10 bonus l b us. n adS, u nam s
bg almlcl Nd n a dra g f a fre
TV sl.

    rmbr t dal, Apr 5; e lk fwrd l
se g u tn.

                    c u

l n g:

encd s my Ck f $1 h, t aml du n pab l u org, cvg mbrSp n t cntrl lrvl clb f t mos o Jan, Feb, n Mar. I h found mbrSp n t clb l b a gral cnv dur g t psl yr. I h usd t cnv emrgncy llfon no on 1 ocaS n Oct n anotr n Nov.

on Fri, Dec 30, I muvd l Lincoln, NE, wr I l rman abl 3 yrs wk g on t rqrms f a dgre n la. I le u ofc no prvrusl, bl obvrusl my lr dd nl reC u ofc n amp lm l prcs t Cang bf u lsl bl g. anotr slm w mald l my old adrs.

l u cnv, pl Ck l b Sr tl my adrs on u rcrds h b Cangd fm 415 Grant ave n Des Moines, IA, l my nu cmpus adrs, 602 Main ave n L.

wn l s cnv, pl snd me a nu mbrsp crd n a nol cnfrm g tl u h recd my pam. Sd u h ny qs rgd g my fnnsl slalus wil d m n clg, d l b m tn hpy l ansr tm.

u v l

Miss Janice Cortez     d Miss C:

tk u f u crlus lr rgd g u rcnl muv. tk u also f u Ck f t aml du l cv u mbrsp n t cnlrl lrvl clb.

e recd u prvus lr m tn a wk ago ll g us tl u hd muvd n Dec. ufllnll, r rcrds w nl updald ull afl u slm w mald.

s u rgsld prvusl, e h Cangd u adrs on r rcrds fm 415 Grant ave n Des Moines l u cmpus adrs, 602 Main ave, n Lincoln. e l snd

(continued)

u slm f t mos o Apr, May, n June
l u nu adrs.

l u cnv, l u pl fl ol t encd fm
gvg u crnl mplm slalus, if u l
b wk g wil u r n scul. u ma us
t cnv nvlop C s also encd.

e r Sr tl u l find u mbrSp n
r lrvl clb a gral cnv wil u r l u
cmpus adrs. Sd u ev ned r srvc,
r if u h ny qs rgd g Fprlas r
lrvl, pl cl t lol-fre no cnvl lsld
on u nu mbrSp crd, C s encd.
rmbr r ofcs r opn ev da, inclg
Sat n Sun.

e wnl l cmnd u on Ng la
scul. wk g l bcm a layr s a v
ambSus Ulak g, n e Uslnd tl
ts s a slp o gral imp n u prfSl
lif. e no u l h a v bril fulr,
Miss C.                              s u

Mr. Jack Warren
Dear Mr. Warren:

/You will remember that on Monday, July 11, your company ordered $1,000 worth of/ supplies for your convenience store from our Park Avenue warehouse. You paid $200 down and signed a note/stating that the remainder would be paid by Tuesday, August 23. We wrote you a courteous reminder in/September and another in October. It is now Wednesday, November 16. Another month has gone by,/and we have not heard from you.

We cannot understand why you have not paid this bill, but we hope that you will take a/few minutes now to write a check for $800 to cover your bill and place it in the mail to our/executive offices at 201 Madison Avenue.

If it is not convenient for you to pay the/complete bill at this time, I suggest that you let us know now. Perhaps it would be more convenient for you to pay/part of the total amount now and the rest later. In any case, one of our courteous representatives/will be happy to provide answers to any questions you may have regarding your bill. However, delaying/any further will do serious damage to your credit rating.

We feel that we have been quite generous,/Mr. Warren, but we can do nothing more. The responsibility of paying your debts is yours. We look forward/to hearing from you before the end of next week. Remember, the status of your credit depends on what you do/now. Yours truly, (263)

To All Customers:

/We are delighted to announce the grand opening of our new suburban department store at 4201/Yale Avenue. The doors will open at 10 a.m. on Thursday, April 5. Without question, the new store is/the largest, most beautiful in the entire area, and the grand opening will be a memorable/occasion.

In our spacious new store, conveniently located at the intersection of Main Street and Yale Avenue,/you will be able to find all the famous, well-organized departments in our principal store on Park/Avenue. In addition, you will find numerous totally new and exciting departments where you can find/everything from imported auto parts to high-quality hand-made furniture and from floor coverings to delicious/cookies and candies.

We know you will appreciate our beautiful new store, which will make shopping more simple/and convenient than ever for you. However, we know that on various occasions you will enjoy the/convenience of shopping at both our downtown and our suburban locations. For your convenience, you may use your charge/card at both stores. As usual, the interest will be only 1 percent of the unpaid balance each month./Regardless of which location you choose, you will receive our courteous, efficient service.

(continued)

As a special bonus/, available only to our present charge customers, you will receive a $10 gift certificate at/our grand opening. Simply present this letter to any member of our courteous sales staff, and the $10/bonus will be yours. In addition, your name is being automatically entered in a drawing for a/free TV set.

Remember the date, April 5; we look forward to seeing you then. Cordially yours, (318)

## DOCUMENT 19-3

Ladies and Gentlemen:

/Enclosed is my check for $100, the amount due and payable to your organization,/ covering membership in the Central Travel Club for the months of January, February, and March. I have/found membership in the club to be a great convenience during the past year. I have used the convenient/emergency telephone number on one occasion in October and another in November.

On Friday,/December 30, I moved to Lincoln, Nebraska, where I will remain about three years working on the requirements/for a degree in law. I let your office know previously, but obviously my letter did not reach your office/in ample time to process the change before your last billing. Another statement was mailed to my old address.

At/your convenience, please check to be sure that my address on your records has been changed from 415 Grant Avenue/in Des Moines, Iowa, to my new campus address, 602 Main Avenue in Lincoln.

When it is convenient,/please send me a new membership card and a note confirming that you have received my payment. Should you have any/questions regarding my financial status while I am at college, I will be more than happy to answer/them. Yours very truly, (224)

## DOCUMENT 19-4

Miss Janice Cortez
Dear Miss Cortez:

/Thank you for your courteous letter regarding your recent move. Thank you also for your check for the amount due/to cover your membership in the Central Travel Club.

We received your previous letter more than a week/ago telling us that you had moved in December. Unfortunately, our records were not updated until/after your statement was mailed.

As you requested previously, we have changed your address on our records from/415 Grant Avenue in Des Moines to your campus address, 602 Main Avenue in Lincoln. We will send your/statement for the months of April, May, and June to your new address.

At your convenience, will you please fill out the/enclosed form giving your current employment status, if you will be working while you are in school. You may use the/convenient envelope which is also enclosed.

We are sure that you will find your membership in our travel club a/great convenience while you are at your campus address. Should you ever need our service, or if you have any/questions regarding transportation or travel, please call the toll-free number conveniently listed on your new/membership card, which is enclosed. Remember, our offices are open every day, including Saturday and/Sunday.

We want to commend you on entering law school. Working to become a lawyer is a very ambitious/undertaking, and we understand that this is a step of great importance in your professional life. We know/you will have a very bright future, Miss Cortez. Sincerely yours, (271)

## SUPPLEMENTARY ACTIVITY

### A Word to the Wise

Your Wardrobe

/The impression you make on others is quite often determined by your clothing. As a business person, you must/consider your clothing very seriously.

There are various sources from which to choose your wardrobe, including/expensive stores on fashionable avenues and budget stores in the suburbs. You should remember, however,/that it is erroneous to believe that you must purchase famous-maker brands to be well dressed. By waiting/for special sales, you will be able to purchase good clothing at reasonable prices.

Don't try to purchase a/complete wardrobe at one time. Focus at first on a few basic items, such as a good suit and a nice pair of/shoes. Then set aside a part of each paycheck to add to your wardrobe. Don't try to follow the latest fads; strike a/balance between what is fashionable and the colors and styles that look good on you.

Vary your clothing from day/to day and from week to week. Do not wear the same things on two consecutive days. Do not wear the same clothing on/the same day each week. For example, do not wear the same suit every Monday or every Wednesday.

If you live in/an area with changing seasons, at a convenient time after warm weather arrives in April or May, have/your winter clothing cleaned and stored. At your convenience in October or November, have your summer clothing cleaned/and stored, and change back to your winter things.

Remember, with proper care and planning, you can have a beautiful/wardrobe and always be well dressed. And you do not have to be wealthy to do so. (274)

# LESSON 20

## PRINCIPLES OF CONSTRUCTION

### Abbreviations

| Words | Abbreviations |
|-------|---------------|
| application, apply (A) | *apl* |
| develop (A) | *dv* |

### Short I Followed by a Vowel

● When a short **i** (pronounced **e**) is followed by another vowel, omit the **i** and write the other vowel.

| Read | Spell | SuperWrite |
|------|-------|------------|
| material | **m-t-e-r-a-l** | *mteral* |
| variance | **v-r-a-n-c** | *vranc* |
| negotiate | **n-g-o-sh-a-t** | *ngoshal* |
| folio | **f-o-l-o** | *folo* |
| premium | **pr-m-u-m** | *prmum* |

### Using Additional Abbreviations

● There are a number of additional abbreviations that may be used. Some are fairly common, such as **sr** for senior. Others are used in a particular business or industry, such as **mkt** for market. Other abbreviations may be devised for your own particular area of interest. For example, **cmpr** could stand for computer.

Abbreviations that are easy to remember, to read, and to write may be incorporated into your writing vocabulary.

Here are some examples that can serve as a guide as you devise a limited number of additional abbreviations, of particular value to you:

| Words | Abbreviations |
|---|---|
| advertisement | *ad* |
| computer | *cmpr* |
| corporation | *corp* |
| established | *est* |
| federal | *fed* |
| government | *govt* |
| incorporated | *inc* |
| merchandise | *mdse* |
| market | *mkt* |
| senior | *sr* |

## APPLICATION

## DOCUMENT 20-1

Miss Sharon Preston    d Miss P:
tk u v mC f u crlus lr o Mon,
June 3, n C u apld f t jb o prncp
acountnl n r Main sl ofc n Boise,
ID. e crlnl d rmbr u fm u wk s a
cmpulr pgmr n r ins depl, wil

(continued)

u w a studnt t Central st clg. e ap u int n join g r org n ts imp pss.

her s t info u rqstd. t jb l cv al areas o acount g. t sccsf cnddat l rep t acount g dept s a mbr o t co exec cmte n l b rsp f drct g t acount g wk f t ntir org. t prsn Cosn l b t mgr o a dept o 10 pep n l b rsp f dvg n org g an acount g prcedrs mnul f t co. n adt, he r se l h t rspt o dvg al ncsry acount g fms n otr mterals f us n al r ofcs.

t u cnv, t u pl fl ot t encd apt fm n rtrn t t r exec mgt ofc t 560 Lincoln ave. pl incl u prvus acount g jbs. wn t s cnv, e wd ap rec g 3 bus rfrncs, incl g tr bus tlfon nos.

tks f u inl, Miss P. e r gld tl
u apld f t jb, n e lk fwrd l
rec g u fml apl sn. wn e rec l,
e l b ab l scdul an Nvu f u
wn a Srl perod o lm.

u s

Mrs Houston:

hw nic l se u dur g my vsl
l CA on Tues, July 21. I w espbll
pld w u rpl on t slalus o u wk.
u h mad xclnl prgrs n a Srl
perod o lm dv g plns f t ofc
lowr, C e pln l bld on Oak ave
n Seattle. u dra gs w mprsv
nded. e Sd b ab l cmp t slrclr
wn t $1 h m bgl. wn t bld g s
cmpd, r nvslm n t sl o WA l b
O $3 b.

(continued)

Mr Rich h gtrd t aprpral mterals n l apl f apruvl o t sil pln w t prpr atr ls n S smlm ts wk. afl he h apld, ty l cns t apl n mak a dcS. e Uslnd ty l le us no tr dcS wn a mo. e d nl rpcl ny serus prblms w t apl bcs e r ask g f no zon g vrancs f t dvm sil.

e h hd numrus nqires abl ofc spac. e h alrdy recd a lnllv cmlm f t les o 3 flors fm t NnSl lnd dvm co n 2 flors fm wslrn Npriss. eC o tes cos h pd a scur l dpsl o $5 t. e ma wl h cmlms f anotr flor r 2 o prmum ofc spac bf t end o t mo. e Sd b ab l h t bld g cmpl lesd bf cnslrcS wk s fnSd.

if u h ny qs rgd g t dvm sil, I sg u cl Mr R l a lm cnv f u. hs ofc hrs r 9 l 5 dal. if I c b o ftr hlp l u, pl le me no. I m av l u cnv.　　Max Keith

Mr Thomas Wade　　　　d Mr W:

e w hpy l rec u crlus lr apl g f a Crg acount l Brooks n asocals depl slor. O t yrs, e h dvd a lng lsl o loyl, slsfid cslmrs. e lk fwrd l Ng u nam on ts lsl.

n od f us l prcs u apl, l u pl fl ol t encd apl fm n rlrn l l us l u cnv. pl lsl 3 cos w hum u h prvusl hd crdl n t aml o u olslnd g blncs, if ny. e wd also lik l no u crnl mplm slalus.

(continued)

aft e rec a favrb crdl rpl, e
l prcs u apl n snd u a Crg crd.
ts crd ma b usd l ny o r cnv
loca&s, incl g r nusl stor on
Jackson ave, n t estrn hls rel
estal dvm, C s ner u hom.

f t &rl perod o lm ull u crd
arivs, hwev, e sg tl u lak advnlg
o t mny sp&l bys av on a c& bass.
r smr sal o fin clot g bgns Wed,
Aug 4. slp n n slcl famus-makr
clot g l dscounls up l 50%.

tks f apl g f crdl w r org,
Mr W. e lk fwrd l h g u s a mbr
o r fml o Crg acounl cslmrs.

cu

Ms Carla Wolfe          d Ms W:

   s u l rmbr, lsl Thurs a rep
fm u org askd r frm l dv an
ollin f an apld ofc prcedrs
mnul f u org. encd f u cns s a
portfolo cnlang t mlerals u askd
us l dv. incld r t ollin f t mnul,
a smp Cplr, numrus dsc& prblms,
svrl dra gs, n vrus apl xrciss.

   l u pl lk O t portfolo, l u cnv,
n le me no if ts s t lyp o mnul
u hd n mind. I wd lik l h u
rac& l t mlerals n psb sgs f
rv& s sn s psb. if l s nl cnv
f u l rvu t mlerals now, pl le
me no wn u l b ab l d so. & l b
wk g l my Grant ave ofc blwen
t hrs o 9 n 5 ev da ull Sept 1.

(continued)

*[shorthand handwriting]*

if u r pld w r wk e l go ahd
n dv a cmp mnul n Iml l l u
bf t end o Oct.
e r hpy l srv u co, Ms W.
v s

---

**DOCUMENT 20-1**

Miss Sharon Preston
Dear Miss Preston:

/Thank you very much for your courteous letter of Monday, June 3, in which you applied for the job of principal/accountant in our Main Street office in Boise, Idaho. We certainly do remember you from your work/as a computer programmer in our insurance department, while you were a student at Central State College./We appreciate your interest in joining our organization in this important position.

Here is the/information you requested. The job will cover all areas of accounting. The successful candidate/will represent the accounting department as a member of the company executive committee/and will be responsible for directing the accounting work for the entire organization. The person/chosen will be the manager of a department of ten people and will be responsible for/developing and organizing an accounting procedures manual for the company. In addition, he or she/will have the responsibility of developing all necessary accounting forms and other/materials for use in all our offices.

At your convenience, will you please fill out the enclosed application form and/return it to our executive management office at 560 Lincoln Avenue. Please include your/previous accounting jobs. When it is convenient, we would appreciate receiving three business references,/including their business telephone numbers.

Thanks for your interest, Miss Preston. We are glad that you applied for/the job, and we look forward to receiving your formal application soon. When we receive it, we will be/able to schedule an interview for you within a short period of time. Yours sincerely, (316)

## DOCUMENT 20-2

Mrs. Houston:

/How nice to see you during my visit to California on Tuesday, July 21. I was especially pleased/with your report on the status of your work. You have made excellent progress in a short period of time/developing plans for the office tower, which we plan to build on Oak Avenue in Seattle. Your drawings were/impressive indeed. We should be able to complete the structure within the $100 million budget. When/the building is completed, our investment in the state of Washington will be over $3 billion./

Mr. Rich has gathered the appropriate materials and will apply for approval of the site plan with the/proper authorities in Seattle sometime this week. After he has applied, they will consider the/application and make a decision. We understand they will let us know their decision within a month. We do not/expect any serious problems with the application because we are asking for no zoning/variances for the development site.

We have had numerous inquiries about office space. We have already/received a tentative commitment for the lease of three floors from the International Land Development Company/ and two floors from Western Enterprises. Each of these companies has paid a security deposit of/ $5,000. We may well have commitments for another floor or two of premium office space before/the end of the month. We should be able to have the building completely leased before construction work is finished./

If you have any questions regarding the development site, I suggest you call Mr. Rich at a time/convenient for you. His office hours are nine to five daily. If I can be of further help to you, please let me know./I am available at your convenience. Max Keith (329)

## DOCUMENT 20-3

Mr. Thomas Wade
Dear Mr. Wade:

/We were happy to receive your courteous letter applying for a charge account at Brooks and Associates/Department Store. Over the years, we have developed a long list of loyal, satisfied customers. We look forward/to entering your name on this list.

In order for us to process your application, will you please fill out the/enclosed application form and return it to us at your convenience. Please list three companies with whom you have/previously had credit and the amount of your outstanding balances, if any. We would also like to/know your current employment status.

After we receive a favorable credit report, we will process your/application and send you a charge card. This card may be used at any of our convenient locations, including our/ newest store on Jackson Avenue, in the Eastern Hills real estate development, which is near your home.

(continued)

For the/short period of time until your card arrives, however, we suggest that you take advantage of the many/special buys available on a cash basis. Our summer sale of fine clothing begins Wednesday, August 4. Stop/in and select famous-maker clothing at discounts up to 50 percent.

Thanks for applying for credit with/our organization, Mr. Wade. We look forward to having you as a member of our family of charge/account customers. Cordially yours, (226)

## DOCUMENT 20-4

Ms. Carla Wolfe
Dear Ms. Wolfe:

/As you will remember, last Thursday a representative from your organization asked our firm to develop/an outline for an applied office procedures manual for your organization. Enclosed for your/consideration is a portfolio containing the materials you asked us to develop. Included are/the outline for the manual, a sample chapter, numerous discussion problems, several drawings, and various/application exercises.

Will you please look over the portfolio, at your convenience, and let me/know if this is the type of manual you had in mind. I would like to have your reaction to the materials/and possible suggestions for revision as soon as possible. If it is not convenient for you to/review the materials now, please let me know when you will be able to do so. I will be working at my/Grant Avenue office between the hours of nine and five every day until September 1.

If you are pleased with/our work, we will go ahead and develop a complete manual and transmit it to you before the end of/October.

We are happy to serve your company, Ms. Wolfe. Very sincerely, (214)

# SUPPLEMENTARY ACTIVITY

## A Word to the Wise

Time Management

/It has been said that each of us has the same amount of time available. This is true, but some people get their/work accomplished with time to spare while others do not. The difference is in the way people manage their time.

Some/people control their time appropriately while others let outside events determine what they will do. Some are/able to be where they are supposed to be and are usually properly prepared. Others rush from one/activity to another, never finishing one before starting the next.

Here is an interesting point:/The person who manages time well never seems to be rushed. In fact, that person has time to relax and enjoy/life. The person who does not manage time well is always busy and never has time to relax.

The principles/of management—planning, organizing, and controlling—apply here. Develop a plan, indicating what needs/to be done, organize your materials appropriately, and control each step to be sure you stay on schedule./

The application of principles of time management can go a long way toward making you successful in/both your business and personal life. (206)

# PART 2

## BEGINNING
## TRANSCRIPTION

# *LESSON 21*

## *SuperWrite REVIEW*

You will use your *SuperWrite* skill to take business letters, memorandums, and other notes that you will later transcribe in the proper business format.

To help you keep the principles firmly in mind, in each of the lessons in the second part of this text there is a review of the principles of constructing *SuperWrite.* In this lesson, we will review a number of abbreviations, a word beginning, and a word ending.

Read the following words, referring to the key if necessary. Then write the words in your own notebook.

### Abbreviations

1. *abt aft m aml n ny*
2. *apl ap r s t av*
3. *ave b bus c co cmp*

### Word Beginning Be-

4. *bgn bcm bwr bnet bst bcs*

### Word Ending -ble

5. *ab tab sizb trb capb wkb*

### Key

1. about; after; am, more; amount; and, in; any

2. application, apply; appreciate; are, or, our; as, is; at, it, to; available

3. avenue; be, been, by; business; can; company; complete

4. begin; become; beware; beneath; beset; because

5. able; table; sizable; trouble; capable; workable

# KEYBOARDING STYLE

## Business Letter Format

There are many styles used to key business letters. In *SuperWrite, Volume One,* we will use the one described here.

**Letterhead.**   In business, letters are keyed on letterhead paper, that is, paper with a company name, address, and other information printed at the top.

**Length.**   Letters are considered to be short, average, long, or two-page according to the number of words in the body. A short letter contains up to 100 words; an average letter, from 101 to 200 words; and a long letter, from 201 to 300 words. If a letter contains more than 300 words, it should be keyed on two pages.

**Margins.**   Margin settings may be adjusted according to the length of a letter. However, in business today many companies use a standard 6-inch line for all letters.

|  | Elite (12-pitch) Type Margins | Pica (10-pitch) Type Margins |
|---|---|---|
| Standard, Long, and 2-page letter | 15-90 | 10-75 |
| Average letter | 20-85 | 15-70 |
| Short letter | 25-80 | 20-65 |

**Vertical spacing.**   To balance a letter on the page, a varying number of vertical spaces are left between the date and the letterhead. (See paragraph on **Date** below.)

**Punctuation.**   No punctuation is used at the end of the beginning and closing lines with two exceptions. A colon is used after the salutation, and a comma is used after the complimentary close.

**Date.**   The current date is keyed beginning at the horizontal center of the page on line 18 for a short letter, line 16 for an average letter, and line 14 for a long or two-page letter.

**Salutation.**   The salutation should correspond to the letter address. Ladies and Gentlemen is an appropriate salutation when the first line of a letter address is the name of a company. The salutation is keyed a double space below the letter address. Double space below the salutation.

**Complimentary close and signature line.**   Key the complimentary close, followed by a comma, a double space below the last line of the body of the letter. Key the signature line a quadruple space below the complimentary close. Include the writer's professional title on the next line.

**Reference initials.**   The reference initials are keyed a double space below the final signature line.

**Enclosure notation.**   The word Enclosure is keyed at the left margin a double space below the reference initials. It is the responsibility of the person keying the letter to determine when an enclosure notation is needed.

## Addresses

Write house and building numbers in figures, except One.

Spell out numbered street names First through Tenth. Write numbered street names over ten in figures.

Do not use commas in house or building numbers.

2270 Dawn Drive                One Trent Boulevard

8900 Fourth Avenue             10103 Lanape Street

Use a hyphen with a space before and after to separate a house number and a street number when both are written in figures. Use th, st, nd (or d), and rd (or d) after a numbered street name.

428 – 82d Street               238 North 180th Street

Type the ZIP Code two spaces after the state abbreviation.

Billings, MT   59231-3398

**The Wellington Organization**
450 State Street
Chicago, Illinois 44544

January 5, 19-- - line 16

QS

Mr. Marvin Anderson, Chief Buyer
Western Office Equipment
829 Carson Drive
Reno, NV 89117-3233
DS
Dear Mr. Anderson:
DS
    Your order for 100 printers reached our office
today. We were very glad to receive your order because
it is our first from your company in more than a year.

    We are sending 50 printers to you today via Over-
land Express. The remaining 50 will be sent to you
within three weeks direct from our factory in Los
Angeles.

    Just initial this letter and return it to us to ap-
prove this slight delay in filling your order. We will
then mark your order top priority and ship it just as
soon as the printers are assembled.

    You may use the same credit terms you have used in
the past. You may deduct a 2 percent discount if full
payment is made within 30 days after delivery. Full
payment is due within 60 days after delivery. The invoice for each shipment will be included with the
printers.

    Welcome back to our organization. Please let us
know whenever we may be of service to you.
DS
                  Cordially yours,

QS

                  Mary McBride
                  Sales Manager

DS
mm
DS
Enclosure

# PUNCTUATION

In a number of the lessons in Part 2 of the text, punctuation rules are given. Read the rules and study the *SuperWrite* examples that follow. Sentences containing uses of the punctuation rules are included in the Application section of the lessons.

The first rule concerns the use of the comma in a compound sentence.

## Compound Sentence

Use a comma to separate two independent clauses joined by coordinating conjunctions <u>and</u>, <u>but</u>, <u>or</u>, or <u>nor</u>. Each independent clause must have a subject and a verb and make sense by itself. Place the comma before the coordinating conjunction.

*e mpl mny wkrs, n r parol*
*ofc s Owkd.*

We employ many workers, and our payroll
office is overworked.

*e h b n bus onl a fu yrs,*
*bt r co h gron qkl.*

We have been in business only a few years,
but our company has grown quickly.

*u ma brng t papr w u,*
*r u ma mal t t us.*

You may bring the paper with you,
or you may mail it to us.

*he cd nt dlvr t splis on tm,*
*nr cd he rtrn t dpst.*

He could not deliver the supplies on time,
nor could he return the deposit.

When a comma is used in a compound sentence, it will be marked in the margin as follows:

, compound
sentence

*he apld f crdt t r stor,*
*n e opnd an acount f hm.*

He applied for credit at our store,
and we opened an account for him.

## APPLICATION

The Application section of each lesson in this part of the text contains a number of business documents. The documents in this lesson are business letters. In later lessons, memorandums and reports are included. Here is a suggested procedure for this lesson:

1. **Read.**   First, read the following documents carefully, referring to the key that follows if necessary.
   **Timed Reading.**   Document 1 is designed to help you read faster. A reading goal is marked at the top of the document. Try to finish reading in the allotted time.

2. **Write.**   After you have read the letters, make one complete copy of each of them in your own notebook.
   **Speed Builder.**   Document 2 is designed to help you build your *SuperWrite* speed. Follow your teacher's instructions as you push to write faster.
   **Punctuation Check.**   Examples of the punctuation rule are included in each of the documents. In the first three documents, these commas are marked; they are not marked in Document 4, which is the Punctuation Check. As you copy, be sure to supply the proper punctuation marks in your own notes. The punctuation marks and the reasons for using them are included in the key.

3. **Type.**   Using your own notes, type the last letter, Document 1-4, in the business letter format shown in this lesson. Note that the letter would be considered average length. A keyboarding time goal is marked at the top of the document.

4.   Follow your teacher's instructions for additional practice with the material in the lesson.

Names and addresses for all letters are included in the Appendix.

Miss Angela Brown d Miss B:

r co s cns g prl s g a nu cmputr sstm, n e wd lik l h u hlp n slcl g t prpr l.

e h b n bus onl a fu yrs, bl r org h gron rpdl. e now h a gral mny wkrs, n r parol ofc s h g dfclly n dg t rqrd wk n fil g t ncsry rpls w t gvrnm. a lsl o t rpls e msl fil s encd.

wd l b psb f smon fm u org l vsl r ofc sn l hlp us evlual r pr sstm n mak rcmndas cncrn g r neds?

e lk fwrd l her g fm u.

v s u

encr

, compound
sentence

, compound
sentence

, compound
sentence

**Goal: 1 minute, 10 seconds (110 words per minute)**

(Word counts begin with the first word of the first paragraph.)

Miss Angela Brown
Dear Miss Brown:

/Our company is considering purchasing a new computer system, and we would like to have your help in/selecting the proper one.

We have been in business only a few years, but our organization has grown/rapidly. We now have a great many workers, and our payroll office is having difficulty in doing the/ required work and filing the necessary reports with the government. A list of the reports we must file is/enclosed.

Would it be possible for someone from your organization to visit our office soon to help us/evaluate our present system and make recommendations concerning our needs?

We look forward to hearing/from you. Very sincerely yours, Enclosure (126)

, compound
sentence

*prblm qkl afl e h cmpd ts xmnas.*

*, compound sentence*

*e ap u pasc n ts mlr, n e prms blr srvc n t fulr. a cpy o r cab gid f nxl mo s encd.*

*u l*

*encr*

---

Mr. William Beatty
Dear Mr. Beatty:

/Thanks for your letter telling us of the trouble you have had in getting proper cable television reception/in your home. We have looked into the matter, but we have not yet determined the source of the trouble.

We will/send a person to your home within the next week to examine the cable both inside and outside your house. We/believe that we will be able to correct the problem quickly after we have completed this examination./

We appreciate your patience in this matter, and we promise better service in the future. A copy/of our cable guide for next month is enclosed. Yours truly, Enclosure (109)

Mrs Emma Bentley   d Mrs B:

u lr ask g f info abl t
ps& e h opn n prsnl arivd
ts mrn g. e r hpy l cns
u an aplcnl f ts ps&.

e ned a capb prsn hu h
hd xperenc wk g n prsnl.
t jb l incl suprvis g svrl
pep s wl s hndl g t prsnl
wk f t co. t slry s opn, n
e r ab l pa a cmpllv ral.

encd s t info u rgsld abl
r co. also encd s an apl
blnk f u l fl ol n rlrn l
us l u cnv.

v s u

encrs

, compound
sentence

## DOCUMENT 21-3

Mrs. Emma Bentley
Dear Mrs. Bentley:

/Your letter asking for information about the position we have open in personnel arrived this/morning. We are happy to consider you an applicant for this position.

We need a capable person who/has had experience working in personnel. The job will include supervising several people as well/as handling the personnel work for the company. The salary is open, and we are able to pay a/competitive rate.

Enclosed is the information you requested about our company. Also enclosed is/an application blank for you to fill out and return to us at your convenience. Very sincerely yours,/Enclosures (121)

## DOCUMENT 21-4                                         *Punctuation Check*

*Keyboarding Goal: 17 minutes (10 words per minute)*

Mr Lee Lopez          d Mr L:

abt a yr ago r co bgn slg alo lirs. e blevd tl tr w a ned f sL a srvc n ts cmun l bl e nvr tl e wd d sL a lrg aml o bus n jsl a yr.

r fin lirs n r dscount prics h mad us t hdqrtrs f lir sals bl l s r loyl cstmrs hu h mad us t most ppulr lir stor n t area.

e wnt l xprs r sncer apS l r mny frnds b ofrg t lrgst slcS o fin lirs l t lost prics o t yr.

(continued)

*r frsl anul lir sal bgns nxl mo n e l b ofr g rmrkb vlus on al maks n sizs o lirs. u l b ab l prls t bsl lirs on t mrkl l xlreml lo prics. cm n l se us durg t sal. e no u l b gld u dd. s u*

**Keyboarding Goal: 17 minutes (10 words per minute)**

Internal punctuation is included, and the reason for using the punctuation is given in parentheses. (Reasons are not included in the word counts.)

Mr. Lee Lopez
Dear Mr. Lopez:

/About a year ago our company began selling auto tires. We believed that there was a need for such a/service in this community, but (*compound sentence*) we never thought we would do such a large amount of business in just a year./

Our fine tires and our discount prices have made us the headquarters for tire sales, but (*compound sentence*) it is our loyal customers who/have made us the most popular tire store in the area.

We want to express our sincere appreciation/to our many friends by offering the largest selection of fine tires at the lowest prices of the year. Our/first annual tire sale begins next month, and (*compound sentence*) we will be offering remarkable values on all makes and/ sizes of tires. You will be able to purchase the best tires on the market at extremely low prices. Come in to/see us during the sale. We know you will be glad you did. Sincerely yours, (150)

# SUPPLEMENTARY ACTIVITY

## A Word to the Wise

Estimating the Length of a Document

/You must learn to estimate the length of a document when you wish to transcribe your *SuperWrite* notes. Your notes are/probably not the same size as the notes in the text. One person will write larger or smaller notes than another,/and each person must learn to estimate the length of his or her own notes.

At the beginning you will not know just/how much space your *SuperWrite* notes will require when they are typed, but you will soon learn to estimate the length of a/document by the amount of space the notes take in your notebook.

The number of words contained in each document/in this text is included in the key. This will help you to place the textbook letters properly on the page. But/you will have to estimate strictly from the length of your notes when you take dictation from material that is/not in the text.

Notice how much space a letter of average length takes in your notebook, and then follow the suggested/placement scale shown in this lesson. Follow the same plan for a long letter and a short letter. You will soon be/able to estimate the correct placement of your letters with considerable accuracy. (198)

# LESSON 22

## *SuperWrite REVIEW*

Read the following words, referring to the key if necessary. Then copy the words in your own notebook.

**Abbreviations**

1. *h hr hw imp incl enc*
2. *info ins inl s le lr*
3. *mgl mgr mo m no r*

**Word Beginning De-**

4. *dsin dprs dlvr dcres dplel ddcl*

**Word Ending -ing**

5. *se g sav g her g lkg wkg mel g*

**Key**

1. has, have; hour; how; importance, important; include; enclose
2. information; insurance; interest; as, is; let; letter
3. management; manager; month; am, more; number; are, or, our
4. design; depress; deliver; decrease; deplete; deduct
5. seeing; saving; hearing; talking; working; meeting

# KEYBOARDING STYLE

## Numbers

In keyboarding business letters, numbers <u>one</u> through <u>ten</u> are written in words; <u>11</u> and above are written in figures.

*tr r 3 nu prnlrs.*

There are three new printers.

*e odd 20 nu rbns f t prnlrs.*

We ordered 20 new ribbons for the printers.

Spell out a number that begins a sentence.

*2 ofcrs alndd t mel g.*

Two officers attended the meeting.

Numbers in a Set

Use figures for related numbers in a set.

*e bl 2 prnlrs, 1 h rbns, n 1 t dsks.*

We bought 2 printers, 100 ribbons, and 1,000 disks.

Use figures and words for rounded millions, billions, etc.

*t ppula$ o t cly s abl 3 m.*

The population of the city is about 3 million.

# PUNCTUATION

## Geographic Expressions

Use a comma in a geographic expression to separate a city from a state.

*Wilmington, DE*

Wilmington, Delaware

(continued)

## PUNCTUATION *continued*

If the state name does not end the sentence, use a comma after it also.

*Se lvs n Detroit, MI, wr Se w brn.*

She lives in Detroit, Michigan, where she was born.

In the Application, the use of the comma in geographic expressions will be noted in the margin of the *SuperWrite* document as follows:

, geographic

*e flu l Baltimore, MD, n tn l Charlotte.*

We flew to Baltimore, Maryland, and then
to Charlotte.

## SPELLING

Beginning with Lesson 22, each lesson contains a number of words that sometimes cause spelling difficulties. Practice spelling each group of words in the following way:

Pronounce and spell each word aloud; then copy it in longhand in your own notebook, being sure that you spell it correctly. When you read the Application section of the lesson, watch for these words.

associates
attempt
catalog
clients
excellent
inheritance
liquidate
microcomputer
probate
received

## APPLICATION

The Application section of this lesson contains four business letters. Follow the same pattern you used in Lesson 21.

1. **Read.**  First read the documents. If you have difficulty reading a word, refer to the key that follows. As you read, watch for the spelling words and the uses of punctuation marks. Time your reading with Document 1, the Timed Reading; try to meet the suggested goal.

2. **Write.** After you have read the material, make one complete copy of it in *SuperWrite* in your own notebook.

Build your writing speed with Document 2, the Speed Builder; follow your teacher's instructions to boost writing speed.

Internal punctuation is not included in Document 22-4, the Punctuation Check. Remember to insert the proper marks of punctuation in this document as you copy it. The punctuation marks and the reasons for using them are included in the key.

3. **Type.** Type the last letter, Document 22-4, from your own notes in the format shown in Lesson 21. Note the number of words contained in the body of the letter, and be sure to place the letter properly on the page. Try to meet the keyboarding time goal shown at the top of the document.

4. Follow your teacher's instructions for additional work with the material in this lesson.

A complete list of names and addresses is included in the Appendix.

## DOCUMENT 22-1 *Timed Reading*

**Goal: 1 minute, 13 seconds (110 words per minute)**

Ms Maxine Graves  d Ms G:

e r dlild l no tl u l b join g t slf o r org sn. u h mad a wis dcs, n I no tl u l njoy wk g her n tl u l d n xclnl jb.

e r v proud o r rcrd l r co. e h b n bus n Columbia, SC, onl 5 yrs, bt e h gron qil rpdl. e now h 25 sals asocals n m tn 2t clints.

, compound sentence

, geographic

, compound sentence

(continued)

*[shorthand text]*

e fel Sr tt u l b ab l hlp us ncres r no o cslmrs. tr r m tn 1 m prspclv clints wn a radus o 1 h mils. tr s ntng ftr f u l d ull u rpl f wk. tr l b a no o ilms tl u l ned l tak cr o on t da u bgn wk.

e lk fwrd l se g u.

v s u

**Timed Reading**

**Goal: 1 minute, 13 seconds (110 words per minute)**

Ms. Maxine Graves
Dear Ms. Graves:

/We are delighted to know that you will be joining the staff of our organization soon. You have made a wise/decision, and I know that you will enjoy working here and that you will do an excellent job.

We are very proud/of our record at our company. We have been in business in Columbia, South Carolina, only five/years, but we have grown quite rapidly. We now have 25 sales associates and more than 2,000 clients./We feel sure that you will be able to help us increase our number of customers. There are more than 1 million/prospective clients within a radius of 100 miles.

There is nothing further for you to do/until you report for work. There will be a number of items that you will need to take care of on the day you/begin work.

We look forward to seeing you. Very sincerely yours. (151)

*Micro Supply Co     l n g:*

*pl snd us 5 h no 24 microcmpulr prnlr rbns. Crg t rbns l r acounl, n dlvr tm l r Dayton, OH, ofc s sn s psb. e l pa f tm wn 30 das afl e rec u slm n od l lak advnlg o t dscounl f prmpl pam.*

*pl snd us a cpy o u lalsl splis cllg, n plac r nam on u lsl f al sC mlerals n t fulr. e pln l d a gral del o bus b mal w u org.*

*e lk fwrd l recg r od sn.*

*C*

*, compound sentence*

*, geographic*

*, compound sentence*

Micro Supply Company
Ladies and Gentlemen:

/Please send us 500 Number 24 microcomputer printer ribbons. Charge the ribbons to our account,/and deliver them to our Dayton, Ohio, office as soon as possible. We will pay for them within 30/days after we receive your statement in order to take advantage of the discount for prompt payment.

Please send us/a copy of your latest supplies catalog, and place our name on your list for all such materials in/the future. We plan to do a great deal of business by mail with your organization.

We look forward to/receiving our order soon. Cordially, (105)

Mrs Carla Hastings    d Mrs H:

encd s a lr I recd fm John Crawford lsl wk. J s ask g f legl advic cncrn g an nhrlnc fm hs ftr.

Mark C did abl 2 mos ago n Atlanta, GA, n lfl sm prprly l J tru a hndrln l.

J wd lik l avoid prbal bcs o t sml siz o t eslal, bl tr r 3 r 4 otr pep hu mil clam a prl o t eslal.

wd u advis J l almpl l lqdal t eslal wol prbal, r wd u sg tl t l b prbald dspil ls siz?

Martha Warren

encr

, compound sentence

, geographic

, compound sentence

, compound sentence

Mrs. Carla Hastings
Dear Mrs. Hastings:

/Enclosed is a letter I received from John Crawford last week. John is asking for legal advice concerning an/inheritance from his father.

Mark Crawford died about two months ago in Atlanta, Georgia, and left some/property to John through a handwritten will.

John would like to avoid probate because of the small size of the estate,/but there are three or four other people who might claim a part of the estate.

Would you advise John to attempt to/liquidate the estate without probate, or would you suggest that the will be probated despite its size? Martha/Warren Enclosure (103)

## DOCUMENT 22-4        *Punctuation Check*

*Keyboarding Goal: 14 minutes (10 words per minute)*

Mr N L Maxwell      d Mr M:

3 mos ago I odd 5 h wCs f rsal l my stors n Cleveland OH bt t wCs h nt yt b dlvrd. a cpy o my od s encd. I h rtn l u co svrl tms bt I h nt recd an ansr cncrng ts imp od.

my prvus ods h alwas b dlvrd prmptl n I h pd my bls on tm. I d nt Ustnd wy l s takg so lng f u l cmp ts Jacs.

(continued)

*my co dpnds on prmpt dlvry o gds fm splirs n qk trnO o stk. pl cncl t od if u cnl mak dlvry wn 10 t 12 das.*

*u t*

*encr*

## DOCUMENT 22-4                    Punctuation Check

### Keyboarding Goal: 14 minutes (10 words per minute)

Mr. N. L. Maxwell
Dear Mr. Maxwell:

/Three months ago I ordered 500 watches for resale at my stores in Cleveland, Ohio, (*geographic-compound sentence*) but the watches/have not yet been delivered. A copy of my order is enclosed. I have written to your company/several times, but (*compound sentence*) I have not received an answer concerning this important order.

My previous orders have/always been delivered promptly, and (*compound sentence*) I have paid my bills on time. I do not understand why it is taking so long/for you to complete this transaction.

My company depends on prompt delivery of goods from suppliers and quick/turnover of stock. Please cancel the order if you cannot make delivery within 10 to 12 days. Yours truly,/    Enclosure (122)

# SUPPLEMENTARY ACTIVITY

## A Word to the Wise

### Proper Writing Materials

/*SuperWrite* may be written in a notebook of almost any design. Some people like to use a stenography/notebook. This small notebook is bound at the top with a spiral. The size makes it easy to carry to meetings,/and the binding makes it easy to turn quickly to a new page.

A pen is usually better than a/pencil for writing because of legibility. Notes written with a pen containing black or dark blue ink are/usually much easier to read than pencil notes. This is particularly true if you need to read them days/or even weeks later.

Your writing instrument must be dependable. Choose a pen that writes easily and does/not skip. A pen that smudges will decrease legibility, and you may get ink stains on your hands and clothing. Good/pens need not be expensive. Take some time to choose a pen that you can use easily, and keep several/available at all times.

Good writing materials are essential to good work. Choose the proper materials, and/ use them correctly. (184)

# *LESSON 23*

## SuperWrite REVIEW

Read the following words, referring to the key if necessary. Then copy the words in your own notebook.

**Abbreviations**

1. *rgd rpl rep rqr rsp sn*
2. *sl sls sg sgs tk tks*
3. *t ty tm v w e*

**Word Beginning In-**

4. *nded ncres nsid ncdnt nclin ncm*

**Word Ending -ly**

5. *onl manl cml slol hpl stdl*

**Key**

1.  regard; report; represent, representative; require; responsible; soon
2.  state, street; states, streets; suggest, suggestion; suggests, suggestions; thank; thanks
3.  the; they; time; very; was, were, with; we
4.  indeed; increase; inside; incident; incline; income
5.  only; mainly; calmly; slowly; happily; steadily

# KEYBOARDING STYLE

## Dates

Type a date in month-day order.

January 4

Note that a cardinal number (4, not 4th) is used.

When the year is included, place a comma between the day and the year.

*t dal w July 4, 1776.*

The date was July 4, 1776.

If the year does not end the sentence, place a comma after the year also.

*Oct 12, 1976, w t da r bus opnd.*

October 12, 1976, was the day our business opened.

If both the day of the week and the day of the month are included, separate them with a comma.

*he lfl on Fri, May 3.*

He left on Friday, May 3.

When a comma is used in a date in the Application, it will be shown in the margin as follows:

, date

*t dal w Wed, June 7, 1989.*

The date was Wednesday, June 7, 1989.

# PUNCTUATION

## Introductory Elements

Use a comma after an introductory element if it improves the clarity of the sentence.

---

Introductory Word

*obvusl, se s t prsn f t jb.*

Obviously, she is the person for the job.

Introductory Phrase

*on t otr hnd, e ned a nu prntr now.*

On the other hand, we need a new printer now.

Introductory Clause

*s u prbl no, t co s no lngr n bus.*

As you probably know, the company is no longer in business.

If the clarity is not improved, do not use a comma.

*l hom I us my on wrd prcsr.*

At home I use my own word processor.

When introductory elements appear in the Application, they will be marked as follows:

, introductory    *s u no, e jsl bl a nu cr.*

As you know, we just bought a new car.

## SPELLING

Here are additional spelling words. Pronounce and spell each word aloud; then copy it in your own notebook, being sure that you spell it correctly. When you read the Application section of the lesson, watch for these words.

assured
atmosphere
banquet
buffet
disrepair
interruption
occasionally
peace
postponed
separate

## APPLICATION

Time your reading speed with Document 1 before reading the remaining documents. Write each document. Remember to insert the needed punctuation in Document 4 before typing it in the correct format. Be sure to note the length of the document and place it properly on the page.

Dr A B Ellis          d Dr E:

, date

   u l rmbr tl on Tues, Apr 3, u prCsd a nu prnlr fm / o t reps o r co n Portland, OR. e

, geographic

r Sr tl u r njoy g ts fin nu prnlr n tl u r ql g xclnl srvc fm l.

   u c b aSrd tl u l h mny yrs o cnlnud srvc fm ts prnlr. hwev, l l ocaSll rqr srvc. r co pvds a nu srvc

, introductory

tl e blev u l find inl g nded.

   e l snd a srvc rep l u ofc ev 3 mos l mak Sr tl u prnlr wks prprl l al lms. if u prnlr Sd ned srvc tl e r uab l pvd l u ofc, e l pvd

, introductory

a smlr prntr wil us s awa
fm u ofc. evn if u h no
prblms, onc a yr e l brng
t prntr l r srvc Sp n
nspcl l nsid n ot.

, introductory

t csl o ts srvc s srpris gl
lo. f onl pnes a da, u c h t
pec o mind tl cms w no g
tl u prntr l opral f mny
yrs wot Nrps.

, introductory

f ftr info abl r srvc plces,
jsl cl us. 1 o r reps l b hpy

, introductory

l xplan r plces n dlal, n
tr l b no oblgas.

, compound sentence

rmbr r co wn u ned dpndb
srvc. e h b n bus n Psnc
Feb 1, 1980.

, date

s u

**Goal: 2 minutes, 24 seconds (110 words per minute)**

Dr. A. B. Ellis
Dear Dr. Ellis:

/You will remember that on Tuesday, April 3, you purchased a new printer from one of the representatives/of our company in Portland, Oregon. We are sure that you are enjoying this fine new printer and that you/are getting excellent service from it.

You can be assured that you will have many years of continued service/from this printer. However, it will occasionally require service. Our company provides a new service/that we believe you will find interesting indeed.

We will send a service representative to your office/every three months to make sure that your printer works properly at all times. If your printer should need service that we/are unable to provide at your office, we will provide a similar printer while yours is away from your/office. Even if you have no problems, once a year we will bring the printer to our service shop and inspect it/inside and out.

The cost of this service is surprisingly low. For only pennies a day, you can have the peace/of mind that comes with knowing that your printer will operate for many years without interruption.

For further/information about our service policies, just call us. One of our representatives will be happy to/explain our policies in detail, and there will be no obligation.

Remember our company when you need/dependable service. We have been in business in Portland since February 1, 1980. Sincerely yours,/(260)

, introductory

, date

, geographic

, compound sentence

, compound sentence

*[shorthand text]*

C

Ms. Olivia Joyce

Dear Ms. Joyce:

/It was indeed nice to know that you would welcome suggestions for improving the service at our annual awards/banquet. I believe that a seated banquet would be much better for our organization. The atmosphere/created by five separate buffet lines detracts from the dignity of the evening.

As I mentioned earlier,/ I have been attending similar annual banquets since July 12, 1986, in Richmond, Virginia,/ and several other cities. This year the event in Richmond was held in a building that is only slightly/larger than ours, and it was a seated dinner. The atmosphere was quite good, and there seemed to be no trouble in/serving the 1,200 people.

Please give this suggestion serious consideration for next year./ I believe that it would improve the entire event. Cordially, (149)

Ms Martha Strong     d Ms S:

I rd n t locl nuspapr on

, date
Mon, Oct 6, tl t cly l bgn

, geographic
rpavg Broad sl her n Cranford,

MO, on Nov 1. I w nded hpy l

no tl t sl l b rpavd. l h b n

a sl o *dsrpr* f nerl a yr. t lsl

, date
rpavg w cmpd on Sept 30, 1985.

, introductory
hwevr, I w grall srprisd l

red abl ts dvm n t papr. s a

, introductory
mrCnl locald on B sl, I fel tl

I Sd h b cnslld abl t bsl lm

f ts majr wk. I cnlcld svrl

, compound
sentence
otr mrCnls on B sl, n nn o

tm w nolfid o t prjcl.

e al fel tl l wd b mC blr l

d ts wk durg a slk Spg sesn

rtr tn l ts lm. if t wk c b

, introductory
*poslpond* onl a fu mos, I m

*Sr tr l b mC ls dsrpS o bus.*
*I hop l her fm u sn.*
*vlu*

## DOCUMENT 23-3

Ms. Martha Strong
Dear Ms. Strong:

/I read in the local newspaper on Monday, October 6, that the city will begin repaving Broad Street/here in Cranford, Missouri, on November 1. I was indeed happy to know that the street will be repaved. It/has been in a state of disrepair for nearly a year. The last repaving was completed on September 30,/ 1985.

However, I was greatly surprised to read about this development in the paper./ As a merchant located on Broad Street, I feel that I should have been consulted about the best time for this/major work. I contacted several other merchants on Broad Street, and none of them were notified of the project./

We all feel that it would be much better to do this work during a slack shopping season rather than at this time./ If the work can be postponed only a few months, I am sure there will be much less disruption of business. I hope/to hear from you soon. Very truly yours, (165) cntrl arlins                    l n g:

on Thurs Nov 20 I flu fm Dallas TX l Los Angeles CA on u arlin. I hd plnd t lrp f m tn a mo n I hd a cnfrmd rsrvaS. l w mad b fon Oct 15. uftnll I dd nl pk up t lkl.

wn I arivd l t ar lrmnl I w told tl t arlin hd no rcrd o my rsrvaS. tr w no av sels bl I w placd on t slndby lsl. l t lsl mnl I w alowd l bord. hwev e wald m tn an hr nsid t plan bf l lfl t lrmnl.

t srvc I recd hrdl reps wl u prms tru u advrlis g. I sncerl hop tl u l mak ev efl l mpruv u srvc n t fulr.

u l

**Keyboarding Goal: 12 minutes (12 words per minute)**

Central Airlines

Ladies and Gentlemen:

/On Thursday, November 20, *(date)* I flew from Dallas, Texas, *(geographic)* to Los Angeles, California, *(geographic)* on your airline./ I had planned the trip for more than a month, and *(compound sentence)* I had a confirmed reservation. It was made by phone October/15. Unfortunately, *(introductory)* I did not pick up the ticket.

When I arrived at the air terminal, *(introductory)* I was told/that the airline had no record of my reservation. There were no available seats, but *(compound sentence)* I was placed on the/standby list. At the last minute I was allowed to board. However, *(introductory)* we waited more than an hour inside the plane/before it left the terminal.

The service I received hardly represents what you promise through your advertising./ I sincerely hope you will make every effort to improve your service in the future.

Yours truly, (133)


# SUPPLEMENTARY ACTIVITY


## A Word to the Wise

Writing Fluency

/Before you begin to take notes, be sure that you have an ample supply of paper and several good pens. If/you should run out of paper or ink, you could inconvenience your employer and others as well. They might have to/wait while you locate additional supplies, and this would put you in a very bad position.

Try to arrange/your materials so that you will have a large flat surface on which to write. If you have a comfortable/writing surface, you will probably take good notes.

As you take notes in *SuperWrite,* write as fluently and/effortlessly as possible. Write all the way across the page, and do not alter your regular writing style. Write as large/or as small as you wish. The size of your notes has very little to do with either speed or legibility./

As you take notes from dictation, write as quickly as necessary. When dictation is rapid, write as quickly/as possible. When dictation is slow, take time to form your letters carefully.

If you have waiting time while you/are taking dictation, look over your notes. Make any corrections or clarifications that are needed.

Use/your dictation time well to produce notes that are easily transcribed. (212)

# *LESSON 24*

## *SuperWrite REVIEW*

Read the following words, referring to the key if necessary. Then copy them in your own notebook.

**Abbreviations**

1. *cnv cns cv depl dv d*
2. *mpl enc ev exec f fm*
3. *r od org ot pd rqr*

**Word Beginning Re-**

4. *rman rtrct rgrup rtir rmuv rlat*

**Word Ending -ment**

5. *trelm pam cm stm grm ncrgm*

**Key**

1. convenience, convenient; consider, consideration; cover; department; develop; do
2. employ; enclose; ever, every; executive; for; from
3. are, or, our; order; organization, organize; out; paid; require
4. remain; retract; regroup; retire; remove; relate
5. treatment; payment; comment; statement; garment; encouragement

## KEYBOARDING STYLE

### Time

Use figures to express time. Separate the hour from the minutes with a colon. Type <u>a.m.</u> or <u>p.m.</u> in small letters with no internal space.

9:25 a.m.                    7:45 p.m.

*t mel g l bgn l 10:30 a m n cnclud l 4:30 p m.*

The meeting will begin at 10:30 a.m. and conclude at 4:30 p.m.

For time on the hour, do not use a colon and zeros.

10 a.m.                    6 p.m.

*t ofc opns l 10 a m.*

The office opens at 10 a.m.

If <u>a.m.</u> or <u>p.m.</u> is not used, use words rather than figures.

*e r opn fm 10 n t mrn g ull 5 n t aflnun.*

We are open from ten in the morning until five in the afternoon.

# PUNCTUATION

## Elements in a Series

Use commas to separate words, phrases, or clauses in a series. Use a comma between the first two (or more) elements as well as before the conjunction.

**Words**

*e pd f rnl, ful, n ins.*

We paid for rent, fuel, and insurance.

**Phrases**

*e wnl l t stor, l t muve, n l t rstrnt.*

We went to the store, to the movie, and to the restaurant.

**Clauses**

*he rd svrl bks, mad cmprhnsv nols, n rol a gd papr.*

He read several books, made comprehensive notes, and wrote a good paper.

When elements in a series occur in the Application, they will be marked in the margin as shown here:

, series        *e ned papr, pncls, n pns.*

We need paper, pencils, and pens.

## SPELLING

Here are additional spelling words. Pronounce and spell each word aloud; then copy it in your own notebook, being sure that you spell it correctly. When you read the Application section of the lesson, watch for these words.

appeared
attorney
congratulations
bulletin
easement
equipment
library
piece
replacement
retract

## APPLICATION

Time your reading speed with Document 1 before reading the remaining documents. Then write all four documents. Remember to insert the necessary punctuation in Document 4 before typing it in the correct format. Be sure to note the length of the document and place it properly on the page.

## DOCUMENT 24-1                                    *Timed Reading*

**Goal: 1 minute, 34 seconds (110 words per minute)**

, date

, series

*Mrs Madeline Melton   d Mrs M: cngrlulass on t prcs o t nu llfon sstm tl e nslld n u ofc on Mon, Feb 5. e no tl u, u mples, n u cstmrs l b v pld w t sstm. e h nslld m tn 1 t sC sstms n ofcs dur g*

(continued)

, compound
sentence

, introductory

, introductory

, introductory

, series

t psl 2 yrs, n r clints r al v hpy w tm.

u l h mny yrs o xclnt srvc fm t eqpm. if u Sd h ny prblm, e l mak t ncsry rpr qkl. if ny pec o eqpm msl b rmuvd fm u ofc f rpr, e l pvd a rplacm fre o Crg ull u h u on eqpm bk.

u mad a wis slcS wn u Cos r co. e pvd onl t bsl eqpm n qll srvc. Sd u ned r srvc, jsl cl us Mon, Wed, r Fri blwen 8:30 a m n 6 p m. on Tues n Thurs e r opn ull 9 p m.

cu

**Goal: 1 minute, 34 seconds (110 words per minute)**

Mrs. Madeline Melton
Dear Mrs. Melton:

/Congratulations on the purchase of the new telephone system that we installed in your office on Monday,/February 5. We know that you, your employees, and your customers will be very pleased with the system./We have installed more than 1,000 such systems in offices during the past two years, and our clients are all/very happy with them.

You will have many years of excellent service from the equipment. If you should have/ any problem, we will make the necessary repair quickly. If any piece of equipment must be removed from/ your office for repair, we will provide a replacement free of charge until you have your own equipment back.

You/made a wise selection when you chose our company. We provide only the best equipment and quality/service. Should you need our service, just call us Monday, Wednesday, or Friday between 8:30 a.m. and 6 p.m./ On Tuesday and Thursday we are open until 9 p.m. Cordially yours, (170)

*[Shorthand content]*

, introductory

, geographic

, series

, compound sentence

(continued)

, introductory

no prblm w typ g dcums r w pag laol. hwev, t ql l o prnl neds mpruvm.

encd s a drfl o a bltn prntd n r AZ ofc. pl rvu l l dlrmn wvl t trb cd b. I l cl u ofc blwen 9 am n 12 nun on

, date

Wed, Mar 6, l gl u cms. t mples n r AZ ofc wnl l mpruv t ql l o t wk bf ty rvis n prnl t finl bltn.

ul

encr

Mr. Harold Moore
Dear Mr. Moore

/As you know, last month we purchased four sets of electronic publishing software to use in our regional/offices. We had used one set of the materials successfully for the past three months in our main office in/Alexandria, Louisiana.

The three other sets were shipped to our offices in Texas, New Mexico,/and Arizona. Two of the sets have been working properly, but our people in Arizona are/having some trouble with the third set. There is no problem with typing documents or with page layout. However, the/quality of print needs improvement.

Enclosed is a draft of a bulletin printed in our Arizona office./Please review it to determine what the trouble could be. I will call your office between 9 a.m. and 12/noon on Wednesday, March 6, to get your comments. The employees in our Arizona office want to improve the/ quality of the work before they revise and print the final bulletin. Yours truly,     Enclosure (172)

Mr James R Potter     d Mr P:

, introductory

s u l rmbr, I prCsd 20 acrs

, geographic

o nvslm prprty ner Wheeling,

, date

WV, on Jan 7, 1988. u srvd s my

alrny l t clos g. l tl lm tr

w a ull l esm acrs 1 prl o t

, introductory

prprly. hwev, t esm w l b

rmuvd Srll afl clos g.

, compound sentence

I now h a byr f t prprly,

n I ned a slm tl t esm h b

rmuvd. alto I rol t prpr ofSls

, introductory

, series

n Mar, n Apr, n agn n May,

I h nl recd a slm.

, introductory

pl rvu t mlr n lry l gl a

slm f me. I l b hpy l pa wlev

fe s ncsry. if u ned l lk w

me, pl cl ny wkda mrn g

afl 9.

v s u

Mr. James R. Potter
Dear Mr. Potter:

/As you will remember, I purchased 20 acres of investment property near Wheeling, West Virginia, on/January 7, 1988. You served as my attorney at the closing. At that time there was a/utility easement across one part of the property. However, the easement was to be removed shortly/after closing.

I now have a buyer for the property, and I need a statement that the easement has been/ removed. Although I wrote to the proper officials in March, in April, and again in May, I have not received a/statement.

Please review the matter and try to get a statement for me. I will be happy to pay whatever fee/is necessary. If you need to talk with me, please call any weekday morning after nine. Very sincerely/yours, (141)

## DOCUMENT 24-4                                    *Punctuation Check*

**Keyboarding Goal: 14 minutes (12 words per minute)**

*Miss Rita Jones          d Miss J:
t nxl mel g o r bus asocas l b
hld on Tues Apr 4 l 3 p m n t clg
librry n Bangor ME. l ts imp mel g
e l her a rpl fm t exec cmle on plns
f t cm g yr. n ads tr l b rpls fm
t bgl cmle t Nlanm cmle n t prjcls
cmle.*

*s u no e h b qil cncrnd abl a slm tl aperd rcnll n t clg nuspapr. t slm qd t acurcy o r fnnSl rpls. e h askd t papr l rlrd t slm n e l dscs ny ftr acS e Sd lak l t mel g.*

*l s o gral imp tl al mbrs alnd ts mel g. if u cnl alnd pl le me no s sn s psb.*

*v l u*

---

**Keyboarding Goal: 14 minutes (12 words per minute)**

Miss Rita Jones
Dear Miss Jones:

/The next meeting of our business association will be held on Tuesday, April 4, *(date)* at 3 p.m. in the/college library in Bangor, Maine. *(geographic)* At this important meeting we will hear a report from the executive/committee on plans for the coming year. In addition, *(introductory)* there will be reports from the budget committee, the/entertainment committee, and the projects committee. *(series)*

As you know, *(introductory)* we have been quite concerned about a statement that/ appeared recently in the college newspaper. The statement questioned the accuracy of our financial/reports. We have asked the paper to retract the statement, and *(compound sentence)* we will discuss any further action we should take at/the meeting.

It is of great importance that all members attend this meeting. If you cannot attend, *(introductory)* please let me/know as soon as possible. Very truly yours (146)

# SUPPLEMENTARY ACTIVITY

## A Word to the Wise

Reading and Writing

/Here are some reminders that will help you in reading and writing *SuperWrite.*

Always read your textbook assignment/before writing it. Read in thought units. Read a phrase, a clause, or a sentence. As you read, look for the meaning. If/a sentence does not seem to make sense, read it again. If you still do not understand, refer to the key.

If you/have trouble reading a particular word, spell it in *SuperWrite.* If you are still not able to read the word,/refer to the key.

When you are writing a document from the text, during dictation keep the book open and/refer to it if you need help.

If you have trouble with a word during dictation of new material, either/look up the spelling in your *SuperWrite* Dictionary or ask your teacher to write it for you when there is/time.

You should label each document clearly so that you will be able to find it quickly if you need to do/so. It is a good idea to leave a few blank lines before starting a new document in your notebook. In/addition, you should date each page so that you can quickly locate the material that you wrote on a certain date./(200)

# LESSON 25

## *SuperWrite REVIEW*

Read the following words, referring to the key if necessary. Then copy them in your own notebook.

**Abbreviations**

1. *pl pr pgm pvd q rec*
2. *wk wks C l lg ls*
3. *b brn buss c co cmp*

**Word Beginning Em-**

4. *mpir mbrs mbrk mblm mfsiz mfss*

**Word Ending -ful**

5. *crf wndrf hlpf brlf hopf af*

**Key**

1. please; present; program; provide; question; receive
2. week, work; weeks, works; which; will; willing; wills
3. be, been, by; business; businesses; can; company; complete
4. empire; embarrass; embark; emblem; emphasize; emphasis
5. careful; wonderful; helpful; beautiful; hopeful; awful

# KEYBOARDING STYLE

## Money

Write amounts of money in figures.

$5.25                  $80

*t lkls csl $35 eC.*

The tickets cost $35 each.

Write round amounts of money of a million or higher in figures and words.

$25 million        $9.5 billion        $2.1 trillion

*t bldg csl $25 m.*

The building cost $25 million.

However, write related numbers in a set in the same form.

*t bgl o $8 m incld $3 h t f manlnnc.*

The budget of $8,000,000 included $300,000 for maintenance.


# PUNCTUATION

## Extra and Vital Information

A word, a phrase, or a clause that is not necessary to the meaning of a sentences is considered extra information.

Use commas to set off extra information.

Extra Word

*l s, hwev, u rspl.*

It is, however, your responsibility.

The word is not necessary to the meaning of the sentence; it is extra information.

**Extra Phrase**

*I feel, of course, that you should go.* (shorthand)

I feel, of course, that you should go.

The phrase is not necessary to the meaning of the sentence; it is extra information.

*Please call me, Mr. Leith, if you need help.* (shorthand)

Please call me, Mr. Leith, if you need help.

Giving the name of the person to whom you are writing is not necessary to the meaning of the sentence; it is extra information.

*Joanna Singleton, my friend, is on vacation.* (shorthand)

Joanna Singleton, my friend, is on vacation.

The phrase is not necessary to identify Joanna Singleton; it is extra information.

**Extra Clause**

*Max Langford, who joined our firm last month, is a good worker.* (shorthand)

Max Langford, who joined our firm last month,
is a good worker.

The clause is not necessary to identify Max Langford; it is extra information.

If the element is necessary to the meaning of the sentence, it is considered vital.

Do not set off vital information with commas.

**Vital Word**

*The word therefore must be included.* (shorthand)

The word therefore must be included.

The word is vital to the meaning of the sentence.

(continued)

## PUNCTUATION *continued*

Vital Phrase

*l s a mlr o cors.*

It is a matter of course.

The phrase is vital to the meaning of the sentence.

Vital Clause

*t prsn hu joind r frm lsl mo s a
gd wkr.*

The person who joined our firm last month is a
good worker.

The phrase is vital; it identifies which person.

*Joe Smith my nabr s her; Joe
Smith t flbl plar s nl.*

Joe Smith my neighbor is here; Joe
Smith the football player is not.

The phrases are vital; they identify which person named Joe Smith.

In the Application, extra elements will be shown in the margin as follows:

, extra        *I l, nvrtls, cl hm.*

        I will, nevertheless, call him.

## SPELLING

Here are additional spelling words. Pronounce and spell each word aloud; then copy it in your own notebook, being sure that you spell it correctly. When you read the Application section of the lesson, watch for these words.

accept
accumulate
assigned
deposit
embarrassing
explanation
financial
percentage
restaurant
specified

## APPLICATION

Time your reading speed with Document 1 before reading the remaining documents. Then write all four documents. Remember to insert the needed punctuation in Document 4 before typing it in the correct format. Be sure to note the length of the document and place it properly on the page.

## DOCUMENT 25-1                                    *Timed Reading*

**Goal: 2 minutes, 7 seconds (110 words per minute)**

*Mr Lawrence Leith        d Mr L:*
*tks f u nqiry cncrn g a*
*rlirm pln f slf-mpld prsns.*
*r bnk ofrs a no o plns tl*
*qlfy U pr fdrl gvrnm gidlins.*
*U / o r plns, u ma b ab l sl*

, introductory

(continued)

, series

asid $10t, $20t, r evn $30t f u rlirm.

, introductory

afl u h dcidd on a pln, u ma dpsl a spcfid prcnlg o u nl ncm eC yr. I msl mfsiz tl t inl ernd on ts mny l acumulal fre o al lxs ull l s wdrn dur g u rlirm yrs. u l pa lx l u ral

, extra

l tl lm, C l prbbl b mC ls tn u crnl ral. ts reps a v powrf wa f u l sav f u fulr.

, introductory

n od l opn a pln, u msl apl f a fdrl mplm idnlfca$ no, C

, extra

u l us on al fms wil t pln s n fc.

, introductory

l dlrmn t rcl aml o u yrl cnlrbu$, u $d cnfr w a fnn$l counslr hu s skld n lx la.

, extra

*pl le us no, Mr L, if e c b o ftr hlp l u s u mbrk on u nu pln l sav f u futr. e wd b dlild l opn 1 o r wndrf rtirm plns f u.*

*c u*

## DOCUMENT 25-1                    *Timed Reading*

**Goal: 2 minutes, 7 seconds (110 words per minute)**

Mr. Lawrence Leith
Dear Mr. Leith:

/Thanks for your inquiry concerning a retirement plan for self-employed persons. Our bank offers a number of/plans that qualify under present federal government guidelines. Under one of our plans, you may be able/to set aside $10,000, $20,000, or even $30,000 for your retirement./

After you have decided on a plan, you may deposit a specified percentage of your net income/each year. I must emphasize that the interest earned on this money will accumulate free of all taxes until/it is withdrawn during your retirement years. You will pay tax at your rate at that time, which will probably be much/less than your current rate. This represents a very powerful way for you to save for your future.

In order to/open a plan, you must apply for a federal employment identification number, which you will use on/all forms while the plan is in force.

To determine the exact amount of your yearly contribution, you should/confer with a financial counselor who is skilled in tax law.

Please let us know, Mr. Leith, if we can be of/further help to you as you embark on your new plan to save for your future. We would be delighted to open one/of our wonderful retirement plans for you. Cordially yours, (228)

Mrs Dorothy Ray      d Mrs R:

, extra

ysrda I w spg n St Paul, C
s abl 1 h mils fm my hom. I
w acod b 2 gd frnds. afl a bsy

, introductory

mrn g, e slpd l u rsrnl f lnC.

, extra

wn Mr William Brown, t walr,

, introductory

brl t Ck, I prd my crdl crd.

, introductory

afl a fu mnls, he told me n
frnl o my frnds tl t crd cd
nl b accpld bcs I hd Ospnl

, introductory

my crdl lml. nedls l sa, ts
w xlreml mbrs g l me. I pd

, extra

t Ck, C amld l $75, w c$. I m,

, extra

hwev, qil upsl b t mcdnl.

, extra

lda I spok w Mr Albert Jones,
an ofcr o t crdl crd co. he vrfid
tl I hd nl xcedd t lml o $1 t,

, extra

C hd b asind l me. I m alwas

, compound
  sentence

qil crf w my fnncs, n I d nl

, introductory

, extra

*[handwritten shorthand/speedwriting text:]*

Uslnd wy t walr cd nt accpl t crd. ftrm, I cnl Uslnd wy I w treld n SC an uplsnl mnr. I h dind l u rstrnl f mny yrs, Mrs R, bcs u alwas srv wndrf fud. bl I m rlclnl l rlrn f fer o mbrsm. c u ofr an xplnas f ts ncdnl? u l

---

## DOCUMENT 25-2            *Speed Builder*

Mrs. Dorothy Ray
Dear Mrs. Ray:

/Yesterday I was shopping in Saint Paul, which is about 100 miles from my home. I was accompanied by/two good friends. After a busy morning, we stopped at your restaurant for lunch. When Mr. William Brown, the waiter, brought/the check, I presented my credit card. After a few minutes, he told me in front of my friends that the card could/not be accepted because I had overspent my credit limit. Needless to say, this was extremely embarrassing to me. I paid the check, which amounted to $75, with cash. I am, however, quite/upset by the incident.

Today I spoke with Mr. Albert Jones, an officer of the credit card company./He verified that I had not exceeded the limit of $1,000, which had been assigned to me. I/am always quite careful with my finances, and I do not understand why the waiter could not accept the card./Furthermore, I cannot understand why I was treated in such an unpleasant manner.

I have dined at your/restaurant for many years, Mrs. Ray, because you always serve wonderful food. But I am reluctant to return for/fear of embarrassment. Can you offer an explanation for this incident? Yours truly, (212)

Principal      d admnstratr:

on Jan 25, 1970, r co mbrkd on a nu bus. e opnd r frst stor n Little Rock, AR, n a rntd bldg w abt $20t n cpll. tr w 2 sals clrks, 1 scrtry, n 1 mgr. tl frst yr e dd abt $1 h t. n bus, C w almost twic t amt e hd prdctd. fm tn on, e xpndd rpdl.

lst yr, r co opnd nu stors n WA, OR, n WY. e now h m tn 3 h stors truot t US, n r yrl gros sals r O $9 h m. n t nxt 2 yrs, e xpct sals t reC $1 b.

t story o r bus s 1 o t tru sccs stores o amrcn fre Npris. e r now makg avl t al sculs n

, introductory

*clgs a fre bkll tl ollins t grot o r sccsf bus. if u wd lik l h cpes o t bkll f u scul, jsl ril us lda. e lk fwrd l herg fm u.*

*s u*

## DOCUMENT 25-3

Principal

Dear Administrator:

/On January 25, 1970, our company embarked on a new business. We opened our/first store in Little Rock, Arkansas, in a rented building with about $20,000 in capital./There were two sales clerks, one secretary, and one manager. That first year we did about $100,000/in business, which was almost twice the amount we had predicted. From then on, we expanded rapidly.

Last year, our company opened new stores in Washington, Oregon, and Wyoming. We now have more than 300/stores throughout the United States, and our yearly gross sales are over $900 million. In the next two/years, we expect sales to reach $1 billion.

The story of our business is one of the true success stories/of American free enterprise. We are now making available to all schools and colleges a free/booklet that outlines the growth of our successful business. If you would like to have copies of the booklet for your school,/just write us today. We look forward to hearing from you. Sincerely yours, (190)

Ms Yoko Nozaki                    d Ms N:

on Mon Dec 3 I vstd u fntr stor n Little Rock AR. I hd prCsd a butf nu sofa tr a fu wks bf n l hd b dlvrd onl a fu das erler.

wn t sofa w dlvrd I found tl t blu clr C I hd slctd v crfl w nt rit n my dn. t sofa C csl m tn $1 t w prCsd on sal. I asumd tl l cd nt b rlrnd.

I askd Mrs Ann Carter u sals rep if t sofa cd b r-cvd n a dfrnt mteral. hwev Se sgd tl I rlrn t sofa n slct anotr. I w v plsntl srprisd tl u wd accpt t sofa bk smpl bcs I hd Cosn t rng clr.

Mrs C w xtreml hlpf n mfsizd tl cstmr stsfc$ w t most imp prdct

*[Shorthand handwriting: o u org. lda t nu sofa arivd n t clr s prfcl.*

*tks l u co f pvdg sc hlpf srvc Ms N. u c b Sr tt I l rtrn l u stor wn I ned adSl fnlr.*

*v s u]*

---

**Keyboarding Goal: 14 minutes (14 words per minute)**

Ms. Yoko Nozaki
Dear Ms. Nozaki:

/On Monday, December 3, *(date)* I visited your furniture store in Little Rock, Arkansas. *(geographic)* I had purchased a/beautiful new sofa there a few weeks before, and *(compound sentence)* it had been delivered only a few days earlier.

When/the sofa was delivered, *(introductory)* I found that the blue color, which I had selected very carefully, *(extra)* was not right/in my den. The sofa, which cost more than $1,000, *(extra)* was purchased on sale. I assumed that it could not be/returned.

I asked Mrs. Ann Carter, your sales representative, *(extra)* if the sofa could be re-covered in a different/material. However, *(introductory)* she suggested that I return the sofa and select another. I was very/pleasantly surprised that you would accept the sofa back simply because I had chosen the wrong color.

Mrs. Carter/was extremely helpful and emphasized that customer satisfaction was the most important product of/your organization. Today the new sofa arrived, and *(compound sentence)* the color is perfect.

Thanks to your company for/providing such helpful service, Ms. Nozaki. *(extra)* You can be sure that I will return to your store when I need additional/furniture.
Very sincerely yours, (186)

# SUPPLEMENTARY ACTIVITY

## A Word to the Wise

Transcribing

/Keyboarding your notes is quite easy with *SuperWrite.* Many students find that it is much easier than typing/from longhand. Here are a few helpful transcribing hints. Always read your notes before transcribing them. This cannot be/overemphasized. When you read your notes, you will be able to correct any errors that were made. You will/also be able to look up the spelling of any words of which you are unsure. You will, in addition, be/able to verify any information that should be checked before the document is typed.

When you begin/typing, try to finish the document without any major interruptions. Your work will be easier if you/do not have to stop for an extended period of time.

Read phrases, clauses, or sentences and hold the words/in your mind as you type. Try to read ahead just a bit so that you understand what is coming next. You should not/type ahead of your reading, assuming you know the next few words. Often errors are made in this way.

As you/finish a document, draw a single diagonal line through the *SuperWrite* notes. When you look through your notebook, this/will tell you that you have transcribed that document. You will, however, still be able to read the notes if you need/to do so.

Read and transcribe for sensibility. When you have finished typing, check your work carefully to be/sure that it is accurate. (245)

# LESSON 26

## SuperWrite REVIEW

Read the following words, referring to the key if necessary. Then copy the words in your own notebook.

**Abbreviations**

1. *info ins inl s le lr*
2. *lrd lrs mgl mgls mgr mgrs*
3. *mo mos mol no nos nod*

**Word Beginning Ex-**

4. *xmn xprl xcl xperenc xrcis xsl*

**Word Ending -ing**

5. *rilg wkg tnkg redg meng mengf*

**Key**

1. information; insurance; interest; as, is; let; letter
2. lettered; letters; management; managements; manager; managers
3. month; months; monthly; number; numbers; numbered
4. examine; expert; exact; experience; exercise; exist
5. writing; working; thinking; reading; meaning; meaningful

# KEYBOARDING STYLE

## Capitalization

**Business organizations and institutions.** Capitalize the first word and other main words in the names of business organizations and institutions. However, watch for unique spellings and capitalization.

Jones and Company              The Silver Eagle Club

**Professional Titles.** Capitalize professional titles when they come before a name.

President M. L. Goodwin

Do not capitalize professional titles when they come after the name or when they appear alone.

*M L Goodwin, prsdnl o t clb, spok l t grup.*

M. L. Goodwin, president of the club, spoke to the group.

*t prsdnl cld t mel g l od.*

The president called the meeting to order.


# SPELLING

Here are additional spelling words. Pronounce and spell each word aloud; then copy it in your own notebook, being sure that you spell it correctly. When you read the Application section of the lesson, watch for these words.

access
assistance
assistants
calendar
copyright
deductible
registration
software
sponsored
useful

# VOCABULARY

The ability to use words effectively is important to all educated people. It is essential that you have a good knowledge of words and that you continue to expand your vocabulary. Each lesson beginning with Lesson 26 contains a vocabulary development section. Study the words as directed, and try to use them regularly.

Here is the first group of words. Study the definitions carefully, and notice how the words are used in the *SuperWrite* examples. Watch for these words in the Application section of the lesson.

access
: *Ability to obtain or make use of.*

*u l h accs l t pgms.*

You will have access to the programs.

deductible
: *Amount that is exempt; an insurance clause that relieves the insurer of responsibility for an initial specified loss.*

*if u Cus a $1 t ddclb, t ins co l nl pa f t frsl $1t o ny ls.*

If you choose a $1,000 deductible, the insurance company will not pay for the first $1,000 of any loss.

pre-existing
: *Existing before; occurring before.*

*t plcy ds nl cv ny pr-nsl g cnds.*

The policy does not cover any pre-existing condition.

prior
: *Earlier; preceding in time.*

*e lkd prir l t mel g.*

We talked prior to the meeting.

(continued)

public domain    *Status of a product not protected under copyright or patent.*

*t cmpulr pgm s n t pblc doman.*

The computer program is in the public domain.

## APPLICATION

Time your reading speed with Document 1 before reading the remaining documents. Then write all four documents. Remember to insert the needed punctuation in Document 4 before typing it in the correct format. Be sure to note the length of the document and place it properly on the page.

## DOCUMENT 26-1      *Timed Reading*

**Goal: 2 minutes, 3 seconds (120 words per minute)**

*Mr Milton Morgan     d Mr M:*

*r u inld n gl g usf cmpulr*

, introductory    *sflwr fre o Crg? if so, u l prbbl b inld n t sflwr xlang pgm spnsrd b cntrl clg.*

, introductory    *abt 2 yrs ago, Dr Jane Edwards,*

, extra    *prsdnt o cntrl clg, n a no o prfsrs l otr st clgs orgd a pgm f area clgs. n t agrem ec clg mad avl t ev otr clg al o ls*

, extra

sflwr tl w nt U cpyril, sflwr tl w n t pblc doman. ts pgm hlpd al t area clgs l xpnd tr librry o cmpulr sflwr.

t pgm s now b q xtndd l incl al sculs n t area. l N t pgm, al u ned d s fl ot t encd

, introductory

fm n rtrn l alng w u rgstra& fe o $50. tn u l h accs l al sflwr tl s av fm t ntwk. t onl

, extra

ad$l csl l b a mol srvc fe o $10, C s pab t frst o eC mo. a cpy o t crnl cllg s encd. an updald cllg splm o al sflwr s mald l al mbrs mol.

e hop u l cns Ng u scul n

, extra

t pgm, Mr M. e no u l find l a vlub educa$l rsorc.

s

encr

**Goal: 2 minutes, 3 seconds (120 words per minute)**

Mr. Milton Morgan
Dear Mr. Morgan:

/Are you interested in getting useful computer software free of charge? If so, you will probably be/interested in the Software Exchange Program sponsored by Central College.

About two years ago, Dr. Jane Edwards,/ president of Central College, and a number of professors at other state colleges organized a/program for area colleges. In the agreement each college made available to every other/college all of its software that was not under copyright, software that was in the public domain. This program helped/all the area colleges to expand their library of computer software.

The program is now being/extended to include all schools in the area. To enter the program, all you need do is fill out the/enclosed form and return it along with your registration fee of $50. Then you will have access to all/software that is available from the network. The only additional cost will be a monthly service fee/of $10, which is payable the first of each month. A copy of the current catalog is enclosed. An/updated catalog supplement of all software is mailed to all members monthly.

We hope you will consider/entering your school in the program, Mr. Morgan. We know you will find it a valuable educational/resource.
Sincerely, Enclosure (245)

, date

, geographic

, extra

, series

, extra

esl cost sals co      l m g:
Rose n co s proud l anounc
t opn g o ls acounl g srvc n
Memphis, TN, on Mon, Mar 4.
R n co, l o t fmosl orgs o ls
kind n ts prl o t naS, now h
ofcs n 25 cles n TN, NC, n GA.
n r nu M ofc, C s locald on
Oak sl, e l ofr cmp acounl g n

lx srvc f ndvduls s wl s f bot lrg n sml buss. r slf incls t gnrl mgr, 3 xprl acountnts, n 2 asstnts.

, series

if u ned r asstnc, r xperencd slf l b gld l hlp u. pl cl r vsl r nu ofc. bgn g Mar 4, e l b opn blwen 9 a m n 6 p m ev wkda. a broSr tl lsls vrus srvcs s encd.

, introductory

, introductory

vs u

encr

*Speed Builder*

East Coast Sales Company
Ladies and Gentlemen:

/Rose and Company is proud to announce the opening of its accounting service in Memphis, Tennessee, on/Monday, March 4.

Rose and Company, one of the foremost organizations of its kind in this part of the/ nation, now has offices in 25 cities in Tennessee, North Carolina, and Georgia.

In our new/Memphis office, which is located on Oak Street, we will offer complete accounting and tax service for individuals/as well as for both large and small businesses. Our staff includes the general manager, three expert/accountants, and two assistants.

If you need our assistance, our experienced staff will be glad to help you. Please call/or visit our new office. Beginning March 4, we will be open between 9 a.m. and 6 p.m. every/ weekday. A brochure that lists various services is enclosed. Very sincerely yours, Enclosure (153)

Mrs Marie Tuttle          d Mrs T:

 t msl ins co w v gld l rec u apl f hlt ins 3 mos ago. u l rmbr l tl lm u tk a fscl xmnaS n tl u w found l b n gd hlt w t xcpS o a strand msl n u bk, C w csd b an alo accdnl 2 mos *prir* l u apl.

 u hlt ins w apruvd w t xcluS o lrelm f ny *pr-xsl g* cndS f a perod o 6 mos. ts, o cors, incld t strand msl n u bk.

 lsl wk e recd u clam f lrelm o a bk njry. n od l pa ts clam, e msl h a slm fm u fsS sa g tl ts njry s nl rlald l

, extra

, extra

, introductory

, introductory

*[handwritten shorthand notes]*

t prvus njry. wn e rec ts
slm, e l rcns u crnl clam.
encd s a fm n an nvlop f
u cnv n hg u fs rply.
vs

encr

Mrs. Marie Tuttle
Dear Mrs. Tuttle:

/The National Insurance Company was very glad to receive your application for health insurance three/months ago. You will remember at that time you took a physical examination and that you were found to/be in good health with the exception of a strained muscle in your back, which was caused by an auto accident two/months prior to your application.

Your health insurance was approved with the exclusion of treatment for any/pre-existing condition for a period of six months. This, of course, included the strained muscle in your back.

Last/week we received your claim for treatment of a back injury. In order to pay this claim, we must have a statement/from your physician saying that this injury is not related to the previous injury. When we/receive this statement, we will reconsider your current claim.

Enclosed is a form and an envelope for your convenience in/having your physician reply. Very sincerely, Enclosure (169)

*Keyboarding Goal: 18 minutes (14 words per minute)*

Miss Natalie Nelson      d Miss N:

t Brady ins co h b n bus f mny yrs. Mary B prsdnt o t co h b a rsdnt o t area al hr life. r org s ddcald l srv g t neds o ndvduls n buss her n Princeton N J.

bcs t B ins co nos t locl ins bus nsid n ol e c srv u ins neds mC blr tn a co tl s locald n a dstnt cty. n ad& e ma b ab l sav u hndrds o dlrs n prmums.

if t ins on u hous r cr l xpir n t cm g mos le / o r acount mgrs cm l u ofc sn l dscrib t plces tl e ofr. l l lak u onl a &rt perod n u l b gld u tkd w us.

encd s a bro&r xplan g r xclnt plces. pl nol crfl hw u c lor u prmum sgnfcnll b slcl g a hir ddclb *amt. ts smpl mens tt u asum an insl rsk eql t t ddclb u Cus.*

*also encd s a cnv clndr C incls r bus adrs n fon no. e hop u l njoy usg l durg t nxt yr.*

*s u*

*encrs*

---

## DOCUMENT 26-4                                    *Punctuation Check*

**Keyboarding Goal: 18 minutes (14 words per minute)**

Miss Natalie Nelson
Dear Miss Nelson:

/The Brady Insurance Company has been in business for many years. Mary Brady, president of the/company, *(extra)* has been a resident of the area all her life. Our organization is dedicated to/serving the needs of individuals and businesses here in Princeton, New Jersey. *(geographic)*

Because the Brady Insurance/Company knows the local insurance business inside and out, *(introductory)* we can serve your insurance needs much better/than a company that is located in a distant city. In addition, *(introductory)* we may be able to save you/hundreds of dollars in premiums.

If the insurance on your house or car will expire in the coming months, *(introductory)* let/one of our account managers come to your office soon to describe the policies that we offer. It will take/only a short period, and *(compound sentence)* you will be glad you talked with us.

Enclosed is a brochure explaining our excellent/policies. Please note carefully how you can lower your premium significantly by selecting a/higher deductible amount. This simply means that you assume an initial risk equal to the deductible/you choose.

Also enclosed is a convenient calendar, which includes our business address and phone number. *(extra)* We/hope you will enjoy using it during the next year.
Sincerely yours, Enclosures (231)

# SUPPLEMENTARY ACTIVITY

## A Word to the Wise

### Making Corrections

/Correcting errors on documents is fairly easy today. If you have access to a word processor,/making corrections is extremely simple. If you make an error, you just backspace and hit the correct key. Corrections/can be made after the document is keyboarded. Even if an error is caught after a document/is printed, the document may be retrieved, the error corrected, and the page reprinted.

Correcting errors/made on typewriters is not as easy or as neat. On many electronic typewriters, a correction ribbon/may be used. Such corrections are usually quite neat. However, the sooner the error is caught, the better the/correction will be. In addition, you must correct the error before the paper is removed from the machine./If a letter is omitted, there may be a spacing problem. You should examine the paper carefully, and/if a correction is not neat, the paper should be typed again.

Correction fluid may be used with some types of/errors. It is very important to cover the error entirely, let the fluid dry, and make a very neat/correction. The fluid must be allowed to dry thoroughly before the correction is made. In some cases where/correction fluid has been used, a good photocopy will look better than the original document. You/must examine the paper critically, and if the correction is not neat, the paper should be typed again.

Erasers/are seldom used to correct typing errors today. In some cases, you may find it necessary to use one./If you do, be extremely careful not to damage the paper.

You and your company are often judged on how/neat your documents appear. Make sure that any corrections that you make are very neat. (317)

# LESSON 27

## SuperWrite REVIEW

Read the following words, referring to the key if necessary. Then copy the words in your own notebook.

### Abbreviations

1. *pr prd prl pgm pgms pgmd*
2. *pvd pvds pvdd q qd q g*
3. *rec recd recg rgd rgdd rgdg*

### Word Beginning En-

4. *ndvr nlir nlirl nlrnc nvy nlill*

### Word Ending -ity

5. *cmun l abl rlib-l oprlun l vri l vri ls*

### Key

1. present; presented; presently; program; programs; programmed
2. provide; provides; provided; question; questioned; questioning
3. receive; received; receiving; regard; regarded; regarding
4. endeavor; entire; entirely; entrance; envy; entitle
5. community; ability; reliability; opportunity; variety; varieties

# KEYBOARDING STYLE

## Copy Notation

If you wish for the recipient of a letter to know that you are sending a copy to a third person, type **c:** and the person's name at the left margin a double space under the last reference line.

```
lpj

Enclosure

c: Mr. Alfredo Lopez
```

# SPELLING

Here are additional spelling words. Pronounce and spell each word aloud; then copy it in your own notebook, being sure that you spell it correctly. When you read the Application section of the lesson, watch for these words.

affirmative
campaign
definitely
expertise
integrity
occupancy
prospective
reception
recommended
soliciting

# VOCABULARY

Study the following words and definitions carefully, and notice how the words are used in the *SuperWrite* examples. Watch for these words in the Application section of the lesson.

expertise

*Specialized knowledge or skill; the skill of an expert.*

*Se h xprtes n t sbjcl.*

She has expertise in the subject.

integrity

*Honesty; incorruptibility; adherence to strict standards.*

*he s a prsn o gral ntgrt.*

He is a person of great integrity.

peers

*Those of equal standing; those belonging to the same group.*

*Se gts alng wl w hr pers.*

She gets along well with her peers.

seminar

*An advanced course featuring discussion.*

*e ofr a smnr n acounlg.*

We offer a seminar in accounting.

soliciting

*Approaching with a request; trying to obtain.*

*e r slclg fnds f t Crt.*

We are soliciting funds for the charity.

# APPLICATION

Time your reading speed with Document 1 before reading the remaining documents. Then write all four documents. Remember to insert the needed punctuation in Document 4 before typing it in the correct format. Be sure to note the length of the document and place it properly on the page.

**Goal: 1 minute, 33 seconds (120 words per minute)**

Mr John J Edwards     d Mr E:

, introductory    dur g t nxt fu mos, a no o

ledrs n r cmun l l b plng n

org g t unild fnd driv f t

cm g yr. r gol s l pvd $1 m

f wrty Crls n t area.

     u h b hil rcmndd b mny o

u frnds n asocals l Brown n

, extra    co, hu sld tt u w a prsn o mlgr l

n rlib l. e fel tt u r dfntl t

prsn e wnt l hd t cmle ts yr.

     if u accpt t rsp l o hdg t

, introductory    cmle, u l mng t ntir org f t

yr n l b rsp f org g n suprvsg

t wk o abl l h pep hu l b

slcl g fnds f t campan.

, introductory    if u h ny qs, pl le us no. e

, date    wd lik l no b Fri, June 1, if

u l b ab l accpl ts pss. e
hop l rec u afrmtv rply sn.
v c u

c: Mr Sam Nelson

---

**DOCUMENT 27-1**                                         *Timed Reading*

*Goal: 1 minute, 33 seconds (120 words per minute)*

Mr. John J. Edwards
Dear Mr. Edwards:

/During the next few months, a number of leaders in our community will be planning and organizing the/United Fund drive for the coming year. Our goal is to provide $1 million for worthy charities in/the area.

You have been highly recommended by many of your friends and associates at Brown and/Company, who stated that you were a person of integrity and reliability. We feel that you are/definitely the person we want to head the committee this year.

If you accept the responsibility/of heading the committee, you will manage the entire organization for the year and will be responsible/for organizing and supervising the work of about 100 people who will be soliciting/funds for the campaign.

If you have any questions, please let us know. We would like to know by Friday, June 1, if you/will be able to accept this position. We hope to receive your affirmative reply soon. Very cordially/yours,     c: Mr. Sam Nelson (185)

Ms Maria Sanchez     d Ms S:

, introductory

eC yr n June, t sci l o mgl
l wstrn clg spnsrs a smnr n

, series

mgl. crnl studnts, grduts, n
locl bus execs r nvitd l atnd.
n t pst ts smnr h atrctd O 3h
prtcpnts. ts yr t smnr l b
hld June 4 n 5.

bcs o u xprtes n t feld o

, introductory

prsnl mgl, e wd lik u l b t
frst spekr ts yr. b accptg ts

, introductory

nvtas, u l b abl l Sr u ideas
w hndrds o crnl n prspctv
mgrs.

t opng adrs l b gvn on June
4 fm 5 pm l 6 pm n fclty hl

, introductory

on t clg cmpus. aft t adrs, a
rcps n bnqt l b hld n Jones

, extra

hl, C s ajacnt l fclty hl. t

*lpc o u lk wd b ntirl up l u.*
*e no tl ny area o mgl wd b*
*o inl l r prtcpnts.*
    *pl le us no if u l b ab l*
*accpl ts nvtaS, Ms S. e lk*
*fwrd l her g fm u.*
                        *vc*

*c: Dr Paul Martin*

, extra

---

Ms. Maria Sanchez
Dear Ms. Sanchez:

/Each year in June, the Society of Management at Western College sponsors a seminar in management./ Current students, graduates, and local business executives are invited to attend. In the past this/ seminar has attracted over 300 participants. This year the seminar will be held June 4 and 5./

Because of your expertise in the field of personnel management, we would like you to be the first speaker this/year. By accepting this invitation, you will be able to share your ideas with hundreds of current and/ prospective managers.

The opening address will be given on June 4 from 5 p.m. to 6 p.m. in/Faculty Hall on the college campus. After the address, a reception and banquet will be held in Jones Hall, which/is adjacent to Faculty Hall. The topic of your talk would be entirely up to you. We know that any/area of management would be of interest to our participants.

Please let us know if you will be able/to accept this invitation, Ms. Sanchez. We look forward to hearing fom you. Very cordially,     c: Dr. Paul Martin (203)

Mr Kenneth Samuels   d Mr S:

Miss Ann Scott rol l me rcntl

, geographic  ll g me tl Se h muvd l Providence,
RI, n h apld f a psS w u co.
Se askd if I wd ril a lr o

, compound sentence  rcmndaS f hr, n I m v hpy
l d so.

I h non Miss S f a no o yrs.
Se bgn wkg f my co afl Se

, date  fnSd hi scul June 30, 1985. Se
w a clrk n t acounlg depl

, geographic  her l Mason sals co n Jackson,

, introductory  MS. afl onl a fu mos, Se bcam
a scrlry n t advrlisg depl.

Miss S Nd nil scul l sout

, extra  cosl clg n 1986, wil Se cnlnud
l wk f my co. lsl yr Se rlrnd

, compound sentence  l clg fl lm, n Se recd hr
dgre lsl mo.

Miss S s a prsnb yng wmn n a v hrd wkr. Se s a prsn o dpndb l n nlgrl. Se s wl likd b hr pers s wl s b mbrs o mgl. I m hpy l gv hr my hisl rcmndaS. if u hir hr, I m Sr tl Se l d an xclnl jb f u.

, introductory

v s u

## DOCUMENT 27-3

Mr. Kenneth Samuels
Dear Mr. Samuels:

/Miss Ann Scott wrote to me recently telling me that she has moved to Providence, Rhode Island, and has applied for/a position with your company. She asked if I would write a letter of recommendation for her, and I/am very happy to do so.

I have known Miss Scott for a number of years. She began working for my/company after she finished high school June 30, 1985. She was a clerk in the accounting department/here at Mason Sales Company in Jackson, Mississippi. After only a few months, she became a/secretary in the advertising department.

Miss Scott entered night school at South Coast College in 1986,/while she continued to work for my company. Last year she returned to college full time, and she received her/degree last month.

Miss Scott is a personable young woman and a very hard worker. She is a person of/dependability and integrity. She is well liked by her peers as well as by members of management. I/am happy to give her my highest recommendation. If you hire her, I am sure that she will do an/excellent job for you. Very sincerely yours, (205)

Miss Alice Murphy              d Miss M:

n t mal lda I recd svrl cpes o t pgm f t strn mgl asoca$ bus cnfrnc l b hld July 26 27 n 28 l t Baxter hotl n Miami FL.

I h alndd ts cnfrnc n t psl n I dfntl rcmnd l f u mples. t cnfrnc ts yr C s dvold ntirl l info mgl prmss l b v gd. I blev tl svrl mbrs o u slf mil lik l h an oprtun l l alnd.

bcs u org s a mbr o t strn mgl asoca$ u r ntilld l snd s mny s 3 o u mples fre o rgstra$ Crg. prtcpnts ma sta l ny o t holls lstd n t pgm f a ral o $75 pr da sngl ocupncy r $90 pr da db ocupncy. holl rsrva$s msl b mad sprll.

encd s a cpy o t cmp pgm. pl fl
ol n rlrn t rgslras fm C s prnld
on t bk cv if ny o u pep wS l alnd.

vs

c: Mrs May Brown

encr

---

DOCUMENT 27-4                                    **Punctuation Check**

**Keyboarding Goal: 15 minutes (16 words per minute)**

Miss Alice Murphy
Dear Miss Murphy:

/In the mail today I received several copies of the program for the Southern Management Association/business conference to be held July 26, 27, and 28 *(series)* at the Baxter Hotel/ in Miami, Florida *(geographic)*.

I have attended this conference in the past, and *(compound sentence)* I definitely recommend/it for your employees. The conference this year, which is devoted entirely to information management, *(extra)*/promises to be very good. I believe that several members of your staff might like to have an/opportunity to attend.

Because your organization is a member of the Southern Management/Association, *(introductory)* you are entitled to send as many as three of your employees free of registration charge./ Participants may stay at any of the hotels listed in the program for a rate of $75 per day/single occupancy or $90 per day double occupancy. Hotel reservations must be made/ separately.

Enclosed is a copy of the complete program. Please fill out and return the registration form,/which is printed on the back cover, *(extra)* if any of your people wish to attend.
Very sincerely,      c:/Mrs. May Brown      Enclosure (224)

# SUPPLEMENTARY ACTIVITY

## A Word to the Wise

Developing Speed and Accuracy

/As you gain skill in *SuperWrite,* you will write faster and more accurately. How can you ensure that you are/practicing correctly? Here are a few reminders for you to remember as you practice.

Your ability to/read quickly is the key to writing quickly. After you have read the entire document and you feel very/comfortable with the content, then write it in your notebook. Read a phrase or a sentence and write as much of it as/possible without referring to the text. If you should have a question about a word, refer to the/*SuperWrite* notes quickly. Spell the word aloud in *SuperWrite,* and write it once or twice on a piece of scratch paper. You will/likely not have trouble with it again.

When you are under pressure to build your writing speed, it is likely that/your notes may become a bit difficult to read. In order to build writing speed, you must push yourself to a speed/that is slightly higher than one at which you are comfortable. Your teacher will give you dictation that will push/you to write faster and faster.

When you are writing notes to use, you should drop back only a few words per minute/ to a comfortable writing speed. You will find that your notes improve, and you will be able to read them easily./

Correct reading and writing practice will ensure that you will develop expertise in *SuperWrite.* (239)

# LESSON 28

## SuperWrite REVIEW

Read the following words, referring to the key if necessary. Then write the words in your own notebook.

### Abbreviations

1. *sl sls sld sg sgs sgd*
2. *tk tks tkf tkd t ty*
3. *lm lml lmd lmg v w*

### Word Beginning Re-

4. *rlir rsum rprs rtnk rgrup rml*

### Word Ending -tion

5. *cS acS frcS mnS lnS fS*

### Key

1. state, street; states, streets; stated; suggest, suggestion; suggests, suggestions; suggested
2. thank; thanks; thankful; thanked; the; they
3. time; timely; timed; timing; very; was, were, with
4. retire; resume; repress; rethink; regroup; remit
5. caution; action; friction; mention; tension; fashion

# KEYBOARDING STYLE

## Subject Line

A subject line may be used in a business letter to help the reader and to assist both the writer and the recipient in filing.

The subject line is typed in capitals a double space below the salutation. The first paragraph begins a double space below the subject line.

```
                    May 5, 19--



     Miss Jane Massey
     1401 University Court
     Boston, MA   33388

     Dear Miss Massey:

     ADVERTISING CONFERENCE

          The advertising conference that was originally
     scheduled to be held in the Madison Hotel on January 21
     will be held on January 23.
```

# SPELLING

Here are additional spelling words. Pronounce and spell each word aloud; then copy it in your own notebook, being sure that you spell it correctly. When you read the Application section of the lesson, watch for these words.

analyzing
appropriate
imperative
liability
management
mandatory
mentioned
retention
retirement
sensible

# VOCABULARY

Study the following definitions carefully, and notice how the words are used in the *SuperWrite* examples. Watch for these words in the Application section of the lesson.

formal
> *According to custom, form, or rule.*
>
> *t fml ddcaS s tmro.*
>
> The formal dedication is tomorrow.

imperative
> *Necessary; not to be avoided; expressing a command.*
>
> *l s mprlv tl u lak acS.*
>
> It is imperative that you take action.

liability insurance
> *Insurance that provides financial protection from a claim by another person.*
>
> *libl ins prtcls u fm fnnSl los if u r sud.*
>
> Liability insurance protects you from financial loss if you are sued.

mandatory
> *Required; obligatory.*
>
> *ins s mndlory n ts sl.*
>
> Insurance is mandatory in this state.

retention
> *The act of keeping or holding in possession.*
>
> *he s n Crg o t rlnS o r rcrds.*
>
> He is in charge of the retention of our records.

# APPLICATION

Time your reading speed with Document 1 before reading the remaining documents. Then write all four documents. Remember to insert the needed punctuation in Document 4 before typing it in the correct format. Be sure to note the length of the document and place it properly on the page.

Mr Wallace Brice          d Mr B:

rcrds rlns sslm

tks f t rpl on r rcrds rlns sslm, C u rcntl cmpd. l arivd l r ofcs lsl wk, n r mgl slded l crfl. t ncluss tl u dru r al v snsb, n e pln l us u sgs s e rvis r rcrds rlns pgm O t nxl fu mos.

e ap t rclnl jb tl u dd anlyz g r sslm, Mr B, n e lk fwrd l wkg w u co n t futr.

e l b hpy l ril a lr o rcmndas f t Wells org if u wd lik us l d so.

vsu

c: Mrs Ann Davis

*Margin notes:*

, extra

, compound sentence

, compound sentence

, compound sentence

, extra

**Goal: 1 minute, 1 second (120 words per minute)**

Mr. Wallace Brice:
Dear Mr. Brice:

RECORDS RETENTION SYSTEM

/Thanks for the report on our records retention system, which you recently completed. It arrived at our/offices last week, and our management studied it carefully. The conclusions that you drew are all very sensible,/and we plan to use your suggestions as we revise our records retention program over the next few months./

We appreciate the excellent job that you did analyzing our system, Mr. Brice, and we look forward/to working with your company in the future.

We will be happy to write a letter of recommendation/for The Wells Organization if you would like us to do so. Very sincerely yours, c: Mrs. Ann/Davis (121)

*Miss Natalie Mason    d Miss M:*

, extra

, date

, introductory

*rlirm o Ann Fry
lsl wk I spok w Mr Anthony Davis, hd o t advrlis g depl o u co. he mnSd tl Miss A F l b rlirg on Fri, July 28. s u l rmbr, Miss F wkd w my co a no o lms Ot psl fu yrs s e rvisd mny o r co pblcass.*

(continued)

, introductory

, introductory

*[shorthand/longhand practice text]*

if u r plng t h a rtirm prty
f Miss F, I wd v mC lik l
alnd. pl le me no if u blev ts
wd b aprpral. n t menlm, I
l lk f a sml gfl l pr l hr
smlm bf hr fml rtirm.

s u

c: Mr H T Kent

---

## DOCUMENT 28-2 Speed Builder

Miss Natalie Mason
Dear Miss Mason:

### RETIREMENT OF ANN FRY

/Last week I spoke with Mr. Anthony Davis, head of the advertising department of your company. He/mentioned that Miss Ann Fry will be retiring on Friday, July 28. As you will remember, Miss Fry worked/with my company a number of times over the past few years as we revised many of our company/publications.

If you are planning to have a retirement party for Miss Fry, I would very much like to attend./Please let me know if you believe this would be appropriate. In the meantime, I will look for a small gift to/present to her sometime before her formal retirement. Sincerely yours, c: Mr. H. T. Kent (113)

Mr Charles Clark        d Mr C:

cr ins xpra$

2 mos ago e rol u tl t ins plcy on u cr wd sn xpir. e dd nl rec a rply, n e mald u a scnd lr 1 mo ago. wn e sll dd nl her fm u, e almpld l cntcl u b llfon. e w, hwev, uab l reC u.

u plcy l xpir on Sept 1 if e d nl her fm u. s u no, alo lib-l ins s mndlory n r sl. if u $d b nvlvd n an accdnl n h no cvg, u cd b sbjcl l a lrg fin.

, compound sentence

, introductory

, extra

, introductory

, introductory

(continued)

, extra

*[handwritten shorthand notes]*

ı s mprlv tl u lak acš now,
Mr C. rnw u plcy b Ck g t
aprpral bx on t encd crd n
rlrng l l us. u c pa lalr.
s u

c: Mr Al Cole
encr

## DOCUMENT 28-3

Mr. Charles Clark
Dear Mr. Clark:

CAR INSURANCE EXPIRATION

/Two months ago we wrote you that the insurance policy on your car would soon expire. We did not receive a/reply, and we mailed you a second letter one month ago. When we still did not hear from you, we attempted to/contact you by telephone. We were, however, unable to reach you.

Your policy will expire on September/1 if we do not hear from you. As you know, auto liability insurance is mandatory in/our state. If you should be involved in an accident and have no coverage, you could be subject to a large fine./

It is imperative that you take action now, Mr. Clark. Renew your policy by checking the appropriate/box on the enclosed card and returning it to us. You can pay later. Sincerely yours, c: Mr./Al Cole (143)

Dr Mary Alice Norton        d Dr N:

adrs Cang

   on Apr 20 I l b muvg l Chicago IL wr I l N la scul. pl Cang my adrs on u rcrds n snd al mal l my cmpus adrs C s encd ull ftr nolfcas.

   u l rmbr tl 3 wks ago I rqsld tl a cpy o my mdcl rcrds b snl l me. uflnll I h nl recd tes rcrds. if ty sd b rlrnd l u ofc I wd ap u sndg tm l my C adrs.

   tks f u asslnc Dr N.

                 v s u

encr

**Keyboarding Goal: 7 minutes (16 words per minute)**

Dr. Mary Alice Norton
Dear Dr. Norton:

ADDRESS CHANGE

/On April 20 I will be moving to Chicago, Illinois, (*geographic*) where I will enter law school. (*extra*) Please change my/address on your records, and (*compound sentence*) send all mail to my campus address, which is enclosed, (*extra*) until further notification./

You will remember that three weeks ago I requested that a copy of my medical records be sent to/me. Unfortunately, (*introductory*) I have not received these records. If they should be returned to your office, (*introductory*) I would/appreciate your sending them to my Chicago address.

Thanks for your assistance, Dr. Norton. (*extra*) Very sincerely yours,/Enclosure (101)

## SUPPLEMENTARY ACTIVITY

### A Word to the Wise

Retention

/While you are taking dictation, you will occasionally fall behind the speaker. If you do, make every effort/to retain the sentence in your mind until you have a moment to finish it.

Most employers will stop/for a moment while speaking. This will be your opportunity to catch up. Keep the material in your mind/and write quickly when you have a chance.

You should not interrupt the speaker during dictation unless it is/absolutely essential. An interruption will most likely break the speaker's concentration and can result in/an omission of vital information. If you ever fall too far behind and feel that you must ask the person/to wait, simply hold up your hand for a moment. This will usually cause the speaker to stop, and you will/not cause further distraction by speaking.

Be ready to read back the last sentence or two after a break. This will/enable the dictator to remember the line of thought.

Practice to increase your retention by reading an/entire sentence and then writing it in your notebook. (189)

# LESSON 29

## SuperWrite REVIEW

Read the following words, referring to the key if necessary. Then write the words in your own notebook.

### Abbreviations

1. *cmp cmp& cnv cnvl cns cnss*
2. *cv cvs rcvd depl depls dv*
3. *dvd dvm d mpl mpld mplm*

### Word Beginning Inter-

4. *Nn&l Nvu Nfer Nvl Nmlnl Nmlnll*

### Word Endings -pal, -ple

5. *prncp prncpl pep amp ap xmp*

### Key

1. complete; completion; convenience, convenient; conveniently; consider, consideration; considers, considerations
2. cover; covers; recovered; department; departments; develop
3. developed; development; do; employ; employed; employment
4. international; interview; interfere; interval; intermittent; intermittently
5. principal; principally; people; ample; apple; example

# KEYBOARDING STYLE

## Attention Line

An attention line may be included in a business letter. It is used to indicate that the letter concerns company business but that the writer wishes to route the letter to a particular person. When an attention line is used, it is typed as the first line of both the envelope mailing address and the inside address.

```
Attention Ms. Sondra Murphy
The Jefferson Company
9800 Main Line Drive
Missoula, MT  59888-1324

Ladies and Gentlemen:
```

Notice that the salutation refers to the second line of the address rather than the attention line.

# SPELLING

Here are additional spelling words. Pronounce and spell each word aloud; then copy it in your own notebook, being sure that you spell it correctly. When you read the Application section of the lesson, watch for these words.

break
copywriter
exceeding
invaluable
precede
principal
resumé
sustained
touch
vehicle

# VOCABULARY

Study the following definitions carefully, and notice how the words are used in the *SuperWrite* examples. Watch for these words in the Application section of the lesson.

exceeding
*Going beyond the limits; surpassing.*

*t drivr w rcedg t sped lml.*

The driver was exceeding the speed limit.

precede
*To come before in time or order; to be in a position in front.*

*t dnr l prced t speC.*

The dinner will precede the speech.

principal
*Main; first; highest.*

*my prncpl gol s l wk n mgl.*

My principal goal is to work in management.

resumé
*A summary of one's history and experience.*

*pl snd a rsma w u lr.*

Please send a resumé with your letter.

sustained
*Endured; withstood.*

*e ssland a gral del o wlr dmg.*

We sustained a great deal of water damage.

# APPLICATION

Time your reading speed with Document 1 before reading the remaining documents. Then write all four documents. Remember to insert the needed punctuation in Document 4 before typing it in the correct format. Be sure to note the length of the document and place it properly on the page.

alnS Miss Sandra Taylor
NnSl pblSrs          l n g :

, extra

yslrda Dr Max Ray, my clg
advisr, mnSd tl n t nxl 6 mos
tr mil b an opn g f a cpyrilr
l NnSl pblSrs. he remndd u
org hil n sgd tl I ril now
ask g f an Nvru.

, introductory

s u l nol on t encd rsma, I
h hd rado n nuspapr xperenc
tl Sd b nvlub l me s a cpyrilr.

, introductory

f xmp, I h rln mny ads f
bot r locl nuspaprs.

n June I l grdual fm sl clg
w a dgre n jrnlsm. my prncp
inl now s n bcm g a cpyrilr
w a lrg co. my evnlul gol s
l bcm a mgr n a pblSg hous.

*I wd ap u scdul g an Nvru f me l u cnv. I l b av blwen t hrs o 9 am n 6 pm ny da durg t wk o Apr 6.*

*vc u*

*c: Dr MR*

*encr*

**Goal: 1 minute, 33 seconds (120 words per minute)**

Attention Miss Sandra Taylor
International Publishers

Ladies and Gentlemen:

/Yesterday Dr. Max Ray, my college advisor, mentioned that in the next six months there might be an opening/for a copywriter at International Publishers. He recommended your organization highly/and suggested that I write now asking for an interview.

As you will note on the enclosed resumé, I have/had radio and newspaper experience that should be invaluable to me as a copywriter./For example, I have written many ads for both our local newspapers.

In June I will graduate from State/College with a degree in journalism. My principal interest now is in becoming a copywriter/with a large company. My eventual goal is to become a manager in a publishing house.

I would/appreciate your scheduling an interview for me at your convenience. I will be available between/the hours of 9 a.m. and 6 p.m. any day during the week of April 6. Very cordially yours,/c: Dr. Max Ray Enclosure (185)

Dr Darlene Taylor      d Dr T:

Madison clg h scduld an NnSl bus cnfrnc n Miami, FL, Feb 21, 22, n 23 nxt yr. e h snt anouncms t O 't pep, n e r xpctg a v gd atndnc.

e r nvit g NnSl ledrs n t feld o bus t b gst spekrs, n e wd lik t xtnd an nvtaS t u t join ts grup. bcs o u xprtes n mgt, e wd lik u t gv t prncp adrs t t cnfrnc.

t prncp adrs t b on t frst evn g, Feb 21, t 9 pm. a rcpS n dnr t prced t speC. if ts t nt Nfer w u v bsy scdul, e hop u t accpt r nvtaS. pl le us no sn if u t b ab t join us.

c

c: Dr Kurt Krause

, geographic

, series

, compound sentence

, compound sentence

, introductory

, extra

, introductory

Dr. Darlene Taylor
Dear Dr. Taylor:

/Madison College has scheduled an international business conference in Miami, Florida,/ February 21, 22, and 23 next year. We have sent announcements to over 1,000 people,/and we are expecting a very good attendance.

We are inviting international leaders in the field/of business to be guest speakers, and we would like to extend an invitation to you to join this group. Because/of your expertise in management, we would like you to give the principal address at the conference.

The/principal address will be on the first evening, February 21, at 9 p.m. A reception and/dinner will precede the speech. If this will not interfere with your very busy schedule, we hope you will accept our/invitation. Please let us know soon if you will be able to join us. Cordially, c: Dr. Kurt Krouse/(160)

---

## DOCUMENT 29-3

, extra

(continued)

, compound sentence

, extra

, introductory

, compound sentence

, compound sentence

t Nsl hiwa. I w almpl g l lrn lfl, n tr w amp lm l d so. t lrk drivr, hu w aprntl xced g t sped lml, hl my vehcl on t psngr sid. t cl& csd m tn $5t n dmg l my cr. alto I w nl hrl, t drivr o t lrk w lakn l t hspil b ambulnc.

lda I recd a lr slg tl I w bg sud f $1 m n cnc& w t accdnl. my lib-l ins s f onl $2 h t, n I fel I Sd rlan a layr l ts lm.

I dd nl brak my lrfc las, n t otr drivr w nlirl l blam. pl ask l o u pep l gl n lC w me s sn s psb.

v l u

c: Miss J K

## DOCUMENT 29-3

Attention Mr. C. T. Courtland
Legal Associates

Ladies and Gentlemen:

/I have been referred to your law company by Miss Joan Kent, who worked for your organization several years/ago. I need the help of a lawyer because of a lawsuit that has been filed against me.

Several weeks/ago I was involved in a major auto accident at the intersection of Broad Street and Main Avenue./I was struck by a truck that had just exited from the interstate highway. I was attempting to turn left, and/there was ample time to do so. The truck driver, who was apparently exceeding the speed limit, hit my/vehicle on the passenger side. The collision caused more than $5,000 in damage to my car. Although/I was not hurt, the driver of the truck was taken to the hospital by ambulance.

Today I received a/letter stating that I was being sued for $1 million in connection with this accident. My/liability insurance is for only $200,000, and I feel I should retain a lawyer at/this time.

I did not break any traffic laws, and the other driver was entirely to blame. Please ask one of your/people to get in touch with me as soon as possible. Very truly yours, c: Miss Joan Kent (213)

## DOCUMENT 29-4         *Punctuation Check*

*Keyboarding Goal: 9 minutes (18 words per minute)*

alnß Miss Susan Marsh
gnrl ins co        l m g:


ins clam
    dur g t hvy rans e hd n ts area
on Apr 5 6 n 7 my hous sfrd a gral
del o dmg. t ruf C w onl 8 yrs old
lekd n svrl placs n tr w dmg l
t flor o t lvg rum n dn.

(continued)

I rpld t prblm l u ins co n I w advisd l go ahd w rprs. t ruf hd l b rplacd n I hd l d a gral del o Nor panl g. t csl o t rpr w $5t. t ins ajslr finll cam l my hom m tn 2 wks lalr n qkl mad a lsl o onl a fu ilms. n t mal lda I recd a Ck f $5h C s onl a frcS o t aml o t ls.

pl snd a prsn l rcns t clam. I fel tl $5h s smpl nl an amp aml f t ls I ssland.

u l

c: Mr Barry White

---

## DOCUMENT 29-4       *Punctuation Check*

**Keyboarding Goal: 9 minutes (18 words per minute)**

Attention Miss Susan Marsh
General Insurance Company

Ladies and Gentlemen:

INSURANCE CLAIM

/During the heavy rains we had in this area on April 5, 6, and 7, (*series-introductory*) my house suffered a great deal/of damage. The roof, which was only eight years old, (*extra*) leaked in several places, and (*compound sentence*) there was damage to the/interior of the living room and den.

I reported the problem to your insurance company, and (*compound sentence*) I was/ advised to go ahead with repairs. The roof had to be replaced, and (*compound sentence*) I had to do a great deal of interior/painting. The cost of the repair was $5,000. The insurance adjuster finally came to my home/more than two weeks later and quickly made a list of only a few items. In the mail today I received a/check for $500, which is only a fraction of the amount of the loss. (*extra*)

Please send a person to/reconsider the claim. I feel that $500 is simply not an ample amount for the loss I sustained./Yours truly, c: Mr. Barry White (146)


# SUPPLEMENTARY ACTIVITY

## A Word to the Wise

Concentrating on Content

/When you are taking dictation, concentrate on content and do not let your mind wander. You will be much more/likely to take the dictation correctly if you concentrate on what is being said, rather than only on/writing isolated words. Your principal job is to get the correct meaning.

Do not let outside interferences/distract you. Keep your mind strictly on the business at hand as you write.

Try to anticipate what will be said/in a document. In this way you will be able to take all the dictation correctly. Occasionally/you will be able to help the person dictating by supplying an appropriate word. However, you should/not interfere unless the person wishes to have assistance.

As you read your notes before you transcribe, you should/ask yourself such questions as Who? What? Where? When? If all relevant points are not covered in your notes, ask for/ clarification before transcribing. If you realize there has been an omission after you have typed your notes, the/missing information should be obtained and inserted, and the paper should be reprinted or retyped.

For/example, if you take a memo scheduling a meeting, you should determine if the following items are/included: Who is to be at the meeting? What is the meeting for? Where is it to be held? When is it scheduled?/Any other relevant information should also be included so that additional correspondence is/not required. (242)

# LESSON 30

## *SuperWrite REVIEW*

Read the following words, referring to the key if necessary. Then copy the words in your own notebook.

**Abbreviations**

1. *abt aft aftwrds m aml amt g*
2. *n my apl apls ap apt*
3. *r t av avl ave aves*

**Word Beginning Over-**

4. *Odu Ocm Otm Onit Osit Ol*

**Word Endings -ious, -eous, -ous, -us**

5. *crtus crtusl vrus vrusl famus status*

**Key**

1. about; after; afterwards; am, more; amount; amounting
2. and, in; any; application, apply; applications, applies; appreciate; appreciation
3. are, or, our; at, it, to; available; availability; avenue; avenues
4. overdue; overcome; overtime; overnight; oversight; overly
5. courteous, courteously; various; variously; famous; status

# KEYBOARDING STYLE

## Envelopes

**Return Address.** Most companies use preprinted letterhead envelopes, which include the company name and return address. In this case, only the writer's name need be typed above the return address. If preprinted envelopes are not available, the complete return address must be typed.

**Recipient's Name and Address.** Type the name and address of the recipient near the center and begin on the twelfth line from the top. The address should be single-spaced and typed in capital letters. No periods or commas should be included. Use the state abbreviations recommended by the United States Postal Service, as shown in the Appendix, and include the ZIP Code.

**Notations.** Mailing notations such as PERSONAL, which are intended for the recipient, should be typed in capital letters a double space below the return address. Mailing notations such as PRIORITY MAIL, which are intended for the Postal Service, should be typed in capital letters a double space below the stamp.

## Envelope

```
B J PEARLSTEIN
DESIGN UNLIMITED
8420 FLEMINGTON EXPRESSWAY
KANSAS CITY MO    27272
      DS
PERSONAL
```

```
                                            DS
                                     PRIORITY MAIL


                 DR ALVIN C CARLTON  | - line 12
                 RESEARCH DIRECTOR
                 THE MILLER-TIDINGS CORPORATION
                 9720 NORTH BURLESON DRIVE
                 FT WORTH TX   78777
```

# SPELLING

Here are additional spelling words. Pronounce and spell each word aloud; then copy it in your own notebook, being sure that you spell it correctly. When you read the Application section of the lesson, watch for these words.

arrangements
discourteous
evaluation
former
insolvent
oversight
personnel
simulator
techniques
viable

# VOCABULARY

Study the following definitions carefully, and notice how the words are used in the *SuperWrite* examples. Watch for these words in the Application section of the lesson.

former      *Coming before in order; occurring earlier in time.*

*he s a fmr mple o my co.*

He is a former employee of my company.

insolvent      *Unable to pay debts; having liabilities greater than assets.*

*e sspd tl u co ma b nslvnl.*

We suspect that your company may be insolvent.

personnel      *People employed by an organization.*

*Se s a mbr o r prsnl.*

She is a member of our personnel.

## VOCABULARY continued

simulator

*One that imitates; an apparatus that generates conditions similar to actual conditions.*

*e prclcd wa llfon smulalr.*

We practiced with a telephone simulator.

viable

*Capable of success; practicable.*

*e ofr a vib pln.*

We offer a viable plan.

## APPLICATION

Time your reading speed with Document 1 before reading the remaining documents. Then write all four documents. Remember to insert the needed punctuation in Document 4 before typing it in the correct format. Be sure to note the length of the document and place it properly on the page.

## DOCUMENT 30-1                          *Timed Reading*

**Goal: 1 minute, 47 seconds (120 words per minute)**

*Mr Oliver Van        d Mr V:*
*"Jones n co. hold on."*
*h u ev recd sC a dscrlus*
*grel g Ot llfon? if so, I'm Sr*

, introductory

*u dd nl ap l l al. u prbbl h*
*a pur opnn o t co u w cl g.*

, extra

*bl, Mr V, d u on ofc wkrs*
*grel clrs n a smlr mnr? if ty*

(continued)

, introductory

d, u c esl imgn hw u cstmrs msl fel abl u bus.

cntrl cmuncaSs s a sml co tl h b n bus jsl O 3 yrs. r onl bus s hlp g cos mpruv tr llfon

, compound sentence

lcneqs, n e lak tl bus v serusl.

hw d e go abl hlp g cos mpruv t slalus o tr llfon mnrs? e snd 1 o r crlus nstrclrs l u ofc f 5 sSs l wk w u ofc prsnl l mpruv tr llfon

, series

lcneqs. e us a llfon smulalr, a vdeolap rcrdr, n vrus otr dvics n r pgm. t csl o ts vlub srvc s v sml, bl t

, compound sentence

bnfls c b xlreml bg.

cl uslda. e l dmnslral l u O t llfon hw e apl wl e leC.

v s u

**Goal: 1 minute, 47 seconds (120 words per minute)**

Mr. Oliver Van
Dear Mr. Van:

/"Jones and Company. Hold on."

Have you ever received such a discourteous greeting over the telephone? If/so, I'm sure you did not appreciate it at all. You probably have a poor opinion of the company/you were calling.

But, Mr. Van, do your own office workers greet callers in a similar manner? If they do,/ you can easily imagine how your customers must feel about your business.

Central Communications is/a small company that has been in business just over three years. Our only business is helping companies/improve their telephone techniques, and we take that business very seriously.

How do we go about helping/companies improve the status of their telephone manners? We send one of our courteous instructors to your/office for five sessions to work with your office personnel to improve their telephone techniques. We use a telephone/simulator, a videotape recorder, and various other devices in our program. The cost/of this valuable service is very small, but the benefits can be extremely big.

Call us today. We/will demonstrate to you over the telephone how we apply what we teach. Very sincerely yours, (213)

*prir l mal*

*Ms Martha Fuentes    d Ms F:*
*evluaß sslm*

*tks f cl g yslrda l arang a lm l cm l r co l sldy r mple evluaß pgm. tr r numrus serus prblms n r evluaß pgm tl e msl Ocm n t ner fulr.*

(continued)

*, compound sentence*

*, date*

*, compound sentence*

*, extra*

*[shorthand/speedwriting handwritten text]*

c: Mr Carlos Lopez

## DOCUMENT 30-2 | Speed Builder

**PRIORITY MAIL**

Ms. Martha Fuentes
Dear Ms. Fuentes:

### EVALUATION SYSTEM

/Thanks for calling yesterday to arrange a time to come to our company to study our employee/evaluation program. There are numerous serious problems in our evaluation program that we must/overcome in the near future. I have talked the situation over with various members of the management/of our company, and they believe that we should proceed with the study as soon as possible. We will be/available to work with you all day Monday, June 4. Is this date satisfactory with you?

I am gathering/all the information you requested, and it will be available when you arrive. Just call if you have/any questions about our evaluation system or if you need any further information.

Please let me/know if these arrangements are satisfactory with you, Ms. Fuentes. Very sincerely yours, c:/Mr. Carlos Lopez (163)

## DOCUMENT 30-3

cnfdnSl

Ms Janet Gross          d Ms G:

rfrnc f Miss Alice Froy
  lsl wk Miss Alice Froy, a fmr

, extra

mple o u co, apld f a jb l my
stor. I rqstd rfrncs fm 2 o hr

, extra

, introductory

fmr mplrs. du l an Osil, hwev,
I dd nl ask f a rfrnc fm u.
I prtculrl wnl l h u opnn o
hr wk bcs u w hr lsl mplr
n t prsn f hum Se wkd t
lngsl perod o lm.

(continued)

, extra

I wd ap l v mC, Ms G, if u
l fl ol t encd fm gvg us info
abl Miss T. pl ansr t vrus
qs n rlrn t fm n t nvlop
tl s also encd.

if e ma rlrn t favr n t
, introductory

fulr, e l b v gld l d so.

u s

encr

**CONFIDENTIAL**

Ms. Janet Gross
Dear Ms. Gross:

**REFERENCE FOR MISS ALICE TROY**

/Last week Miss Alice Troy, a former employee of your company, applied for a job at my store. I requested/references from two of her former employers. Due to an oversight, however, I did not ask for/a reference from you. I particularly want to have your opinion of her work because you were her last/employer and the person for whom she worked the longest period of time.

I would appreciate it very/much, Ms. Gross, if you will fill out the enclosed form giving us information about Miss Troy. Please answer the/various questions and return the form in the envelope that is also enclosed.

If we may return the/favor in the future, we will be very glad to do so. Yours sincerely, Enclosure (130)

*Keyboarding Goal: 10 minutes (18 words per minute)*

prsnl

Mr Sumio Saga      d Mr S:

on Thurs Oct 5 e rot u a crtus lr slg tl t pam f u od o Aug 10 w Odu. e asumd tl u hd nl pd u bl bcs o an Osil. e stl dd nl her fm u n e rot u agn on Nov 1. l tl lm e prpoosd a vib pln tl incld an xlns o 3 mos f u l pa t bl.

now anotr mo h gn b. e h nl recd u pam nr h u ofrd ny xplnas. e r qil cncrnd abl t prblm n e sspcl tl u co cd b nslvnl. e d nl ws l lrn u acounl O l a layr bl e ma h no otr Coic. if e d nl her fm u b Dec 15 e l b fcd l d so. lak slps now l prlcl u vlub crdl Mr S. snd us u Ck f $9 h lda.

                           u l

c: Mrs Mable Morris

*Keyboarding Goal: 10 minutes (18 words per minute)*

PERSONAL

Mr. Sumio Saga
Dear Mr. Saga

/On Thursday, October 5, *(date)* we wrote you a courteous letter stating that the payment for your order of/August 10 was overdue. We assumed that you had not paid your bill because of an oversight. We still did not hear/from you, and *(compound sentence)* we wrote you again on November 1. At that time we proposed a viable plan that included/an extension of three months for you to pay the bill.

Now another month has gone by. We have not received your/payment, nor *(compound sentence)* have you offered any explanation. We are quite concerned about the problem, and *(compound sentence)* we suspect that your/company could be insolvent. We do not wish to turn your account over to a lawyer, but *(compound sentence)* we may have no/ other choice. If we do not hear from you by December 15, *(introductory)* we will be forced to do so. Take steps now to/protect your valuable credit, Mr. Saga *(extra)*. Send us your check for $900 today. Yours truly, c: Mrs. Mable Morris (163)

# SUPPLEMENTARY ACTIVITY

## A Word to the Wise

Handling Special Instructions

/When you take a document, your employer may give special instructions. He or she may say, "Send this Express," "This/letter is confidential," or "This is a rush job." The special information may be for the Postal Service,/for the person receiving the letter, or for you.

When your employer gives special instructions, mark them in your/notebook at the beginning of the document. Even if the instructions are given after the document/has been dictated, you should mark the special notation at the beginning.

If your employer specifies/overnight delivery, you should write this at the top of your notes. Later you will type EXPRESS MAIL, or the name of/one of the various other delivery services, both on the letter and on the envelope. If you/are asked to mark a letter "personal," you should write this at the top of your notes. Later you will type PERSONAL/both on the letter and on the envelope. If your employer says, "Please type this letter now," you should write/"immediate" or "rush" at the top of your notes. Then you will remember to type the letter first.

Whatever special/instructions are given, mark them clearly at the beginning of your notes and then follow the instructions. (218)

# *LESSON 31*

## *SuperWrite REVIEW*

Read the following words, referring to the key if necessary. Then write the words in your own notebook.

### Abbreviations

1. *f fm h hr hrs hrl*
2. *enc encd encr ev exec execs*
3. *yr yrs yrl u us e*

### Word Beginnings For-, Fore-, Fur-

4. *furd fc fml fclos fse fwrn*
5. *fnS fnSd fnlr ftr ftrm fnc*

### Key

1. for; from; has, have; hour; hours; hourly
2. enclose; enclosed; enclosure; ever, every; executive; executives
3. year; years; yearly; you, your; yours; we
4. forward; force; formal; foreclose; foresee; forewarn
5. furnish; furnished; furniture; further; furthermore; furnace

# KEYBOARDING STYLE

## Memorandum Format

When a person in a business wishes to send a message to another person in the same organization, a memorandum is usually prepared. A memorandum is similar to a business letter with the following exceptions:

1. To, From, Date, and Subject lines are included at the top.

2. No salutation or complimentary close is used.

3. The writer usually initials or signs the memorandum close to his or her typed name at the top.

Many offices use preprinted memorandum forms that are designed to make typing easy. If no forms are available, the same information may be typed at the top of a page.

The person who types the memorandum must often supply an appropriate subject line.

# MEMORANDUM FORMAT

```
        TO:  Ms. Myoko Ito, Administrative Services  - line 10

        FROM:  Joe Billings, Personnel  JB

        DATE:  February 23, 19--

        SUBJECT:  Approval of New Employee

  1"    The new line for hiring an additional employee in administrative      1"
        services was approved yesterday afternoon by the personnel
        committee.  The justification you provided was considered more
        than adequate for adding a new person in the information
        processing area.  A copy of the minutes from the meeting is
        enclosed.

        Please gather the information needed in order for us to advertise
        the position and schedule interviews.  As soon as I hear from
        you, I will proceed with the necessary paperwork in this
        department.

        rlm

        Enclosure

        c: Ann Saunders
```

## SPELLING

Here are additional spelling words. Pronounce and spell each word aloud; then copy it in your own notebook, being sure that you spell it correctly. When you read the Application section of the lesson, watch for these words.

bankruptcy
candidate
confidence
exemplary
financier
foreclose
oversee
recourse
unforeseen
vacated

## VOCABULARY

Study the following definitions carefully, and notice how the words are used in the *SuperWrite* examples. Watch for these words in the Application section of the lesson.

bankruptcy

*State in which one is legally declared incapable of paying debts; insolvency.*

*he askd t corl l estbl$ bnkrpcy.*

He asked the court to establish bankruptcy.

exemplary

*Worthy of imitation; serving as a model.*

*Se dd hr wk n an xmplry mnr.*

She did her work in an exemplary manner.

financier

*One who is expert in financial matters.*

*he srvd as fnncer f t co.*

He served as financier for the company.                    (continued)

## VOCABULARY continued

foreclose    *To deprive a borrower of the right to mortgaged property, as when payments are not made.*

*un t bror cd nl mel t pams,*
*t bnk hd l fclos t prprly.*

When the borrower could not meet the payments,
the bank had to foreclose the property.

vacated    *Ceased to occupy.*

*t bldg w vacald lsl mo.*

The building was vacated last month.

## APPLICATION

Time your reading speed with Document 1 before reading the remaining documents. Then write all four documents. Remember to insert the needed punctuation in Document 4 before typing it in the correct format. Be sure to note the length of the document and place it properly on the page.

## DOCUMENT 31-1                                    *Timed Reading*

*Goal: 34 seconds (130 words per minute)*

*l Mr Elvin Grider        fm Maria Sanchez*
*mrklg depl                fnnc depl*

*fnnc g t Jefferson bldg*
*e w hpy l h b ab l srv s*
*fnncer f Mrs Jane Jefferson,*
, extra  *u clinl, wn Se prCsd a nu ofc*

, geographic

*bldg n Portland, ME. if Mrs*
*J Sd ned ftr fnds f bldg r*

, introductory

*f ny ufsen crcmstncs, pl ask*
*hr l cl us.*

*if e ma b o ftr asstnc l u*

, introductory

*r ny o t otr mbrs o u depl,*
*pl le us no. e lk fwrd l*
*wkg w u n t futr.*

## DOCUMENT 31-1

*Timed Reading*

**Goal: 34 seconds (130 words per minute)**

To: Mr. Elvin Grider, Marketing Department

From: Maria Sanchez, Finance Department

Date: —

Subject: Financing the Jefferson Building

/We were happy to have been able to serve as financier for Mrs. Jane Jefferson, your client, when she purchased/a new office building in Portland, Maine. If Mrs. Jefferson should need further funds for building or for any/unforeseen circumstances, please ask her to call us.

If we may be of further assistance to you or any of/the other members of your department, please let us know. We look forward to working with you in the future. (74)

l Mr Tom Granger    fm Alice Simms
legl dept              fnnc dept

, introductory

fcloSr o prprty l 8820 Industrial ave
s e dscsd ystrda, r bnk s
fcd l fclos t prprty locald l
8820 ndstral ave. t onr o t prprty,

, extra

Mr Ben Jones, h mad no pam

, introductory

on hs lon f m tn 6 mos. ftrm,
he vacald t stor lst July. lrs

, compound sentence

l t bus h b rtrnd, n e h no
fwrd g adrs. e fer he ma sn
dclr bnkrpcy. r onl rcors l ts
lm s l prced w fml fcloSr.

, compound sentence

pl lak wlev legl acS s ncsry,
n le me no t slalus o u wk.

To: Mr. Tom Granger, Legal Department

From: Alice Simms, Finance Department

Date: —

Subject: Foreclosure of Property at 8820 Industrial Avenue

/As we discussed yesterday, our bank is forced to foreclose the property located at 8820/ Industrial Avenue. The owner of the property, Mr. Ben Jones, has made no payment on his loan for more/than six months. Furthermore, he vacated the store last July. Letters to the business have been returned, and we have/no forwarding address. We fear he may soon declare bankruptcy. Our only recourse at this time is to proceed/with formal foreclosure.

Please take whatever legal action is necessary, and let me know the status of/your work. (101)

## DOCUMENT 31-3

*l Ms Grace Stern   fm Paul Moore*

*Parker co cntrcl*
*encd s a cpy o a lr I recd fm*
*Miss Mary Parker. s u l mol,*

, introductory

*Miss P h askd us l fnd hr nu*
*ofc l 4 h Madison ave.*
*ts reps a v lrg aml o bus f*

, compound
sentence

*r org, n e msl d an xmplry*

, introductory

*jb. s u no, t P co s l o t lrgsl*
*prsnl agnces n ts area. mny*

(continued)

| | |
|---|---|
| , extra | |
| , series | |
| , extra | |
| , compound sentence | |
| , compound sentence | |

*prspdv clints, incl g bus onrs, mgrs, n wkrs, N t ofc dal. l l b qil gd f r bus l h fnSd ts imp ofc.*

*I wd lik u l Ose ts jb, Ms S. u h dn an xclnl jb n smlr ofcs n t psl, n I no tl u l onc agn d a jb tl l rep r org n an olslndg wa. I h gral cnfdnc n u abl, n I lk fwrd l hg u rply.*

*encr*

## DOCUMENT 31-3

To: Ms. Grace Stern

From: Paul Moore

Date: —

Subject: Parker Company Contract

/Enclosed is a copy of a letter I received from Miss Mary Parker. As you will note, Miss Parker has asked/us to furnish her new office at 400 Madison Avenue.

This represents a very large amount/of business for our organization, and we must do an exemplary job. As you know, the Parker Company/is one of the largest personnel agencies in this area. Many prospective clients, including/business owners, managers, and workers, enter the office daily. It will be quite good for our business to have/furnished this important office.

I would like you to oversee this job, Ms. Stern. You have done an excellent job/in similar offices in the past, and I know that you will once again do a job that will represent our/ organization in an outstanding way. I have great confidence in your ability, and I look forward/ to having your reply. Enclosure (165)

## DOCUMENT 31-4       *Punctuation Check*

**Keyboarding Goal: 9 minutes (20 words per minute)**

l Mrs May Edwards      fm Rosa Lopez

rfrnc f Gary Kent

    encd s a cpy o t prsnl rcrd o Mr Gary Kent. s u l se Mr K bgn wk f us July 8 1987 wn he fn&d hi scul. he bgn wk s an hrl mple n t mal rum bt he w prmotd on Feb 7 1988 l hd o t mal rum. Mr K recd no ftr prmo&s ull lst yr wn he w tfrd l t scur l dept. snc tn he h srvd s asstnt l t Cef scur l ofcr.

    Mr K recd v gd fml evlua&s n eC o t ps&s he hld w r co. ftrm he s wl likd b hs suprvisrs n hs pers.

(continued)

*I fel tl he s a gd cnddal f t nu pss s hd o scur l n t NnSl dvs. if u Sd ned ftr info pl le me no.*

*encr*

*DOCUMENT 31-4*            *Punctuation Check*

**Keyboarding Goal: 9 minutes (20 words per minute)**

To: Mrs. May Edwards

From: Rosa Lopez

Date: —

Subject: Reference for Gary Kent

/Enclosed is a copy of the personnel record of Mr. Gary Kent. As you will see, *(introductory)* Mr. Kent began/work for us July 8, 1987, *(date)* when he finished high school. He began work as an hourly employee/in the mail room, but *(compound sentence)* he was promoted on February 7, 1988, *(date)* to head of the mail room./Mr. Kent received no further promotions until last year when he was transferred to the security department./Since then, *(introductory)* he has served as assistant to the chief security officer.

Mr. Kent received very good/formal evaluations in each of the positions he held with our company. Furthermore, *(introductory)* he is well liked/by his supervisors and his peers. I feel that he is a good candidate for the new position as head of/security in the international division. If you should need further information, *(introductory)* please let me know./Enclosure (162)

# SUPPLEMENTARY ACTIVITY

## A Word to the Wise

Your Desk

/In the office the principal item of furniture is the office desk. Chances are you will spend the major/part of every workday sitting at your desk. Your desk is your home while you are at work. It should be a comfortable/and attractive place to work. It should be orderly and neat, and there should be ample room for everything you/need during the workday. The drawers should not be stacked with items that you seldom use.

Many office desks have a large/drawer where pens, pencils, scissors, correction fluid, clips, and so on are kept. You should make a real effort to keep this drawer/in proper order. Items should be arranged so that they can be found quickly. When an item is used, it should be/ returned to the same area of the drawer. For example, such items as pencils should be kept at the front of/the drawer so that they can be reached quickly. Scissors may be placed a bit farther back in the drawer. Some office workers/find it helpful to place a number of small open boxes in the drawer. For example, one small box may contain/rubber bands while another contains postage stamps.

The stationery drawer should contain letterhead paper, memo/forms, and envelopes. It should also contain any form that you use on a daily basis. Stationery/items that are not used regularly should be kept in a supply closet. Any items that you seldom use should/not take space in your stationery drawer.

Many desks have one large file drawer. This drawer should not be used for the/general files in a large office. Most papers should be kept in some type of file cabinet or shelf file. Such a file is/often open to any worker who needs the information. Other workers should have no occasion to open/the file drawer of your desk. This drawer may be used to file items of a confidential or personal nature./

Work to manage your desk properly. You will find that your work will be much easier. (335)

# LESSON 32

## SuperWrite REVIEW

Read the following words, referring to the key if necessary. Then write the words in your own notebook.

**Abbreviations**

1. *hw imp impl incl incld incls*
2. *o od ods odd org uorgd*
3. *ol pd upd pl pld plg*

**Ou**

4. *flour hous houss proud ounc trousrs*

**Ow**

5. *lowr powr now cow down town*

**Key**

1. how; importance, important; importantly; include; included; includes
2. of; order; orders; ordered; organization, organize; unorganized
3. out; paid; unpaid; please; pleased; pleasing
4. flour; house; houses; proud; ounce; trousers
5. tower; power; now; cow; down; town

# PUNCTUATION

## Requests Phrased as Questions

In a business letter, requests may seem very blunt.

*snd t rpl l me nxl wk.*

Send the report to me next week.

If you wish to soften the tone, a request may be written as a question. However, if compliance is expected, use a period rather than a question mark.

*l u pl snd t rpl l me nxl wk.*

Will you please send the report to me next week.

If you wish to soften the tone still further, a question mark may be used. However, this may appear to give the person an option of whether or not to comply.

*l u pl snd t rpl l me nxl wk?*

Will you please send the report to me next week?

In the Application, when a request is phrased as a question and is followed by a period, it will be noted in the margin as follows:

. request    *l u pl mal t paprs l me.*

Will you please mail the papers to me.

# SPELLING

Here are additional spelling words. Pronounce and spell each word aloud; then copy it in your own notebook, being sure that you spell it correctly. When you read the Application section of the lesson, watch for these words.

| | |
|---|---|
| advisory | questionnaire |
| completing | rotated |
| coupon | tune-up |
| entrepreneurs | |
| informal | |
| innovative | |
| lubrication | |

# VOCABULARY

Study the following definitions carefully, and notice how the words are used in the *SuperWrite* examples. Watch for these words in the Application section of the lesson.

associate's degree     *A degree conferred after two years of work, often at a community or junior college.*

*he recd an asocal's dgre.*

He received an associate's degree.

entrepreneurs     *Business persons; those who assume the duties and responsibilities of a business.*

*r org hlps nu ntrprnurs.*

Our organization helps new entrepreneurs.

informal     *Casual, ordinary, or familiar; marked by absence of ceremony.*

*e l h svrl nfml mel gs.*

We will have several informal meetings.

innovative     *Characterized by new ideas or methods.*

*e h an invalv ins pgm.*

We have an innovative insurance program.

rotated     *Revolved; exchanged in a set pattern.*

*u lirs Sd b rolald prodcl.*

Your tires should be rotated periodically.

# APPLICATION

Time your reading speed with Document 1 before reading the remaining documents. Then write all four documents. Remember to insert the needed punctuation in Document 4 before typing it in the correct format. Be sure to note the length of the document and place it properly on the page.

alnS Ms Christine Doran

org o rlird execs                    lng:

   n a fu wks I l b opn g a nu clot g Sp n t downtown area, n I ned sm hlp n sl g up my acount g sstm. I recd my asocal's dgre fm cntrl clg n June. I Ustnd t clot g bus v wl, bt I h hd no xperenc n acount g. I w told tl u org now pvds asstnc n advic l nu ntrprnurs fre o Crg.

   l wd b a grat hlp l me l h an xperencd bus exec advis me on hw l hndl t acount g wk tl l b ncsry n my nu bus. I m prtculrl cncrnd

, compound
sentence

, compound
sentence

(continued)

, series

, introductory

. request

*abl cmpg t rpls mndald b cly, sl, n fdrl las. if u c sply ts lyp o asslnc, l u pl cl me l 555-1809 nylm afl t hr o 9n t mrng. I sncerl ap u hlp.*

*vcu*

---

## DOCUMENT 32-1          *Timed Reading*

**Goal: 1 minute, 15 seconds (130 words per minute)**

Attention Ms. Christine Doran
Organization of Retired Executives

Ladies and Gentlemen:

/In a few weeks I will be opening a new clothing shop in the downtown area, and I need some help in/setting up my accounting system. I received my associate's degree from Central College in June. I/understand the clothing business very well, but I have had no experience in accounting. I was told that your/organization now provides assistance and advice to new entrepreneurs free of charge.

It would be a great/help to me to have an experienced business executive advise me on how to handle the accounting/work that will be necessary in my new business. I am particularly concerned about completing the/reports mandated by city, state, and federal laws. If you can supply this type of assistance, will you please/call me at 555-1809 anytime after the hour of nine in the morning. I sincerely/appreciate your help. Very cordially yours, (166)

l al mples          fm Joan Morrison
                         mple bnfls

rlirm pgm

, introductory

bgn g Jan 1, t Mason acounl g
co l pvd ls wkrs w an imp
nu rlirm pgm. e r v proud
o ts invalv pgm, n e blev

, compound
sentence

tl ev mple l b qil hpy w t
mny xtra bnfls av.

, introductory

n t nxl mo, eC mple l rec
a prsnlizd bkll tl incls al t
felrs o t nu pgm. wn t bkll
arivs, l u pl rvu al t prvbs

, introductory
. request
, introductory

crfl. if u h my qs abl ny o tm,
pl cl t prsnl ofc. e l b gld l
hlp u.

, introductory

if l s nedd, e l scdul an
nfml mel g l go O t prvbs o t
pgm smlm n t ner futr.

To: All Employees

From: Joan Morrison, Employee Benefits

Date: —

Subject: Retirement Program

/Beginning January 1, the Mason Accounting Company will provide its workers with an important/new retirement program. We are very proud of this innovative program, and we believe that every employee/will be quite happy with the many extra benefits available.

In the next month, each employee will/receive a personalized booklet that includes all the features of the new program. When the booklet arrives, will/you please review all the provisions carefully. If you have any questions about any of them, please call the/personnel office. We will be glad to help you.

If it is needed, we will schedule an informal meeting to/go over the provisions of the program sometime in the near future. (130)

## DOCUMENT 32-3

, geographic

, extra
, introductory

, series
. request

, introductory

dscount on ny srvc on u frst vsl l r nu Sp.

also encd s a bkll o cupns tl u ma us durg t ntir mo o Aug. wn u us 10 tes cupns f t spcfid srvc, u l rec a dscount up l 30% of t rgulr pric. f rmp, cm n f a cmp lubrca& n oil Cang n sav 25% of t rgulr pric. if u w& l h u lirs rotald n blncd, u l sav 30%. u l also sav 30% on t csl o a cmp tun-up. n ts s n ad& l t $20 dscount u l rec b mal.

e lk fwrd l recg u qnr n l se g u n r srvc cntr ofn.

s u

encrs

Mr. J. T. Ball
Dear Mr. Ball:

/We are pleased to announce the opening of the new Central Auto Service Shop at 400 Main Street in/downtown Clarke, Mississippi. We want to offer exactly the type of service that you need, Mr. Ball. Therefore, we/have a very special request of you.

Will you please take a few moments now to fill out, sign, and return the enclosed/questionnaire. When we receive the questionnaire, we will mail you a coupon that will allow you to take a/ $20 discount on any service on your first visit to our new shop.

Also enclosed is a booklet of/coupons that you may use during the entire month of August. When you use one of these coupons for the specified/service, you will receive a discount up to 30 percent off the regular price. For example, come in for/a complete lubrication and oil change and save 25 percent off the regular price. If you wish to have/ your tires rotated and balanced, you will save 30 percent. You will also save 30 percent on the cost of/a complete tune-up. And this is in addition to the $20 discount you will receive by mail.

We look/forward to receiving your questionnaire and to seeing you in our service center often. Sincerely yours,/Enclosures (222)

## DOCUMENT 32-4      *Punctuation Check*

**Keyboarding Goal: 8 minutes (20 words per minute)**

l Mr Max Bloom      fm Lila Blake

prsnl advisry cmte apointm
l t Mar 14 mel g t bord o drctrs
o t Black co vold l st up an advisry
cmte l assl t bord n ls prsnl wk.
t bord mbrs fll tl u wd b t bsl Coic
l hd ts cmte.

*t dules o t cmte l b l rvu co-prsnl plcy n mak rcmndass cncrng al prsnl mtrs. t cmte l b prmnt n l cnssl o 5 mbrs. tr l b 1 prsn fm ec o t majr depts n t co. t mbrs l b apointd b t bord f trms o 2 yrs.*

*e wnt u t no Mr B tt e h gral cnfdnc n u abt. d u blev u dules l alow u tm t accpt ts imp rsp t?*

*l u pl le me her fm u s sn s psb.*

---

**DOCUMENT 32-4**                                    *Punctuation Check*

**Keyboarding Goal: 8 minutes (20 words per minute)**

To: Mr. Max Bloom

From: Lila Blake

Date: —

Subject: Personnel Advisory Committee Appointment

/At the March 14 meeting, *(introductory)* the board of directors of the Black Company voted to set up an/advisory committee to assist the board in its personnel work. The board members felt that you would be the best choice to/head this committee.

The duties of the committee will be to review company personnel policy and/make recommendations concerning all personnel matters. The committee will be permanent and will consist/of five members. There will be one person from each of the major departments in the company. The members will/be appointed by the board for terms of two years.

We want you to know, Mr. Bloom, *(extra)* that we have great confidence in/your ability. Do you believe your duties will allow you time to accept this important/responsibility?

Will you please let me hear from you as soon as possible. *(request)* (149)

# SUPPLEMENTARY ACTIVITY

## *A Word to the Wise*

Managing Your Notebook

/Your notebook should be kept in a handy place so that you will be able to reach it easily. You may receive/a telephone call, someone may drop by and leave a message, or your employer may wish to dictate a memo./Your notebook should not be kept in a place where it can be seen easily by others or in a place where it could/be picked up accidentally and carried away by a visitor.

When you pick up your notebook, you should be/able to find a blank page quickly. In order to locate a blank page in your notebook, you may leave it open/to the page following the last document. Other ways are to mark the page with a paper clip or place a/rubber band around the used pages. A pen should be kept with your notebook.

Leave several blank lines after one document/before you begin writing another. Identify each document clearly at the beginning either/with a name or a subject. If you are using a notebook that is bound at the top, date each page at the bottom./If the notebook is bound at the left, date each page at the top. You will be glad that you have taken the time to/identify documents by name or subject and date when you need to find your notes in a hurry.

While you are in/school, you may wish to keep two notebooks, one for classwork and one for homework. In this way you can locate your classwork/or your homework very easily. At work you may find having two notebooks is handy, particularly if/you work for two people. (264)

# LESSON 33

## SuperWrite REVIEW

Read the following words, referring to the key if necessary. Then write the words in your own notebook.

**Abbreviations**

1. *rpl rpld rpls rep repd urepd*
2. *rqr rqrd rqrm rsp rspl sn*

**Word Beginning Im-**

3. *mprs mprnt mport mprsnl mpct mpasl*

**Word Beginning Enter-**

4. *N Nd Npris Npriss Nlan Nlanm*

**Word Beginning Under-**

5. *U Unet Uground Upowrd Ucv Usld*

**Key**

1. report; reported; reports; represent, representative; represented; unrepresented
2. require; required; requirement; responsible; responsibility; soon
3. impress; imprint; import; impersonal; impact; impatient
4. enter; entered; enterprise; enterprises; entertain; entertainment
5. under; underneath; underground; underpowered; undercover; understood

# PUNCTUATION

## Semicolon with Independent Clauses and No Conjunction

Use a semicolon between two closely related independent clauses if there is no coordinating conjunction.

*Mark dd nl fel wl; he wnl hom erl.*

Mark did not feel well; he went home early.

If a transitional word, such as <u>therefore</u>, introduces the second independent clause, it is followed by a comma.

*Mark dd nl fel wl; trf, he wnl hom erl.*

Mark did not feel well; therefore, he went home early.

In the Application when two independent clauses are separated by a semicolon rather than by a conjunction, the following notation will appear in the margin:

; no conjunction

*he slded f t xm; he mad a gd grad.*

He studied for the exam; he made a good grade.

# SPELLING

Here are additional spelling words. Pronounce and spell each word aloud; then copy it in your own notebook, being sure that you spell it correctly. When you read the Application section of the lesson, watch for these words.

beneficiary
contingent
impatient
maximum
perturbed
projections
rejection
resolved
revision
tender

# VOCABULARY

Study the following definitions carefully, and notice how the words are used in the *SuperWrite* examples. Watch for these words in the Application section of the lesson.

beneficiary

*One who benefits; the designated person to receive monies from a trust or from insurance.*

*t bnfSary o t ins plcy*
*l rec a Ck.*

The beneficiary of the insurance policy
will receive a check.

contingent

*Depending upon; conditional; for use in circumstances not completely planned for.*

*hs rec g t pam s cnlngnl*
*on svrl fclrs.*

His receiving the payment is contingent
on several factors.

perturbed

*Disturbed greatly; made uneasy or anxious.*

*Se w prlrbd b t sluaS.*

She was perturbed by the situation.

resolved

*Settled; concluded; found a solution.*

*t cnflcl msl b rslvd sn.*

The conflict must be resolved soon.

tender

*A formal offer; a bid.*

*r lndr o $1m w accpld.*

Our tender of $1 million was accepted.

Time your reading speed with Document 1 before reading the remaining documents. Then write all four documents. Remember to insert the needed punctuation in Document 4 before typing it in the correct format. Be sure to note the length of the document and place it properly on the page.

## DOCUMENT 33-1 — *Timed Reading*

**Goal: 1 minute, 50 seconds (130 words per minute)**

l al mples            fm Amanda Cole
                         prsnl depl

rlirm pln

encd s u prsnl cpy o t nu
NnSl Npriss rlirm pln. l u pl
lak sm lm s sn s psb l red t
bkll trol. u l nol tl t pln h
Ugn majr Cangs snc t lsl rvs
n 1985.

pl nolc on pag 4 t prjcss o
u prsnl rlirm ncm. I msl mprs
on u tl tes fgurs r onl eslmls;
ty r basd on u crnl anul slry
n cnlnud mplm. t aclul amls
ma b mC hir; ty cd b lor.

*(margin notes:)*
. request
; no conjunction
; no conjunction

, series

; no conjunction
, introductory

, compound
  sentence

. request

. request

, extra

, introductory

notc on pags 23, 24, n 25 t
prvds f cntnud ins f u n u
fml aft rtirm. u l b abl cntnu
u hlt ins wol Nrpds, hwev, u
l b rqrd l asum fl rspl f
pam. u lif ins ma b cntnud,
bl t mxmm aml l b hf tl o u
finl yr o mplm. l u pl b dr
tl t nam o t prsn lstd s
primry bnfdary s crcl. l u
also pl Ck t nam o u cntngnl
bnfdary.

if, aft u h hd a Cnc l rvu
al t prvds, u h qs abl u
prtculr sluad, pl cl t prsnl
ofc.


encr

**Goal: 1 minute, 50 seconds (130 words per minute)**

To: All Employees

From: Amanda Cole, Personnel Department

Date: —

Subject: Retirement Plan

/Enclosed is your personal copy of the new International Enterprises retirement plan. Will you please/take some time as soon as possible to read the booklet thoroughly. You will note that the plan has undergone/major changes since the last revision in 1985.

Please notice on page 4 the projections of your/personal retirement income. I must impress on you that these figures are only estimates; they are based on your/current annual salary and continued employment. The actual amounts may be much higher; they could be/lower.

Notice on pages 23, 24, and 25 the provisions for continued insurance/for you and your family after retirement. You will be able to continue your health insurance without/interruption; however, you will be required to assume full responsibility for payment. Your life/insurance may be continued, but the maximum amount will be half that of your final year of employment. Will/you please be sure that the name of the person listed as primary beneficiary is correct. Will you/also please check the name of your contingent beneficiary.

If, after you have had a chance to review/all the provisions, you have questions about your particular situation, please call the personnel office./Enclosure (242)

l al co mples     fm Harold Cox

prsdnl

agsſ o Moore Spg co

on Mar 20 gnrl Npriss Nd

nl an agrem l prCs t M

Spg co f $1 b. r lndr o $1 t pr

Sr f 1 m Srs o slk w accpld.

U a rqrm o t fdrl gvrnm,

, introductory

; no conjunction
, introductory

, introductory

; no conjunction

; no conjunction

*[shorthand writing]*

## DOCUMENT 33-2

To: All Company Employees

From: Harold Cox, President

Date: —

Subject: Acquisition of Moore Shipping Company

/On March 20 General Enterprises entered into an agreement to purchase Moore Shipping Company/for $1 billion. Our tender of $1,000 per share for 1 million shares of stock was accepted./

Under a requirement of the federal government, we must await approval of this purchase by federal/officials, however, we feel there is no reason for rejection.

(continued)

When the purchase is formally approved,/there will be few changes in the operation of either company. I want to impress on each of you that/there will be no cutbacks in personnel and no layoffs. The transition will be a slow and gradual one; no/job is in jeopardy.

We extend a warm greeting to the members of Moore Shipping Company; welcome to our/family of workers. (143)

## DOCUMENT 33-3

prir l mal
alns Mr Kenneth Taylor
Jenson, Taylor, and Cline l ng:

anul rpt
rcntl I recd my anul stm
fm u crdt co. I ap hg t stm;
I us l l prpr my ncm tx fms.
tr r a fu itms tl I d nt fll
Ustnd, hwev. l u pl ansr sm
qs n od l cler up a fu points.
tr r 2 nos mprntd l t tp
o t stm. 1 s my acount no; wt
s t otr?
U t Dec hd g tr r 3 rfrncs

*; no conjunction*

*, extra*

*. request*

*; no conjunction*

*l ndl Npriss. I h no rcrd o bus w sc an org. l u pl ll me wy ts nam apers on my acount smry.*

. request

*my crdl lin s $5t; l Sd b $3t.*

; no conjunction

*l u pl le me her fm u sn.*

. request

*s u*

## DOCUMENT 33-3

PRIORITY MAIL

Attention Mr. Kenneth Taylor
Jenson, Taylor, and Cline
Ladies and Gentlemen:

ANNUAL REPORT

/Recently I received my annual statement from your credit company. I appreciate having the statement;/I use it to prepare my income tax forms. There are a few items that I do not fully understand, however./Will you please answer some questions in order to clear up a few points.

There are two numbers imprinted at the/top of the statement. One is my account number; what is the other?

Under the December heading there are three/references to National Enterprises. I have no record of business with such an organization./Will you tell me why this name appears on my account summary.

My credit line is shown as $5,000;/it should be $3,000.

Will you please let me hear from you soon. Sincerely yours, (131) l Mr Carl Lindsey        fm Ann Murphy

Miss Janice Davis
        alCd s a lr I recd fm Miss J
D l o r cslmrs n t sl o ME. s u l
nol Miss D s qil prlrbd w us. Se
prCsd a hom Nlanm cnlr n r Portland
ME slor lsl mo. uflnll l dd nl pvd t
qll sound tl Se lpcld. wn Se almpld
l rlrn l Se w lold tl l cd nl b accpld
l r slor.
        Miss D sls tl t sals rep w mpasl
n lreld hr n a v mprsnl mnr. Se
rminds us tl Se h b a cslmr o r
slor f m tn 5 yrs.
        U tes cndSs I blev tl u Sd cl hr
n ofr l h t Nlanm cnlr pkd up n
gv hr a fl rfnd. Se s a gd cslmr

*trf e Sd lry l kep hr gdl. l u pl le me no hw t prblm s rslvd.*

*encr*

---

DOCUMENT 33-4                                    *Punctuation Check*

**Keyboarding Goal: 8 minutes (22 words per minute)**

To: Mr. Carl Lindsey

From: Ann Murphy

Date: —

Subject: Miss Janice Davis

/Attached is a letter I received from Miss Janice Davis, one of our customers in the state of Maine. *(extra)* As you/will note, *(introductory)* Miss Davis is quite perturbed with us. She purchased a home entertainment center in our Portland, Maine, *(geographic)* store/last month. Unfortunately, *(introductory)* it did not provide the quality sound that she expected. When she attempted to/return it, *(introductory)* she was told that it could not be accepted at our store.

Miss Davis states that the sales representative/was impatient and treated her in a very impersonal manner. She reminds us that she has been a/customer of our store for more than five years.

Under these conditions, *(introductory)* I believe that you should call her and offer/to have the entertainment center picked up and give her a full refund. She is a good customer, *(no conjunction)* therefore, *(introductory)* we/should try to keep her goodwill. Will you please let me know how the problem is resolved. *(request)* Enclosure (152)

# SUPPLEMENTARY ACTIVITY

## A Word to the Wise

Proofreading and Editing

/When you mail a letter, only the document in the envelope is available to represent you, your/employer, and your company. If the document is complete and accurate, the impression on the reader/will be good. If the document contains errors, the reader may not understand the contents; he or she may/even lose confidence in your company.

When you enter a document on the keyboard, it is your/responsibility to be sure that it is accurate. Proofreading or editing your work is an essential part of/your job; do not overlook this important function.

In business offices today there are many aids to help/you create accurate documents. There are spell-checkers with many word processors that can help you catch those/typographical and spelling errors. If you have such a device available, it is a good idea to use/it with each document that you prepare. Many times a spell-checker will point out an error that you may have missed,/even if you have proofread the paper several times.

However valuable electronic devices/may be, they cannot ensure that each sentence makes sense and contains the information that it should. They cannot ensure/that all details have been included and are in the correct order. They cannot verify that the dates/included in a document are the correct dates.

If there is time after you have completed a document, set/it aside briefly while you do another assignment. When you read the document later, you will see it in/a new light. Questions will occur to you, and you will be able to check to see if they are answered in the/document. You will be able to verify any information that may appear to be questionable. Read/for overall content, and then read for small details. Work carefully and do not rush as you proofread.

Proofreading/or editing your work is vital; take this important part of your work very seriously. (357)

# LESSON 34

## SuperWrite REVIEW

Read the following words, referring to the key if necessary. Then write the words in your own notebook.

**Abbreviations**

1. *e wk wks wkl C l*
2. *lg ulg yr yrs yrl u*

**Word Beginning Ex-**

3. *xtra xmn xtrem xpnd xpns xpnss*

**Word Beginning Pro-**

4. *prtcl prduc prdc$ prfl prtst prf$l*

**Word Beginning Un-**

5. *utl uls utold uncsry usold uab*

**Key**

1. we; week, work; weeks, works; weekly; which; will
2. willing; unwilling; year; years; yearly; you, your
3. extra; examine; extreme; expend; expense; expenses
4. protect; produce; production; profit; protest; professional
5. until; unless; untold; unnecessary; unsold; unable

# PUNCTUATION

## Coordinate Adjectives

Use a comma to separate two coordinate adjectives in a series if each independently modifies the following noun.

*he s a dpndb, capb prsn.*

He is a dependable, capable person.

There are two ways to tell if the adjectives each independently modify the noun.

1. If the word <u>and</u> can be inserted between the adjectives.

   He is a dependable and capable person.
   (The word <u>and</u> can be inserted.)

2. If the two adjectives can be interchanged.

   He is a capable, dependable person.
   (The adjectives can be interchanged.)

Do not use a comma if the word <u>and</u> cannot be inserted between the adjectives.

*Se wor a bulf blu sul.*

She wore a beautiful blue suit.
(Not beautiful and blue)

Do not use a comma if the words cannot be interchanged.

She wore a beautiful blue suit.
(Not blue beautiful suit)

When coordinate adjectives appear in the Application, they will be marked as follows:

, coordinate
adjectives

*Se s a dlgnl, capb wkr.*

She is a diligent, capable worker.

## SPELLING

Here are additional spelling words. Pronounce and spell each word aloud; then copy it in your own notebook, being sure that you spell it correctly. When you read the Application section of the lesson, watch for these words.

| | | | |
|---|---|---|---|
| although | hinder | manual | recommended |
| excessive | incurring | professional | |
| exciting | lengthy | profitable | |

## VOCABULARY

Study the following definitions carefully, and notice how the words are used in the *SuperWrite* examples. Watch for these words in the Application section of the lesson.

excessive

*More than what is proper or reasonable.*

*t rpnss h b xcsv.*

The expenses have been excessive.

fiscal

*Relating to financial matters.*

*fscl rspl s a ncsl.*

Fiscal responsibility is a necessity.

incurring

*Becoming subject to; bringing liability upon yourself.*

*e wnl l rduc csls wol ncr g prblms.*

We want to reduce costs without incurring problems.

profit margin

*Return on business investment after expenses are paid.*

*r prfl mrgn msl b ncresd.*

Our profit margin must be increased.

(continued)

## VOCABULARY continued

tax audit

*An examination of tax records; a check
of the accuracy of an account.*

*e r prpr g f a tx adt.*

We are preparing for a tax audit.

## APPLICATION

Time your reading speed with Document 1 before reading the remaining documents. Then write all four documents. Remember to insert the needed punctuation in Document 4 before typing it in the correct format. Be sure to note the length of the document and place it properly on the page.

## DOCUMENT 34-1                                    *Timed Reading*

*Goal: 1 minute, 26 seconds (130 words per minute)*

*Mr Wayne Paul     d Mr P:*

, introductory

, introductory

, introductory

, coordinate adjectives

*if u r msg fon cls wn u r awa fm u fon, u r likl msg bus. if u fon s tid up n clints cnt gt tru, u r prbl lusg prfts. if u r abl spek w onl / bus asocat t a tm, u ma b usg u tm mprprl. t maks no sns t try t cndct bus tda w an oldald tlfon sstm. bus tda dmnds mdrn, efSt cmuncass.*

, introductory

, series

, introductory

, coordinate
  adjectives

; no conjunction

*[Shorthand/speedwriting text:]*

wn u r awa fm u ofc, a gd
sstm l alow u l fwrd u cls
ull u rtrn. l l alrt u wn a
scnd clr s tryg l reC u. l l
also alow u l spek w 2, 3, r
evn m prsns l 1 tm.

if u sstm s nt pvdg tes
xtra fetrs, cl us tda. e l b
gld l dmnstrat tes n mny
m intlg, xcitg fetrs tt c hlp
u bus opral m efctvl. e r
opn fm 9 a m ull 6 p m wkdas;
e r opn fm 9 a m ull 1 p m
Sats.

u s

## DOCUMENT 34-1        *Timed Reading*

**Goal: 1 minute, 26 seconds (130 words per minute)**

Mr. Wayne Paul
Dear Mr. Paul:

/If you are missing phone calls when you are away from your phone, you are likely missing business. If your phone is tied/up and clients cannot get through, you are probably losing profits. If you are able to speak with only one/business associate at a time, you may be using your time improperly.

(continued)

It makes no sense to try to/conduct business today with an outdated telephone system. Business today demands modern, efficient communications./

When you are away from your office, a good system will allow you to forward your calls until you/return. It will alert you when a second caller is trying to reach you. It will also allow you to speak/with two, three, or even more persons at one time.

If your system is not providing these extra features, call us/today. We will be glad to demonstrate these and many more interesting, exciting features that can help your/business operate more effectively. We are open from 9 a.m. until 6 p.m. weekdays; we are/open from 9 a.m. until 1 p.m. Saturdays. Yours sincerely, (189)

## DOCUMENT 34-2 . *Speed Builder*

*l Mr Max Peters fm Jackie Stevens*

*mal g prcedrs*

, coordinate
adjectives

*r bus dpnds on prmpt, tml dlvry o mal. r cstmrs xpct l rec tr mterals qkl, n e h*

, compound
sentence

, coordinate
adjectives

*bll r rpulaS on fst, dpndb srvc.*

, extra

*Durg t pst fscl perod, hwev, e h xperencd an xtreml lrg ncres n r mal g n dlvry xpnss. r csts h gn fm $5 h pr wk l wl O $1 t pr wk.*

, introductory

nedls l sa, ts h lndd l dcres r prfl mrgn.

, introductory

l ts lm, l s ncsry l mak sgnfcnl Cangs n r mal g prcedrs n od l sav mny.

, introductory

frsl, onl ilms tl r cnsd

, introductory

urgnl l b snl xprs. scnd, locl dlvry srvc l b usd onl wn a cslmr fmll rqsls dlvry

, introductory

on t sam da. trd, al otr mal l b snl tru rgulr mal srvc.

le me mfsiz tl I d nl wnl

; no conjunction

l hndr r opras; I smpl wS l rduc r xcsv mal csls. I fel tl e c acmplS a rdcS n xpnss wol ncrg majr prblms. if

, introductory

u wS l dscs ts w me, pl cl me l u cnv.

(continued)

*. request*

*l u pl dstrbul a cpy o t nu ruls l al mbrs o r slf. pl ask tm l nsrl t ruls n tr prcedrs mnuls.*

---

## DOCUMENT 34-2                                    *Speed Builder*

To: Mr. Max Peters

From: Jackie Stevens

Date: —

Subject: Mailing Procedures

/Our business depends on prompt, timely delivery of mail. Our customers expect to receive their materials/quickly, and we have built our reputation on fast, dependable service.

During the past fiscal period,/however, we have experienced an extremely large increase in our mailing and delivery expenses. Our/costs have gone from $500 per week to well over $1,000 per week. Needless to say, this has/tended to decrease our profit margin.

At this time, it is necessary to make several significant/changes in our mailing procedures in order to save money.

First, only items that are considered urgent/will be sent Express. Second, local delivery service will be used only when a customer formally/requests delivery on the same day. Third, all other mail will be sent through regular mail service.

Let me emphasize/that I do not want to hinder our operation; I simply wish to reduce our excessive mail costs. I feel/that we can accomplish a reduction in expenses without incurring major problems. If you wish to/discuss this with me, please call me at your convenience.

Will you please distribute a copy of the new rules to all/members of our staff. Please ask them to insert the rules in their procedures manuals. (230)

Mr Louis Mattingly     d Mr M:

anul apointm

, introductory

lsl yr abl ts lm, u scduld
an apointm w us l dscs u
nvslms. u l rmbr tl e
rcmndd tl u nvsl n svrl

, coordinate
adjectives

prflb, xcil g slks. e also sgd
tl u rduc u nvslm n bnds.

, introductory

b flo g r advic, u w abl
mpruv u prfls wil prlcl g
u rsorcs.

l s now lm l xmn u
nvslms agn. r prfSl slf c
rcmnd a no o imp slks n
bnds tl e fel ma prduc evn
gralr prfls f u ts yr.

e r lak g t lbrly o scdul g

, date

an apointm f u f Wed, June
3, l 4 pm. ts s t sam da n

(continued)

; no conjunction

. request

*lm u cam n lst yr ; e hop l l b cnv f u agn. e l hold ts apointm f u ull June 1. l u pl cnfrm t lm n dal s sn s psb.*

*u l*

*c : Miss Rose Lopez*

## DOCUMENT 34-3

Mr. Louis Mattingly
Dear Mr. Mattingly:

**ANNUAL APPOINTMENT**

/Last year about this time you scheduled an appointment with us to discuss your investments. You will remember that/we recommended that you invest in several profitable, exciting stocks. We also suggested that/you reduce your investment in bonds. By following our advice, you were able to improve your profits while/protecting your resources.

It is now time to examine your investments again. Our professional staff can/recommend a number of important stocks and bonds that we feel may produce even greater profits for you this year./

We are taking the liberty of scheduling an appointment for you for Wednesday, June 3, at 4 p.m. This/is the same day and time you came in last year; we hope it will be convenient for you again. We will hold this/appointment for you until June 1. Will you please confirm the time and date as soon as possible. Yours truly, c: Miss Rose Lopez (163)

**Keyboarding Goal: 11 minutes (22 words per minute)**

Mr A B Peterson       d Mr P:

encd r u cmpd ncm lx paprs f t psl fscl yr. l u pl ril u sgntr n t dal l t btm o t scnd pag.

bcs tr w an Opam l l b uncsry f u l mak ny ad$l pam l ts lm. s u l nol e h apld t fl aml o t Opam l u frsl eslmald pam f ts yr. trf u l nl h l mak an eslmald pam f ts yr ull June. rmbr l snd a Ck f $3 h on June 15 Sept 15 n Dec 15.

eC yr u msl fil a lngty dlald rpl on u prsnl rlirm pgm. ts rpl f t crnl yr s also encd. alto l s nl du ull July I sg tl u snd l now. t fm h b cmpd if al fgurs r crcl jsl sin dal n mal l.

t info on tes fms s basd on t info u gav us. l u pl rmn t fms

(continued)

*crfl l b Sr tl tr r no errs. e sg tl u kep al t rcrds o bus xpnss f a mnmm o 7 yrs n cas tr Sd b a lx adt. if u h ny prblm Ustnd g ny o t fms pl cntcl us.*

*s*

*encrs*

---

## DOCUMENT 34-4                    *Punctuation Check*

**Keyboarding Goal: 11 minutes (22 words per minute)**

Mr. A. B. Peterson
Dear Mr. Peterson:

/Enclosed are your completed income tax papers for the past fiscal year. Will you please write your signature and the/date at the bottom of the second page. *(request)*

Because there was an overpayment, *(introductory)* it will be unnecessary for/you to make any additional payment at this time. As you will note, *(introductory)* we have applied the full amount of the/overpayment to your first estimated payment for this year. Therefore, *(introductory)* you will not have to make an/estimated payment for this year until June. Remember to send a check for $300 on June 15, September/15, and December 15. *(series)*

Each year you must file a lengthy, detailed *(coordinate adjectives)* report on your personal retirement/program. This report for the current year is also enclosed. Although it is not due until July, *(introductory)* I/suggest that you send it now. The form has been completed; *(no conjunction)* if all figures are correct, *(introductory)* just sign, date, and mail *(series)* it.

The/information on these forms is based on the information you gave us. Will you please examine the forms carefully/to be sure that there are no errors. *(request)* We suggest that you keep all records of business expenses for a minimum/of seven years in case there should be a tax audit. If you have any problem understanding any of/the forms, *(introductory)* please contact us. Sincerely, Enclosures (226)

# SUPPLEMENTARY ACTIVITY

## A Word to the Wise

Checking the Facts

/Before you type a document, you must determine if all the information included is accurate. The/words must be spelled correctly, of course, and the punctuation must be correct. But you must not overlook errors/in content. Verify all important facts by looking carefully at each sentence, assuming that it might/contain an error.

Dates and times often are sources of errors in business documents. For example, if your notes/read "The meeting will last until ten," determine if it is 10 a.m. or 10 p.m.

If your notes contain the/date "Tuesday, January 4," check your calendar to see if January 4 falls on a Tuesday.

If you/have written "The meeting will be in Portland," verify if the city is Portland, Oregon, or Portland, Maine./

If a document is to be sent to several people, be sure that the list of names is complete and accurate./An omitted name can cause a great deal of embarrassment.

The details in a business document are/extremely important. They affect goodwill as well as profits. Although both you and your employer are responsible/for producing accurate, complete documents, you must assume that you will be the person making the/final check. (222)

# *LESSON 35*

## *SuperWrite REVIEW*

Read the following words, referring to the key if necessary. Then write the words in your own notebook.

**Word Beginning Be-**

1. *blwen bcs bnet blev blra bgn g*

**Word Beginning Trans-**

2. *Tpir Tpos Tml Tcrib Tport Tprlas*

**Ow**

3. *now flowr lowr lowl down town*

**Ou**

4. *hous ounc ouncs proud proudl doul*

**Qu**

5. *ql qil qz aqir aqird nqir*

**Key**

1. between; because; beneath; believe; betray; beginning
2. transpire; transpose; transmit; transcribe; transport; transportation
3. now; flower; tower; towel; down; town
4. house; ounce; ounces; proud; proudly; doubt
5. quit; quite; quiz; acquire; acquired; inquire

# PUNCTUATION

## Compound Adjectives

When two or more words function as a single adjective <u>before</u> a noun, they are called a compound adjective.

Hyphenate a compound adjective before a noun.

*l s a wl-non bld g.*

    It is a well-known building.

If the same words come <u>after</u> the noun, they are not a compound adjective. Do not use a hyphen.

*t bld g s wl non.*

    The building is well known.

If the first word is an adverb ending in <u>ly</u>, do not use a hyphen whether the words come before or after the noun.

*Se s a hil rgdd spekr.*

    She is a highly regarded speaker.

When a compound adjective appears in the Application, it will be marked as follows:

— compound    *e recd an up-l-t-mnl rpl.*
adjective

    We received an up-to-the-minute report.

# SPELLING

Here are additional spelling words. Pronounce and spell each word aloud; then copy it in your own notebook, being sure that you spell it correctly. When you read the Application section of the lesson, watch for these words.

| | |
|---|---|
| absence | employees |
| accommodate | expedite |
| acquiring | impede |
| compound interest | repeatedly |
| deliberation | transferred |

# VOCABULARY

Study the following definitions carefully, and notice how the words are used in the *SuperWrite* examples. Watch for these words in the Application section of the lesson.

certificate of deposit
: *A printed statement from a financial institution saying that a named person has a specified sum on deposit for a stated period.*

*crlfd o dpsl* pd 9% inl.

certificate of deposit **paid 9 percent interest.**

compound interest
: *Interest computed on the accumulated interest as well as on the principal.*

*e recd cmpnd inl on r dpsl.*

**We received** compound interest **on our deposit.**

deliberation
: *Weighing in mind; thoughtful consideration for action.*

*afl dlbra$, I dcidd l rlrn l scul.*

**After** deliberation, **I decided to return to school.**

expedite
: *To carry out promptly; to accelerate.*

*a gd cmunca$s sslm l hlp l xpdil u wk.*

**A good communications system will help to** expedite **your work.**

impede
: *To slow progress; interfere with.*

*a pur sslm l mped u wk.*

**A poor system will** impede **your work.**

# APPLICATION

Time your reading speed with Document 1 before reading the remaining documents. Then write all four documents. Remember to insert the needed punctuation in Document 4 before typing it in the correct format. Be sure to note the length of the document and place it properly on the page.

## DOCUMENT 35-1

**DOCUMENT 35-1** — *Timed Reading*

*Goal: 1 minute, 4 seconds (130 words per minute)*

Miss Beverley Medlin d Miss M:
her r sm tngs f u l tnk abt
cncrn g a llfon sslm.

a wl-dsind sslm alows
cslmrs l reC u wol b g Ffrd
rpeldl. l alows u mples l rdil
cls qkl b lCg / bln. l aclll
alows u l se t no o t clr bf u
ansr t fon.

ds ts sound lik u llfon sslm?
s u sslm mdrn n up l dal? r u
proud o u sslm? s l a hndy lul
tl hlps u rpdil u evda bus, r
ds l smlms sem l mped bus?

*– compound adjective*

*, compound sentence*

(continued)

, introductory

, coordinate adjectives

— compound adjective

*if u sslm neds l b updald, cl 1 o r reps lda n le us So u r mdrn, up-l-dal fon sslms. u l prbbl b qil srprisd l hw rsnbl ty r pricd.*

*cu*

## DOCUMENT 35-1      *Timed Reading*

**Goal: 1 minute, 4 seconds (130 words per minute)**

Mrs. Beverley Medlin
Dear Mrs. Medlin:

/Here are some things for you to think about concerning a telephone system.

A well-designed system allows/customers to reach you without being transferred repeatedly. It allows your employees to redial calls quickly/by touching one button. It actually allows you to see the number of the caller before you answer the/phone.

Does this sound like your telephone system? Is your system modern and up to date? Are you proud of your system?/Is it a handy tool that helps you expedite your everyday business, or does it sometimes seem to impede/business?

If your system needs to be updated, call one of our representatives today and let us show you our/modern, up-to-date phone systems. You will probably be quite surprised at how reasonably they are priced./Cordially yours, (141)

## DOCUMENT 35-2      *Speed Builder*

*l Ms Maureen McGee fm Nathan Cain*

*apoinlm l Iprlad depl*
*u mo ask g me if I wd accpl*
*an apoinlm l mng t Iprlad*

, coordinate
adjectives

, introductory

depl arivd lda. I m v proud l
h b slcld l hd sC a lrg, imp
depl. uflnll, I cnl accpl.

f sm lm I h b cns g rqsl g
a lev o *absnc* fm t co so tl I mil
cnlnu grdul wk n brus l _sl_ clg

– compound
adjective

, introductory

on a fl-lm bass. afl a qral del
o *dlbraS,* I h dcidd l prced w
ts cors o acS. trf, I l b uab l

, introductory

accpl t asinm s mgr o t IprlaS
depl.

– compound
adjective

, compound
sentence

I m v hpy l h wkd n sC a
wl-mngd org, n I l b rlrng l
wk her n abl a yr. I sncerl
hop tl t bord l cns alow g me
l srv n ts r sm smlr cpcl l
tl lm. l u pl rprs my apS l t
mbrs o t bord f tr cns.

To: Ms. Maureen McGee

From: Nathan Cain

Date: —

Subject: Appointment to Transportation Department

/Your memo asking me if I would accept an appointment to manage the transportation department arrived/today. I am very proud to have been selected to head such a large, important department. Unfortunately,/I cannot accept.

For some time I have been considering requesting a leave of absence from the/company so that I might continue graduate work in business at State College on a full-time basis. After a/great deal of deliberation, I have decided to proceed with this course of action. Therefore, I will be/unable to accept the assignment as manager of the transportation department.

I am very happy/to have worked in such a well-managed organization, and I will be returning to work here in about a/year. I sincerely hope that the board will consider allowing me to serve in this or some similar/capacity at that time. Will you please express my appreciation to the members of the board for their/consideration. (181)

## *DOCUMENT 35-3*

- compound adjective

- compound adjective

, introductory

- compound adjective

; no conjunction
pl- l clos ts acount; e wnt l

, introductory
lev abt $3t tr. hwev, e wnt l
tak advntg o t hir inl ral tt
s now av fm a crtfd o dpst. e
l b ab l gt an inl ral o 9% if e
lev r mny on dpst f 6 mos. n

, introductory
ad$, e l rec cmpound inl rtr
tn smp inl. ts l mak gil a dfrnc

; no conjunction
n t amt o inl e ern; r pr acount
pas onl 5%.

l u pl slp b t bnk s sn s

. request
psb n mak t Tfr. tks f u hlp.

c: Mr Harold Jenkins

## DOCUMENT 35-3

To: Mrs. Nadine Short

From: Sam Wolfson

Date: —

Subject: Transfer of Funds

/Last evening the executive board of the Central Investment Club voted to transfer $5,000 from/our day-to-day savings account at the International Bank to a six-month certificate of deposit/at the same bank.

(continued)

As you know, we now have about $8,000 in our day-to-day savings account. We do/not plan to close this account; we want to leave about $3,000 there. However, we want to take advantage/of the higher interest rate that is now available from a certificate of deposit. We will be/able to get an interest rate of 9 percent if we leave our money on deposit for six months. In addition,/we will receive compound interest rather than simple interest. This will make quite a difference in the amount of/interest we earn; our present account pays only 5 percent.

Will you please stop by the bank as soon as possible and/make the transfer. Thanks for your help. c: Mr. Harold Jenkins (169)

## DOCUMENT 35-4                                    *Punctuation Check*

**Keyboarding Goal: 7 minutes (24 words per minute)**

*l Mr Mark Peters            fm J D Jones*

*Madison ofc towr*
*l t exec bord metg on Fri May 4 e*
*dscsd aqirg t Madison ofc towr a wl*
*non bld g locald n downtown M. e ned*
*t xtra spac bcs r co h gron rpdl O t*
*psl 5 yrs.*
*t towr h 9 flors o ofc spac. t ofcs r*
*wl dsind n I h no doul tl t bld g wd*
*acmdal r neds f l lesl 20 yrs.*
*wn e nqird lsl yr t pr onrs w*
*ask g f $10 m f t towr. e fll tl t bld g*
*w smwl Opricd. l u pl gl n lc w tm*

*[handwritten shorthand notes]*

agn l dlrmn tr ask g pric now. wn u
h ts info l u pl Fml l l Mr Doyle n
snd a cpy l me. e l tn dcid on r nxl
slp.

c: Mr D

---

## DOCUMENT 35-4            *Punctuation Check*

**Keyboarding Goal: 7 minutes (24 words per minute)**

To: Mr. Mark Peters

From: J. D. Jones

Date: —

Subject: Madison Office Tower

/At the executive board meeting on Friday, May 4, *(date)* we discussed acquiring the Madison Office Tower, a/well-known *(compound adjective)* building located in downtown Madison. *(extra)* We need the extra space because our company has grown/rapidly over the past five years.

The tower has nine floors of office space. The offices are well designed, and *(compound sentence)* I have/no doubt that the building would accommodate our needs for at least 20 years.

When we inquired last year, *(introductory)* the present/owners were asking for $10 million for the tower. We felt that the building was somewhat overpriced. Will you/please get in touch with them again to determine their asking price now. *(request)* When you have this information, *(introductory)* will you please/transmit it to Mr. Doyle and send a copy to me. *(request)* We will then decide on our next step. c: Mr./Doyle (141)

# SUPPLEMENTARY ACTIVITY

## A Word to the Wise

Expediting Information in the Electronic Office

/You will find that your ability to use *SuperWrite* will help you to expedite the flow of information/in the electronic office.

Of course, you will use your ability to write quickly as you take dictation/of letters, memos, and reports. You will save your time and that of your employer because you can write notes quickly/and transcribe them later.

You will also use your *SuperWrite* ability to write instructions and messages./You will likely receive many telephone calls during the course of the day, and you will have to take messages/for one or more business associates. It is your responsibility to take a complete, accurate/telephone message, and you will be able to do so using *SuperWrite.* You will then type a well-organized/message and leave it for the person who was called.

You will also use your skill to make notes to yourself in the office./As you outline your work for the day, you will do so in *SuperWrite.* You will use your skill when you make lists of/needed supplies. Your employer may ask you to take care of three or four items. You will be able to jot down the/work easily in your notebook and then do the work in order of priority.

In the electronic/office of today, being able to make quick, legible notes is a great asset. You will find that you will use your/*SuperWrite* skills to help you expedite information throughout the day. (252)

# LESSON 36

### SuperWrite REVIEW

Read the following words, referring to the key if necessary. Then write the words in your own notebook.

**Short I Before a Vowel**

1. *mleral mlerals ado folo rado vranc*

**Word Beginning Pre-**

2. *prpr prprd prdcl prdcld prvu prfr*

**Word Ending -tion**

3. *moᏕ sluaᏕ rlaᏕ fuᏕ nolaᏕ snsaᏕ*

**Sh**

4. *Se Sl Srl Sgr Sp Sap*
5. *cᏕ brᏕ crᏕ clᏕ plᏕ iSu*

**Key**

1. material; materials; audio; folio; radio; variance
2. prepare; prepared; predict; predicted; preview; prefer
3. motion; situation; relation; fusion; notation; sensation
4. she; shall; shirt; sugar; ship; shape
5. cash; brush; crush; clash; plush; issue

# KEYBOARDING STYLE

## Report Format

In business short reports are often used to present information. There are many acceptable formats; one is explained here.

**Margins.** The report is typed using one-inch side margins. It may be single-spaced or double-spaced.

**Title.** The title is centered in capitals on the tenth line from the top. A quadruple space is left below the title.

**Subtitles.** A double space is left above and below a first- or second-level subtitle.

A first-level subtitle is centered with the first letter of each word capitalized.

A second-level subtitle is typed at the left margin with the first letter of the first word and the first letter of all other main words capitalized. This subtitle is underlined.

A third-level subtitle is indented and typed on the same line with the paragraph. The first letter of the first word is capitalized. This subtitle is underlined and followed by a period and two spaces. The paragraph begins at this point.

**Second page.** The second page begins with the page number on the sixth line from the top of the paper. Double space below the page number to the text.

**An Example of Report Format**

TITLE OF REPORT  -line 10

QS

    In business, reports are often used to present information. The report is double-spaced.  If you wish to conserve paper, however, you may single-space the report and double space between the paragraphs.  Paragraphs are indented five spaces.

    A business report is usually typed with one-inch side margins.  The title begins on the tenth line from the top edge of the paper.  Other pages in the body of the report begin on the seventh line.  A margin of about six lines is left at the bottom.

First-Level Subtitle

1"
    A first-level subtitle is preceded and followed by a double space and is centered.  The first letter of the first word and the first letter of other main words are capitalized.
  1"

<u>Second-Level Subtitle</u>

    Second-level subtitles are typed at the left margin and underscored.  The first letter of the first word and the first letter of other main words are capitalized.

    <u>Third-level subtitle</u>.  A third-level subtitle is indented and typed on the line with the paragraph.  It is underscored and followed by a period.  Only the first letter of the first word is capitalized.

## SPELLING

Here are additional spelling words. Pronounce and spell each word aloud; then copy it in your own notebook, being sure that you spell it correctly. When you read the Application section of the lesson, watch for these words.

| | |
|---|---|
| dispensed | physician |
| eligible | portfolio |
| generic | reimbursed |
| maintenance | spouse |
| pharmacy | underwritten |

## VOCABULARY

Study the following definitions carefully, and notice how the words are used in the *SuperWrite* examples. Watch for these words in the Application section of the lesson.

dispensed        *Prepared and distributed, as in medication.*

*t drgs l b dspnsd tru u locl frmcy.*

The drugs will be dispensed through your local pharmacy.

generic        *General; not bearing a company name.*

*f sav gs, r frmcy uss gnrc drgs.*

For savings, our pharmacy uses generic drugs.

reimbursed        *Paid back; repaid an equal amount.*

*t co rmbrsd us f r xpnss.*

The company reimbursed us for our expenses.

spouse        *A wife or husband.*

*u spous s cvd b r ins.*

Your spouse is covered by our insurance.

## VOCABULARY continued

underwritten      *Assumed liability for; agreed to pay for.*

*r ins s Urtn b t co.*

Our insurance is underwritten by the company.

## APPLICATION

The Application contains an extended business report. First read it carefully. Then copy it in *SuperWrite* in your notebook, inserting the necessary punctuation. From your notes, type it in the business report format shown in this lesson.

**NOTE:** Business documents in the Application section of Lessons 36-40 are Punctuation Checks. Therefore, no reasons for using punctuation will appear in the *SuperWrite* documents. Punctuation marks and reasons for using the punctuation will continue to appear in the key for each document.

## DOCUMENT 36
## Extended Business Report           Punctuation Check
*Keyboarding Goal: 24 minutes (24 words per minute)*

*t Pace co hlt ins pgm*

*al wkrs hu r mpld fl tm b t P co
r elgb f cvg U 1 o t co hlt ins plns.
tr r 2 plns av. t frsl s t basc pln n
t scnd s t hlt manlnc pln. U etr pln
t fl tm wkr s cvd l no ol o pkt xpns.
t spous n Cldrn o an mple ma b cvd
U etr pgm f a sl mol fe.*

(continued)

t basc pln

fss n hsplls

U t basc pln u ma Cus ny fss r hspll u ws. if t splir ds nl accpl asinm o rpnss fm us u l b rsp f cs pam f t srvc. u r rqrd l prpr a fm n sbml l l us f pam. u l tn b rmbrsd l r prscribd rals f rpnss tl u ncr. if t splir Crgs m tn r prscribd rals u r rsp f t dfrnc.

prscrps drgs

prscrps drgs ma b prcsd fm ny frmcy. ty r cvd l a ral o 50% o tr aclul csl. u ma us etr brnd nam r gnrc drgs. hwev u msl prpr n mal a fm l us n od l rec rmbrsm.

csl

t csl o t <u>basc</u> pln s Urln b t co f t fl lm wkr. t csl o inclg a spous s $25 pr mo. t csl f eC Cild s an adSl $25 pr mo. hwev a fml l nl b rqrd l pa m tn $1 h pr mo f cvg.

t hlt manlnnc pln

fs&s n hsplls

U t <u>hlt</u> manlnnc pln u u spous n u Cldrn msl us fs&s n hsplls lsld n t co porlfolo. tes r t co apruvd splirs. ny rxpnss ncrd l b pd n fl drcl l t fs& r hspll. u l nl b rsp f pa g c& f ny bls n u ned nl fl ol ny fms.

prscrp& drgs

prscrp& drgs r dspnsd tru t co frmcy.

(continued)

gnrc drgs. n od l nSr savgs gnrc
drgs l b usd wnev psb.

brnd nam drgs. brnd nam drgs
l b dspnsd onl n tos cass wr t
fsS so drcls.


csl

mple onl. t csl o t hlt manlnnc
pln s Urln b t co f t fl lm mple.

fml mbrs. t csl o incl g al mbrs o
t imedal fml s $50 pr mo.


slcS


wn mples r hird on a fl lm bass
ty r gvn t opS o slcl g 1 o t plns.
eC yr n Jan al fl lm mples ma elcl
l Cang fm 1 pln l anotr. afl Feb 1 no
Cangs otr tn t adS r dleS o a fml
mbr ma b mad ull t flo g Jan.

*adsl info*

*f adsl info n a co portfolo o ins cvg pl cl t prsnl ofc durg rgulr wk g hrs. f ny otr mterals pl slp b t prsnl ofc.*

## DOCUMENT 36
### Extended Business Report                    *Punctuation Check*

**Keyboarding Goal: 24 minutes (24 words per minute)**

THE PACE COMPANY HEALTH INSURANCE PROGRAM

/All workers who are employed full time by the Pace Company are eligible for coverage under one of/the company health insurance plans. There are two plans available. The first is the Basic Plan, and *(compound sentence)* the second/is the Health Maintenance Plan. Under either plan, *(introductory)* the full-time *(compound adjective)* worker is covered at no out-of-pocket *(compound adjective)* expense./The spouse and children of an employee may be covered under either program for a set monthly fee.

The/Basic Plan

### Physicians and Hospitals

Under the Basic Plan, *(introductory)* you may choose any physician or hospital you/ wish. If the supplier does not accept assignment of expenses from us, *(introductory)* you will be responsible for cash/payment for the service. You are required to prepare a form and submit it to us for payment. You will then be/reimbursed at our prescribed rates for expenses that you incur. If the supplier charges more than our prescribed/rates, *(introductory)* you are responsible for the difference.

### Prescription Drugs

Prescription drugs may be purchased from any pharmacy./They are covered at a rate of 50 percent of their actual cost. You may use either brand-name *(compound adjective)* or/ generic drugs. However, *(introductory)* you must prepare and mail a form to us in order to receive reimbursement.

(continued)

### Cost

The cost/of the Basic Plan is underwritten by the company for the full-time *(compound adjective)* worker. The cost of including/a spouse is $25 per month. The cost for each child is an additional $25 per month./However, *(introductory)* a family will not be required to pay more than $100 per month for coverage.

### The/Health Maintenance Plan

### Physicians and Hospitals

Under the Health Maintenance Plan, *(introductory)* you, your spouse, and your children *(series)* must use/physicians and hospitals listed in the company portfolio. These are the company-approved *(compound adjective)* suppliers./Any expenses incurred will be paid in full direct to the physician or hospital. You will not be/responsible for paying cash for any bills, and *(compound sentence)* you need not fill out any forms.

### Prescription Drugs

Prescription/drugs are dispensed through the company pharmacy.

Generic drugs.   In order to ensure savings, *(introductory)* generic drugs/will be used whenever possible.

Brand-name *(compound adjective)* drugs.   Brand-name *(compound adjective)* drugs will be dispensed only in those cases where the/physician so directs.

### Cost

Employee only.   The cost of the Health Maintenance Plan is underwritten by the/company for the full-time *(compound adjective)* employee.

Family members.   The cost of including all members of the/immediate family is $50 per month.

### Selection

When employees are hired on a full-time *(compound adjective)* basis, *(introductory)* they/are given the option of selecting one of the plans. Each year in January, *(introductory)* all full-time *(compound adjective)* employees may/elect to change from one plan to another. After February 1, *(introductory)* no changes other than the addition/or deletion of a family member may be made until the following January.

### Additional/Information

For additional information and a company portfolio of insurance coverage,/*(introductory)* please call the personnel office during regular working hours. For any other materials, *(introductory)* please stop/by the personnel office. (564)

# SUPPLEMENTARY ACTIVITY

## A Word to the Wise

Body Position

/A lounge chair may be a good place to take a nap, but it is not a good place to work.

In an office you should be/constantly aware of your posture. If you lounge in your office chair, there will be two major consequences.

1. When/you do not sit erect with your feet on the floor, you will become tired fairly quickly. You put a strain on your/back muscles, and you develop back pain and become tired.

2. When you have poor posture, you present a very poor/image to those who see you. You project the image of someone who is not taking work very seriously/when you sit with your legs crossed or when you lean far back in your chair.

Choose a chair that is the right height for you. A tall/person needs a higher chair than someone who is short. It is a good idea to select an adjustable chair/so that you will be able to raise or lower the height to just the position that you prefer.

Find an adequate/surface when you take notes so that your notebook will lie flat. If you have to place your notebook on top of other materials/on the desk, you will prepare poor notes. Conditions should be ideal when you are at your desk, but you will often need/to take notes when you are away from your desk. If you have to take notes in the office of a business associate,/try to locate a proper writing surface. However, you should not write on the edge of another person's desk/without permission.

Sofas and large chairs are often found in executive offices. However, you should not/choose these because they are quite often very low. It is difficult to write when sitting on a sofa or a low chair. You will probably have to place your notebook on your knee or on the arm of the chair, and neither choice is a/good one. If you must take notes while sitting on a low chair, sit erect near the front edge of the seat and keep your feet/close to the chair, not extended forward.

Proper body position not only makes your work easier, it also/helps you to project the right image. (365)

# *LESSON 37*

## *SuperWrite REVIEW*

Read the following words, referring to the key if necessary. Then write the words in your own notebook.

Oi

1. *oil soil soild boil boilr toil*

Oy

2. *boy boys loyl loylly royl njoym*

Ch

3. *Cef Cer Ck Cild Crm Cnc*
4. *reC teC teCrs aproC srC bnC*

Th

5. *tem tl bot pt rtr brtr*

**Key**

1. oil; soil; soiled; boil; boiler; toil
2. boy; boys; loyal; loyalty; royal; enjoyment
3. chief; cheer; check; child; charm; chance
4. reach; teach; teachers; approach; search; bench
5. theme; that; both; path; rather; brother

# PUNCTUATION

## Titles of Publications

Enclose the title of a part of a published work in quotation marks.

*[handwritten cursive]*

The title of the chapter is "Getting Ahead."

*[handwritten cursive]*

The article was entitled "Working for Yourself."

Underscore or key in all capitals the titles of books, magazines, newspapers, or other separately published works.

*[handwritten cursive]*

We will read the text, World History.

*[handwritten cursive]*

The article appeared in Time.

*[handwritten cursive]*

Our local newspaper is The Daily Reporter.

# SPELLING

Here are additional spelling words. Pronounce and spell each word aloud; then copy it in your own notebook, being sure that you spell it correctly. When you read the Application section of the lesson, watch for these words.

abandon
already
choose
function key
initiate
opening menu
prompt
screen
scrolling
stacks

## VOCABULARY

Study the following definitions carefully, and notice how the words are used in the *SuperWrite* examples. Watch for these words in the Application section of the lesson.

function key

*A key on a computer keyboard that when struck causes the computer to perform a series of predetermined steps.*

*t fnc& ky css t cmpulr l prnl a dcum.*

The function key causes the computer to print a document.

initiate

*To cause to begin.*

*strik g 1 ky l insal a src o t dala bas.*

Striking one key will initiate a search of the database.

opening menu

*The beginning section of a computer program that allows the user to choose a desired application.*

*u ma slcl an apl fm t opn g mnu.*

You may select an application from the opening menu.

prompt

*A symbol on the computer screen that reminds the user to take some type of action.*

*strik t prpr ky wn t prmpl apers on t scren.*

Strike the proper key when the prompt appears on the screen.

## VOCABULARY continued

stacks

*The area in a library in which reading matter is shelved.*

*u msl find t bk n t slks.*

You must find the book in the stacks.

## APPLICATION

The Application contains an extended business report. First read it carefully. Then copy it in *SuperWrite* in your notebook, inserting the necessary punctuation. From your notes, type it in a business report format.

### DOCUMENT 37
### Extended Business Report
Punctuation Check

*Keyboarding Goal: 30 minutes (26 words per minute)*

*hw l us t librry cmpulr cllg*

*blwen Jan 5 1988 n Aug 25 1989 t sl unvrs l librry Ifrd t crd cllg rfrnc sslm l a cmpulr basd rfrnc sslm. t flo g info l hlp u n find g mleral n t librry.*

*find g a bk*

*t nu sslm s smlr l t old sslm. l local a bk n t librry u l lk f a lill*

(continued)

a sbjcl r an atr. hwev u l insal a
srC tru t cmpulr dala bas rtr tn
tru crds.

frsl local a cmpulr lrmnl tl s nl
n us. swC l on if l s nl alrdy on. t
swC s locald l t bk o t lrmnl on t
lfl sid. an opng mnu l aper on t
scren.

u l nolc tl tr s a fl alfblc kybord
tr r also a no o spSl kys l t lp o t
kybord. eC o tes kys h a spSl fncS
n s cld a fncS ky. t kys r clerl labld
n u Sd b abl us tm esl afl u h rd ts
info.

local g a bk b lill
wn u no t lill o a bk hl fncS ky
no 1. wal f t prmpl on t scren lyp t
lill n hl t N ky. t dala bas l b srCd
n t fl bblogrfc rfrnc l aper on t
scren. jl down t rfrnc n us l l local

t bk n t slks us g t mps locald on
eC flor.

f xmp if u wS l find t bk nlilld
xrcis g f njoym lyp t lill n fl. t
cmpulr l rspnd w t fl bblogrfc
rfrnc incl g t atr nam t pblSr n t
plac n dal o pblcaS s wl s t rfrnc
no.

local g a bk b sbjcl
if u wd lik l local a bk on a crln
sbjcl slrik fncS ky no 2. wal f t
prmpl lyp t sbjcl n slrik t N ky.

if t cmpulr rspnds tl no bk w
found Ck t sbjcl w t rfrnc lrl nlilld
sbjcl hd gs. a cpy s locald ner eC
bnk o cmpulr lrmnls. if t wrd u Cos
s nl a lslld sbjcl tr l b a crs-rfrnc
tl l sg a no o smlr wrds l us l
srC t dala bas.

(continued)

wn u h typd an apruvd sbjcl nam t cmpulr l lsl a no o bks tl cnlan ts sbjcl mlr. jl down t rfrnc nos n local t bks n t slks.

f xmp if u wS l find a bk on t sbjcl o xplor g f oil t rfrnc lxl l gv a no o sbjcl hd gs tl u ma us. u ma find a lxl w a Cpdr nlilld drlg f oil r anotr nlilld local g oil. etr Sd cnlan t info u wnl.

local g a bk b atr

if u no t atr o a bk u wS l local slrik fncS ky no 3. wal f t prmpl lyp t lsl nam o t atr n slrik t N ky. if t lsl nam s frl cmn lyp t frsl nam also.

t cmpulr l rspnd w al t bks b tl prlculr atr. jl down t rfrnc nos n find t bk u wnl n t slks.

adsl fncss

tr r a no o adsl fncss tl u ma us s u srC f a ltl.

scrol g
if u h Cosn a sbjcl tl incls a gral mny rfrncs u ma ned l slp t rfrncs fm scrol g of t scren so tl u ma cpy tm.

slpg a scrol. red t mleral fm t vrus rfrncs s l apers on t scren. wn u se a rfrnc u wsl l cpy slrik fncs ky no 4. ts l slp t scren fm scrol g.

rsum g a scrol. wn u h cped t mleral fm t scren n wsl l se otr rfrncs slrik fncs ky no 4 onc agn. ts l cs t cmpulr l rsum scrol g.

(continued)

slp g

   if u ws l abndn t fncs u r now us g strik fncs ky no 5. ts l cs t fncs l slp n t opn g mnu l aper agn. u ma trn Cus anotr fncs.


ql g

   wn u h fnsd us g t trmnl n ws l ql strik fncs ky no 5 C l cs t cmpulr l slp t crnl fncs. u ma lev t trmnl on r u ma swC l of.


       ql g adsl hlp


   ny mbr o t librry slf l b gld l hlp u n local g mteral. if u h my trb find g wt u ned jsl ask. e r her l hlp u.

*Keyboarding Goal: 30 minutes (26 words per minute)*

HOW TO USE THE LIBRARY COMPUTER CATALOG

/Between January 5, 1988, and August 25, 1989, *(dates)* the State University/library transferred the card catalog reference system to a computer-based *(compound adjective)* reference system./The following information will help you in finding material in the library.

Finding a Book

The/new system is similar to the old system. To locate a book in the library, *(introductory)* you will look for a/title, a subject, or an author. *(series)* However, *(introductory)* you will initiate a search through the computer data base/rather than through cards.

First, *(introductory)* locate a computer terminal that is not in use. Switch it on if it is not already/on. The switch is located at the back of the terminal on the left side. An opening menu will/appear on the screen.

You will notice that there is a full alphabetic keyboard; *(no conjunction)* there are also a number of/special keys at the top of the keyboard. Each of these keys has a special function and is called a function key. The keys/are clearly labeled, and *(compound sentence)* you should be able to use them easily after you have read/this information.

Locating a Book by Title

When you know the title of a book, *(introductory)* hit function key number 1. Wait for the prompt on/the screen, type the title, and hit the enter key. *(series)* The data base will be searched, and *(compound sentence)* the full bibliographic/reference will appear on the screen. Jot down the reference, and *(compound sentence)* use it to locate the book in the stacks, using the/maps located on each floor. *(extra)*

For example, *(introductory)* if you wish to find the book entitled Exercising for Enjoyment,/*(underscore book title-extra)* type the title in full. The computer will respond with the full bibliographic reference, including/the author name, the publisher, and the place and date of publication *(extra-series)*, as well as the reference number./*(extra)*

Locating a Book by Subject

If you would like to locate a book on a certain subject, *(introductory)* strike function key number/2. Wait for the prompt, type the subject, and strike the enter key. *(series)*

If the computer responds that no book was found, *(introductory)* check/the subject with the reference text entitled Subject Headings. *(underscore book title)* A copy is located near each bank of/computer terminals. If the word you chose is not a listed subject, *(introductory)* there will be a cross-reference that will/suggest a number of similar words to use to search the data base.

(continued)

When you have typed an approved subject name, *(introductory)* the/computer will list a number of books that contain this subject matter. Jot down the reference numbers, and *(compound sentence)*/locate the books in the stacks.

For example, *(introductory)* if you wish to find a book on the subject of exploring for oil, *(extra)* the/reference text will give a number of subject headings that you may use. You may find a text with a chapter/entitled "Drilling for Oil" *(quote chapter title)* or another entitled "Locating Oil." *(quote chapter title)* Either should contain the information you want./

### Locating a Book by Author

If you know the author of the book you wish to locate, *(introductory)* strike function key/number 3. Wait for the prompt, type the last name of the author, and strike the enter key. *(series)* If the last name is fairly/common, *(introductory)* type the first name also.

The computer will respond with all the books by that particular author. Jot/down the reference numbers, and *(compound sentence)* find the book you want in the stacks.

### Additional Functions

There are a number of/additional functions that you may use as you search for a text.

### Scrolling

If you have chosen a subject that/includes a great many references, *(introductory)* you may need to stop the references from scrolling off the screen so that you/may copy them.

Stopping a scroll.   Read the material from the various references as it appears on the/ screen. When you see a reference you wish to copy, *(introductory)* strike function key number 4. This will stop the screen from scrolling./

Resuming a scroll.   When you have copied the material from the screen and wish to see other references, /*(introductory)* strike function key number 4 once again. This will cause the computer to resume scrolling.

### Stopping

If you wish to/abandon the function you are now using, *(introductory)* strike function key number 5. This will cause the function to stop, and *(compound sentence)* the/opening menu will appear again. You may then choose another function.

### Quitting

When you have finished using/the terminal and wish to quit, *(introductory)* strike function key number 5, which will cause the computer to stop the current/function. *(extra)* You may leave the terminal on, or *(compound sentence)* you may switch it off.

### Getting Additional Help

Any member of the/library staff will be glad to help you in locating material. If you have any trouble finding what you/need, *(introductory)* just ask. We are here to help you. (785)

# SUPPLEMENTARY ACTIVITY

## A Word to the Wise

Confidential Material

/It is very important to keep confidential material confidential. In an office you will have/ access to information of such a nature.

When a business is negotiating to purchase property,/for example, the figures should not be made available to the public. Matters of a legal nature should/be kept strictly confidential. Payroll and tax records are generally not public knowledge.

When you deal with/confidential material, you should be very careful. If you are working on a confidential/document and someone stops at your desk, take steps to ensure that the person does not read the material. If you are/working on a word processor, the screen may be visible to visitors. Should someone stop at your desk, quietly/turn off the monitor. It is important, of course, to do this in an inoffensive way. If you rush to/cover up documents or shove papers into a drawer, the person will feel that you doubt his or her loyalty. One way/to direct a person's attention away from materials you are working on is to rise and greet the/caller and direct him or her politely to a chair away from your desk.

If you must leave your desk while you are/working on a confidential document on a word processor, you should not leave the computer on. Transfer the/document to a memory device and switch the computer off before leaving the desk. You will be able/to retrieve the document quickly when you return. If you leave the monitor on, anyone who comes into/ your office will be able to read the material. If you simply turn the monitor off, another/ person may switch it back on and read the material. If you store your document but leave the computer on, a/dishonest visitor could view your directory and retrieve a confidential item.

Whenever you leave your/desk, it is a good idea to lock it. In addition, file cabinets containing sensitive documents should/be kept locked.

You are responsible for many items that are of a confidential nature. Take this/responsibility very seriously. (387)

# LESSON 38

## SuperWrite REVIEW

Read the following words, referring to the key if necessary. Then copy the words in your own notebook.

**Mem**

1. *mbr mbrs mriz mrzas rmbr rmbrs*
2. *rmbrd mry mrb cmral cmrald cmras*

**Word Ending -ment**

3. *jgm muvm nvlvm asinm gvrnm lrelm*

**Word Ending -ble**

4. *rlib rlib-l slab slb-l ralb snsb*

**Word Ending -ity**

5. *cmd l cmd ls sulb-l psb-l psb-ls vri ls*

**Key**

1. member; members; memorize; memorization; remember; remembers
2. remembered; memory; memorable; commemorate; commemorated; commemoration
3. judgment; movement; involvement; assignment; government; treatment
4. reliable; reliability; stable; stability; ratable; sensible
5. commodity; commodities; suitability; possibility; possibilities; varieties

# KEYBOARDING STYLE

## Citations

In business reports, you may wish to refer to information from a published source such as textbook, a reference book, or a journal article. In many business documents today, citations are used instead of footnotes. A citation is a direct reference to the bibliography or list of references.

A citation is typed in parentheses following the information for which the reference is supplied. The author's last name is included, followed by the year of publication and the page number(s) where the information was found. For example, if the material in this paragraph were from page 92 of a text by Gerald A. Smith, the citation would look like this: (Smith, 1987, 92). Note that the last name of the author is used, followed by a comma, the year of publication, followed by a comma, and the page reference.

A list of all references, including complete bibliographic information, will be typed at the end of the report.

# SPELLING

Here are additional spelling words. Pronounce and spell each word aloud; then copy it in your own notebook, being sure that you spell it correctly. When you read the Application section of the lesson, watch for these words.

charities
eventuality
indefinitely
intestate
jurisdiction
levied
livelihood
nonprofit
possessions
priority

## VOCABULARY

Study the following definitions carefully, and notice how the words are used in the *SuperWrite* examples. Watch for these words in the Application section of the lesson.

eventuality      *A possible occurrence; outcome.*

*t evnlul l s th u l lv*
*f mny yrs.*

The eventuality is that you will live
for many years.

inheritance tax      *An assessment imposed on property willed*
*to another; a tax on an estate.*

*t la rqrs th t nhrlnc lx*
*b pd frsl.*

The law requires that the inheritance tax
be paid first.

intestate      *Having no legal will.*

*if u di nlslal, otrs l*
*dlrmn hw u prprly l*
*b dslrbuld.*

If you die intestate, others will
determine how your property will
be distributed.

jurisdiction      *Authority or control; the right or power*
*to govern and apply the law.*

*t mlr s U t jrsdc$ o t*
*corl.*

The matter is under the jurisdiction of the
court.

## VOCABULARY continued

levied                    *Collected a tax or assessment.*

*t sl lved t lx on t prprly.*

The state levied the tax on the property.

## APPLICATION

The Application contains an extended business report. First read it carefully. Then copy it in *SuperWrite* in your notebook, inserting the necessary punctuation. From your notes, type it in a business report format.

## DOCUMENT 38
## Extended Business Report                    *Punctuation Check*

*Keyboarding Goal: 29 minutes (26 words per minute)*

*pln g u eslal*

*no / liks l spek o sC tngs bl evon msl pln f dt. t evnlul l s tl l l ocr n t dslnl fulr tr s also a psbl tl l ma ocr sn. t wis prsn maks crf cmp plns abl hw hs r hr ps$s l b dslrbuld afl dt. if tr r tos hu dpnd on u f tr livlhd u l wnl l b Sr tl ty r prlcld agnsl fnnSl ls. if u wS l lev mny l crln pep r orgs u Sd mak u wSs non legll n t fm o a l. if u di nlslal otrs nl u l dlrmn hw u*

(continued)

prprly l b dstrbuld. (Jones, 1989, 34)

her r sm tngs u Sd kep n mind wn u r plng u estal.

u imedat fml

u frst cncrn s prbbl u imedat fml. if u r lik most otr pep u spous n u Cldrn r u frst prirt. u spous Sd b ab l cntnu t crnt styl o lif wol bg fcd l mak Cangs. Cldrn hu r n scul Sd b ab l cntnu n t sam sculs wol NrpS. tr Sd b adql ncm l cr f al mbrs o u imedat fml. u ma wnt l pvd f u spous ndfntl n f u Cldrn utl ty r slf-sport g.

lif ins

t mjrt o yng slf sport g pep mst sply tes neds w lif ins. tr r a no o

typs o ins eC ofr g spsl fetrs. t idea
s t gt enf ins t tak cr o basc neds
t t most rsnb cst. a gd lif ins plcy
s a basc elm n most estats.

otr itms o vlu

otr itms C u mst cns r u hous u
cr n ny otr prprty o majr vlu s t
s prsnl prprty. tes itms usull r
lft t mbrs o t imedat fml.

u xtndd fml

u ma wsl t lev prprty t mbrs o u
xtndd fml. u xtndd fml mit incl
grndprnts ants uncls csns n otr rltvs.
n most cass sply g ncsts s nt rqrd
f t xtndd fml. if sC a prsn s a mbr
o u houshold hwev u mit ned t cns
ts prsn wn u prcs lif ins. n sm cass

(continued)

majr ilms r prsnl prprly ma b lfl l a mbr o t xlndd fml.

Crls n nnprfl nsllu$s

most pep h 1 r m Crls l C ty gv sm lyp o sporl. mny pep w$ l gv mny l a rlgus r so$l org. wn pln g an eslal a prsn $d cns wl ilms r hw mC mny $d b lfl l sC an org.

ncm prprly
n sm cass a pec o prprly tl prducs ncm s an xclnl Coic l gv l a Crl r nnprfl org. a rnll hous s a gd xmp. hwev sC a dc$ $d b dscsd w an ofcr o t nsllu$ l C u w$ l mak t gfl. t ofcr l b ab l ll u if t gfl s aprpral. (Brown, 1988, 92)

otr ilms o vlu

sm pep wS l gv otr arlcls o vlu
l Crls r nnprfl agnces. ts mil incl
arlwk a rr bk r a pec o julry.

otr cnss

tr r mny otr ilms tl u Sd kep
n mind wn u r plng u eslal. her
r 2 o tm.

lxs

a majr cns wn plng an eslal s
an nhrlnc lx. lxs r lved l vry g
rals fm l lxg jrsdcS l anotr. mosl
pep wS l kep al nhrlnc lxs s lo s
psb. gd plng c hlp a prsn asr tl
prprly s dslrbuld prprl n tl tr s
adql cS l pa al ncsry lxs.

(continued)

*pln erl*

*most cnss l b o an ndvdul natr n no 2 estats r likl l b xcll t sam. t cmn elm hwevr s tl plng Sd b dn erl. l c esl b lu lat l pln l c nvr b lu erl. tr s no sbsllul f wl mad plns.*

---

**DOCUMENT 38**
**Extended Business Report**                    **Punctuation Check**

*Keyboarding Goal: 29 minutes (26 words per minute)*

### PLANNING YOUR ESTATE

/No one likes to speak of such things, but *(compound sentence)* everyone must plan for death. The eventuality is that it will/occur in the distant future; *(no conjunction)* there is also a possibility that it may occur soon. The wise person makes/careful, complete *(coordinate adjectives)* plans about how his or her possessions will be distributed after death. If there are those who/depend on you for their livelihood, *(introductory)* you will want to be sure that they are protected against financial loss. If/you wish to leave money to certain people or organizations, *(introductory)* you should make your wishes known legally in/the form of a will. If you die intestate, *(introductory)* others, not you, *(extra)* will determine how your property will be/distributed. (Jones, 1989, 34)

Here are some things you should keep in mind when you are planning your estate./

### Your Immediate Family

Your first concern is probably your immediate family. If you are like/most other people, *(introductory)* your spouse and your children are your first priority. Your spouse should be able to continue/the current style of life without being forced to make changes. Children who are in school should be able to continue/in the same schools without interruption. There should be adequate income to care for all members of your/immediate family. You may want to provide for your spouse indefinitely and for your children until/they are self-supporting.

Life Insurance

The majority of young, self-supporting *(coordinate adjectives)* people must supply these needs/with life insurance. There are a number of types of insurance, each offering special features. *(extra)* The idea/is to get enough insurance to take care of basic needs at the most reasonable cost. A good life insurance/policy is a basic element in most estates.

Other Items of Value

Other items which you/must consider are your house, your car, and any other property of major value, *(series-extra)* as well as personal/property. These items usually are left to members of the immediate family.

### Your Extended/Family

You may wish to leave property to members of your extended family. Your extended family/might include grandparents, aunts, uncles, cousins, and other relatives. *(series)*

In most cases, *(introductory)* supplying necessities/is not required for the extended family. If such a person is a member of your household, *(introductory)* however,/*(extra)* you might need to consider this person when you purchase life insurance. In some cases major items or/personal property may be left to a member of the extended family.

### Charities and Nonprofit/Institutions

Most people have one or more charities to which they give some type of support. Many people wish/to give money to a religious or social organization. When planning an estate, *(introductory)* a person should/consider what items or how much money should be left to such an organization.

Income Property

In some/cases, *(introductory)* a piece of property that produces income is an excellent choice to give to a charity/or nonprofit organization. A rental house is a good example. However, *(introductory)* such a decision should/be discussed with an officer of the institution to which you wish to make the gift. The officer will be/able to tell you if the gift is appropriate. (Brown, 1988, 92)

Other Items of Value/

Some people wish to give other articles of value to charities or nonprofit agencies. This might/include artwork, a rare book, or a piece of jewelry. *(series)*

### Other Considerations

There are many other items/that you should keep in mind when you are planning your estate. Here are two of them.

(continued)

### Taxes

A major consideration/when planning an estate is an inheritance tax. Taxes are levied at varying rates from one taxing/jurisdiction to another. Most people wish to keep all inheritance taxes as low as possible. Good/planning can help a person assure that property is distributed properly and that there is adequate/cash to pay all necessary taxes.

### Plan Early

Most considerations will be of an individual/nature, and *(compound sentence)* no two estates are likely to be exactly the same. The common element, however, *(extra)* is that/ planning should be done early. It can easily be too late to plan; *(no conjunction)* it can never be too early. There is no/substitute for well-made *(compound adjective)* plans. (765)

## SUPPLEMENTARY ACTIVITY

### A Word to the Wise

Responsibility

/When your employer gives you a job to do, it is your responsibility to complete it. If you do not/finish the work, you have not met your responsibility. If you do not do the work accurately, you have/not met your responsibility. If you do not do the work in the allotted time, you have not met your/responsibility. Occasionally almost everyone will have trouble meeting a goal, but if it happens/repeatedly, you may well be looking for employment elsewhere.

If your employer gives you an assignment and/for any reason you do not complete it, it is very likely that your employer will have to do the job./No employer wants to have to complete work that was delegated to an employee.

Responsibility/does not include only those jobs that your employer assigns to you; it also includes those jobs that you assign/yourself. When you see a job that needs to be done, you should take the responsibility of doing it before/someone points it out to you.

Accept responsibility willingly. Remember to do the jobs that are/assigned to you completely and in a timely fashion. Look for other jobs that need to be done and complete them on/your own. Soon you will develop the reputation that you are indeed a responsible person. (238)

# *LESSON 39*

## *SuperWrite REVIEW*

Read the following words, referring to the key if necessary. Then write the words in your own notebook.

**Word Beginning Under-**

1. *Ulak Ulo Udvd Uslm Uslnd Usld*

**Word Endings -ious, -eous, -ous, -us**

2. *famus slalus crlus crlusl vrus vrusl*

**Word Ending -ly**

3. *onsll soll lrmndusl cÅull panslak gl Srl*
4. *hrdl brl grall opnl crfl rdl*

**Word Beginning De-**

5. *dvol dvold dlil dlild dlilf dplel*

**Key**

1. undertake; undertow; underdeveloped; understatement; understand; understood

2. famous; status; courteous; courteously; various; variously

3. honestly; solely; tremendously; casually; painstakingly; surely

4. hardly; barely; greatly; openly; carefully; readily

5. devote; devoted; delight; delighted; delightful; deplete

# KEYBOARDING STYLE

## List of References

A list of references or a bibliography is a complete list of all sources used in a report. The sources are alphabetized according to the last name of the author. The bibliography may be typed on the last page of the body of the report, or it may be typed on a separate page and placed at the end.

A title such as REFERENCES, LIST OF REFERENCES, or BIBLIOGRAPHY is typed in capitals at the horizonal center of the page. The first reference is typed a quadruple space below the title. The first line of each reference is typed at the left margin, and subsequent lines are indented five spaces. Each reference is single-spaced, and there is a double space between references.

## Reference Page

REFERENCES  -line 10

QS

Brown, William Carl.  "Insuring Your Family."  Insurance Today,
    September 1988, 34-36.

Green, Miller C.  Your Future.  Denver:  Mountain State
    Publishers, 1984

Jones, Anna S.  "Excavation in America."  Exploring the World, May
    1988, 24.

Menendez, Rafaella.  Oil Exploration in New Mexico.  Santa Fe:
    The Western Press, 1987.

Smith, Gerald A.  Exploring for Gold.  Boston:  National
    Publishing Company, 1986.

# SPELLING

Here are additional spelling words. Pronounce and spell each word aloud; then copy it in your own notebook, being sure that you spell it correctly. When you read the Application section of the lesson, watch for these words.

| | | | |
|---|---|---|---|
| burden | impractical | rectify | tremendously |
| duration | incumbent | severity | |
| expedient | queue | time-consuming | |

# VOCABULARY

Study the following definitions carefully, and notice how the words are used in the *SuperWrite* examples. Watch for these words in the Application section of the lesson.

duration

*A period of time; until the end.*

*t wal w 1 mnl n duraS.*

The wait was one minute in duration.

expedient

*Appropriate for achieving a goal quickly.*

*e msl find an xpedenl sluS.*

We must find an expedient solution.

incumbent

*Taken as an obligation or duty.*

*l s ncmbnl on us l rduc csls.*

It is incumbent on us to reduce costs.

queue

*A system whereby those in line are accommodated in order; a waiting line.*

*tr s no qu f olgog cls.*

There is no queue for outgoing calls.

rectify

*To correct; adjust.*

*e msl rclfy t sluaS.*

We must rectify the situation.

## APPLICATION

The Application contains an extended business report. First read it carefully. Then copy it in *SuperWrite* in your notebook, inserting the necessary punctuation. From your notes, type it in a business report format.

***Keyboarding Goal: 21 minutes (28 words per minute)***

rpt on t Smith llfon sstm

t S llfon sstm w nstld n t vrus ofcs o t cntrl sals co bgn g Jan 2 1970. (Carson, 1980, 42) t flog s a rvu o t slatus o t sstm s wl s rcmndats f t fulr.

cntrl swCbord

al ncm g cls n eC ofc r rould tru a cntrl swCbord. l s nt ucmn f a clr l h l wal f an xlndd perod bf t cl s ansrd. t lngt o t wal dpnds on t lm o t cl. t most lrblsm hrs r fm 9 a m ull 11 a m n fm 4 p m ull 5 p m.

Ifrd cls

bcs al cls r ansrd b an opralr eC cl msl b Ifrd ts also rqrs xtra tm. O a 2 wk perod t avrg ncmg cl tk almosl 2 mnls bf t clr recd t crcl prsn. t locl ndstry stndrd s ls tn 1 mnl. (Williams, 1988, 3)

olsid lins

alto olsid cls c b mad wol t ncs l o dil g t opralr olgo g cls d go tru t cnlrl sslm. r pep ofn h l wal f an olsid lin l bcm av. ocasll t wal s m tn a mnl n duras. tr s no qu sslm n t prsn smpl msl pk up t fon wn a lin s av. ts c b an anoy g xperenc n l c b lrmndusl tm- cnsum g.

(continued)

lng-dstnc cls

al lng-dstnc cls r placd O t rgulr lng-dstnc ntwk l t pr tm. evn cls l r otr ofcs msl b hndld n ts mnr. r lng-dstnc tlfon bls r n xcs o $1 t pr mo n eC o r ofcs. ts csl cnt b jstfid now n l apers tl l l ncres n t fulr uls a Cang s mad.

fwrd g cls

wn l o r pep s awa fm hs r hr dsk t opralr h no wa l fwrd cls almtcll. n ad& l s mprctcl f eC o r pep l cl t opralr n rqsl tl cls b fwrdd. l wd creal an xlra brdn on t opralr s wl. an xpedenl allrntv msl b found.

lm usd n dil g

mC o r bus dpnds on llfon sals n r slf msl spnd a gral del o lm dil g cls n rdil g cls wn a lin s bsy. r pr sslm h no sped dil g r rdil g felr.

rcmnda$

t $ sslm w a dpndb efSl sslm wn l w nslld bl l s hrdl capb o gv g us t lyp o srvc e ned lda. l s ncmbnl on us l rclfy t prblms e r now fac g.

t cnlrl sals co Sd cnlcl a no o splirs n oblan bds on rplac g t nlir llfon sslm. bcs o t svr l o t pr slua$ ts Sd b dn w al du hasl.

(continued)

*rfrncs*

*Carson, Forrest R. hstry o t cntrl sals co. Milwaukee: globl pblsg co, 1980.*

*Williams, Reba A. ndstry stndrds n Medford. Chicago: cntrl prs, 1988.*

## DOCUMENT 39
### Extended Business Report                    *Punctuation Check*

**Keyboarding Goal: 21 minutes (28 words per minute)**

REPORT ON THE SMITH TELEPHONE SYSTEM

/The Smith telephone system was installed in the various offices of the Central Sales Company beginning/January 2, 1970. *(date)* (Carson, 1980, 42) The following is a review/ of the/status of the system as well as recommendations for the future.

Central Switchboard

All incoming/calls in each office are routed through a central switchboard. It is not uncommon for a caller to have to wait/for an extended period before the call is answered. The length of the wait depends on the time of the call./The most troublesome hours are from 9 a.m. until 11 a.m. and from 4 p.m. until 5 p.m./

Transferred Calls

Because all calls are answered by an operator, *(introductory)* each call must be trans-ferred; *(no conjunction)* this also requires/extra time. Over a two-week *(compound ad-jective)* period, *(introductory)* the average incoming call took almost two minutes before the/caller reached the correct person. The local industry standard is less than one minute. (Williams, 1988, 3)/

Outside Lines

Although outside calls can be made without the necessity of dialing the operator,/*(in-troductory)* outgoing calls do go through the central system. Our people often have to wait for an outside line to become/available. Occasionally, *(introductory)* the wait is more than a minute in duration. There is no queue system, and *(compound sentence)* the/person simply must pick up the phone when a line is available. This can be an annoying experience,/and *(compound sentence)* it can be tremendously time-consuming.

### Long-Distance Calls

All long-distance calls are placed over the regular/long-distance network at the present time. Even calls to our other offices must be handled in this/manner. Our long-distance telephone bills are in excess of $1,000 per month in each of our offices./This cost cannot be justified now, and *(compound sentence)* it appears that it will increase in the future unless a change is made./

### Forwarding Calls

When one of our people is away from his or her desk, *(introductory)* the operator has no way to forward/calls automatically. In addition, *(introductory)* it is impractical for each of our people to call the/operator and request that calls be forwarded. It would create an extra burden on the operator as well./An expedient alternative must be found.

### Time Used in Dialing

Much of our business depends on telephone/sales, and *(compound sentence)* our staff must spend a great deal of time dialing calls and redialing calls when a line is busy. Our present/system has no speed dialing or redialing feature.

### Recommendation

The Smith system was a dependable,/efficient *(coordinate adjectives)* system when it was installed, but *(compound sentence)* it is hardly capable of giving us the type of service we/need today. It is incumbent on us to rectify the problems we are now facing.

The Central Sales Company/should contact a number of suppliers and obtain bids on replacing the entire telephone system./Because of the severity of the present situation, *(introductory)* this should be done with all due haste.

### REFERENCES

Carson,/Forrest R. History of the Central Sales Company. Milwaukee: Global Publishing Company, 1980./

Williams, Reba A. Industry Standards in Medford. Chicago: Central Press, 1988. (578)

## SUPPLEMENTARY ACTIVITY

### A Word to the Wise

Office Talk

/"Have you heard . . . ?" "Did you know that . . . ?" "Wait till you hear what I just heard." Do these words sound familiar? They are all too often/heard in business today.

When you work in an office, you will hear many things that may be of interest to you/ and your friends. However, information that is heard in an office is often of a confidential nature./In addition, information that may not be classified as confidential is sometimes of a sensitive/nature. Even business that would not be considered sensitive is often considered private. You should not/discuss the business that goes on in your office with outsiders or with others who work in the same company. It/is a serious mistake to do so.

If you discuss all the previous day's business, no matter how sensitive,/with your friends, you will soon become known as someone who may not be trustworthy. A person who develops this/kind of reputation in business will seldom be promoted into a position of greater responsibility./

How do you keep your friends from questioning you about office matters that should be kept confidential?/When a question is asked, simply reply, "I'm sorry, I cannot discuss that." Just one time is usually/enough to stop that type of questioning. When your friends understand that you will not discuss business transacted in your/office, they will respect you. In addition, your employer will respect you, and you will position yourself as/a person who is responsible—one who can be trusted with even more responsibility. (278)

# *LESSON 40*

## *SuperWrite REVIEW*

Read the following words, referring to the key if necessary. Then copy the words in your own notebook.

**Word Beginning Trans-**

1. *Tporl Tprla8 T8 T8l Tml Tmld*

**Word Beginning Pro-**

2. *prduc prtcl prtc8 prced prcedr prcs*

**Word Beginning Pre-**

3. *prdcl prclud prcludd prsum prrgstr prlmnry*

**Oi**

4. *nois noisy join soil boil void*

**Oy**

5. *loyl royl boy boys toy njoy*

1.  transport; transportation; transition; transitional; transmit; transmitted
2.  produce; protect; protection; proceed; procedure; process
3.  predict; preclude; precluded; presume; preregister; preliminary
4.  noise; noisy; join; soil; boil; void
5.  loyal; royal; boy; boys; toy; enjoy

# SPELLING

Here are additional spelling words. Pronounce and spell each word aloud; then copy it in your own notebook, being sure that you spell it correctly. When you read the Application section of the lesson, watch for these words.

adequate
adjacent
amenable
conform
integral
plain
preclude
site
transmitted
zoning

# VOCABULARY

Study the following definitions carefully, and notice how the words are used in the *SuperWrite* examples. Watch for these words in the Application section of the lesson.

adjacent

*Close to; lying near; next to.*

*t lnd s ajacnl l a prk.*

The land is adjacent to a park.

amenable

*Willing to follow advice or suggestion.*

*e r amenb l u prposls.*

We are amenable to your proposals.

flood plain

*An area bordering a body of water, subject to flooding.*

*t lnd s nl n a fld plan.*

The land is not in a flood plain.

integral

*Necessary for completeness.*

*lndscapg s an nlgrl prl o
r plns.*

Landscaping is an integral part of
our plans.

preclude

*To make impossible by previous action;
to prevent.*

*gd plng Sd prclud majr
prblms.*

Good planning should preclude major
problems.

## APPLICATION

The Application contains an extended business report. First read it carefully. Then copy it
in *SuperWrite* in your notebook, inserting the necessary punctuation. From your notes, type
it in a business report format.

prposl f Spg cnlr
8t fft ave
Lexington, PA

t Gilbreth co locald l 121 Baker sl
n L PA prposs l bld a Spg cnlr l
8t fft ave C s l t NscS o fft ave n
Green sl n sbrbn L. t prlmnry plns
C wr mad b Yale asocals r cmpd n
h b Imld sprll l t zong bord.

siz o cnlr

t inSl plns r f a loll o 30 slors.
t cnlr wd incl a grocry slor a lrg
dscounl cnlr n 28 otr Sps. t cnlr wd
cnlan l h t sqr fel o flor spac n
3 h t sqr fel o prkg spac.

crclr o cnlr

a Sp g vlg

t cnlr s dsind s a Sp g vlg w
Nnl brk wkwas. l wd nl b a slrp
Sp g cnlr w prk g onl n frnl o t
ndvdul slors. al Sps wd b sluald
l lesl 2 h fel fm t sl n adql of sl
prkg wd b pvdd.


cmun l slndrds

t bld gs wd cnfm l cmun l slndrds
o slyl n slrclr n prfSl lndscap g wd
b an nlgrl prl o t cnlr. l wd b dsind
f t cnv n njoym o t rsdnls o t
cmun l.


drang


t drang n t area s cnsd abv avrg.
1 crnr o t prposd cnlr s wn 1t fel

(continued)

o a crnl fld plan. (cly o L, 1985, 842)
hwev nn o t area h ev hd my serus
wlr dmg.

lrfc n Iprla& pln

erler tr w sm q s l wtr t cnlr wd
creal a lrfc prblm f t nabrhd. bcs
nlrncs l t cnlr wd b alowd onl l
loca&s spcfid b t sl gvrnm tr &d b
no lrfc prblms.
tr s no Iprla& lrmnl n t vcn l bl
2 bus rouls srv t nabrhd.
t dvrs r amenb l t &rg o cnslrc&
csls o al ncsry sl mpruvms n t
imedal area.
nois

bcs no slor wd b locald wn 2 h
fel o my rsl q bldq tr &d b no nois
prblm. n ad& a 10 fl brk fnc wd

spral t bk o t cnlr fm ajacnl prprly.

tr wd b no rcreasl fcl ls n t cnlr l wd b cmposd o rlal Sps n rslrnls onl.

csl

t csl o t cnlr inclg lnd sil mpruvms n al cnslrcS wd b n xcs o $50 m. t fnncg wd b tru eslrn nSl bnk.

lm fram

sil prpraS
prpr g t sil C incls clerg t lnd n nsll g wlr gs n drang pips wd lak aprxmll 6 mos.

cnslrcS
t aclul cnslrcS wd lak abl 1 yr if no ufsen prblms dv.

les g

les g wd bgn wn aclul cnslrc&
cmncs. t plm s l h t cnlr l lesl 75%
lesd wn t frsl bld g s rdy l opn.

cnclu&

if t cnlr s apruvd l l b a majr
ad& l t cly. dur g cnslrc& l l pvd mny
jbs f locl rsdnls. wn t cnlr s cmpd
l l pvd prmnl mplm f m tn 3 h
wkrs. n ad& l l pvd mC nedd srvcs
l t rsdnls o t area. tr r no smlr
fcl ls wn 5 mils.

e h dn evtng n r powr l prlcl t
nabrhd nvirnm. e fel r ac&s l
prclud ny majr prblms tl mil ocr.

if t plns r apruvd s Fmld e l
prced w r plns l cler t lnd n bgn
cnslrc& imedall.

*rfrnc*

*cly o L. cly rgslr. L, PA: main prs, 1985.*

## DOCUMENT 40
## Extended Business Report                    Punctuation Check

**Keyboarding Goal: 25 minutes (28 words per minute)**

PROPOSAL FOR SHOPPING CENTER
8000 FIFTH AVENUE
LEXINGTON, PENNSYLVANIA

/The Gilbreth Company, located at 121 Baker Street in Lexington, Pennsylvania, *(extra-geographic)* proposes/to build a shopping center at 8000 Fifth Avenue, which is at the intersection of Fifth Avenue/and Green Street in suburban Lexington. *(extra)* The preliminary plans, which were made by Yale and Associates, *(extra)* are/completed and have been transmitted separately to the zoning board.

Size of Center

The initial plans are/for a total of 30 stores. The center would include a grocery store, a large discount center, and 28/other shops. *(series)* The center would contain 100,000 square feet of floor space and 300,000 square feet/of parking space.

Character of Center

A Shopping Village

The center is designed as a shopping village with/internal brick walkways. It would not be a strip shopping center with parking only in front of the individual/stores. All shops would be situated at least 200 feet from the street, and *(compound sentence)* adequate off-street *(compound adjective)* parking/would be provided.

Community Standards

The buildings would conform to community standards of style and/structure, and *(compound sentence)* professional landscaping would be an integral part of the center. It would be designed for the/convenience and enjoyment of the residents of the community.

Drainage

The drainage in the area is/considered above average. One corner of the proposed center is within 1,000 feet of a current flood/plain. (City of Lexington, 1985, 842) However, *(introductory)* none of the area/has ever had any serious water damage.                    (continued)

### Traffic and Transportation Plan

Earlier there was some/question as to whether the center would create a traffic problem for the neighborhood. Because entrances to the/center would be allowed only at locations specified by the state government, *(introductory)* there should be no traffic/problems.

There is no transportation terminal in the vicinity, but *(compound sentence)* two bus routes serve the neighborhood.

The/developers are amenable to the sharing of construction costs of all necessary street improvements in the/immediate area.

### Noise

Because no store would be located within 200 feet of any/existing building, *(introductory)* there should be no noise problem. In addition, *(introductory)* a ten-foot *(compound adjective)* brick fence would separate the back of/the center from adjacent property.

There would be no recreational facilities in the center; *(no conjunction)* it/would be composed of retail shops and restaurants only.

### Cost

The cost of the center, including land, site improvements,/and all construction, *(extra-series)* would be in excess of $50 million. The financing would be through the Eastern/National Bank.

### Time Frame

Site Preparation

Preparing the site, which includes clearing the land and installing/water, gas, and drainage pipes, *(extra-series)* would take approximately six months.

Construction

The actual construction would take/about one year if no unforeseen problems develop.

Leasing

Leasing would begin when actual construction/commences. The plan is to have the center at least 75 percent leased when the first building is ready to/open.

### Conclusion

If the center is approved, *(introductory)* it will be a major addition to the city. During/construction, *(introductory)* it will provide many jobs for local residents. When the center is completed, *(introductory)* it will provide/permanent employment for more than 300 workers. In addition, *(introductory)* it will provide much-needed *(compound adjective)* services to/the residents of the area. There are no similar facilities within five miles.

We have done everything/in our power to protect the neighborhood environment. We feel our actions will preclude any major/problems that might occur.

If the plans are approved as transmitted, *(introductory)* we will proceed with our plans to clear the land and/begin construction immediately.

REFERENCE

City of Lexington. City Register. Lexington, Pennsylvania:/Main Press, 1985. (706)

## *SUPPLEMENTARY ACTIVITY*

### *A Word to the Wise*

Getting Ready for an Interview

/You will probably be planning for an interview sometime in the near future. When you find a company where/you really want to work, you will want the interview to be excellent. There are a number of things you can do/to prepare for that all-important job interview.

You will have sent your letter of application and personal/data sheet to the company several weeks earlier. If the company does not call you, you may wish/to send a follow-up letter, one in which you give updated or additional information. When you are/called, be ready to go.

Have your clothing cleaned and ready for the interview. Wear clothing that is appropriate/ for office wear. Choose neutral colors and a conservative style. Your shoes should be unsoiled. Your hair should be neat and/styled in a becoming way. Do not wear excessive jewelry. A good rule to follow is, "If you have a doubt/about a piece of jewelry, don't wear it."

Be prepared to answer questions concerning your professional goals, both your/immediate goals and your long-term goals. Be ready to handle a question such as "How much money do you wish/to make here?" A noncommittal answer such as, "That is open to discussion" is probably the best type of/response. Be able to present your education, your particular skills, and your experience in a/positive light.

Be able to ask intelligent questions about the company where you are interviewing./ Interviewers often ask, "Is there anything you would like to ask?" No is a very poor answer. There are probably/a number of items about which you would like to have information. Have a few good, thoughtful questions/ready.

In addition, you should practice interviewing. Ask a friend to play the role of the interviewer and go/through a practice interview several times. This will help you to feel more comfortable when the actual/interview takes place.

Give yourself every possible chance. When you find the company where you want to work, make the interview/pay off. (363)

# APPENDIX

# ADDRESSES FOR TRANSCRIPTION

*SuperWrite, VOLUME ONE*

*PART 2 (LESSONS 21-35)*

The addresses for all documents in *Volume One,* Part 2, are included in this list. In addition, addresses are included for all related documents, which appear in the Teacher's Manual.

## Lesson 21

**Document 21-1**

Miss Angela Brown
Brown Office Systems
4200 Broadway
Albuquerque, NM 87503-1324

**Related to Document 21-1**

Mr. Charles Casey
Casey and Company
500 Main Street
Albuquerque, NM 87509-1442

**Document 21-2**

Mr. William Beatty
1609 Hancock Avenue
Macon, GA 35667-2312

**Related to Document 21-2**

Mr. Ronald Casey
Central Cable TV
100 Fourth Avenue
Macon, GA 35669-1102

**Document 21-3**

Mrs. Emma Bentley
803 - 21st Avenue
Salem, MA 01924-3214

**Related to Document 21-3**

Mrs. Emma Bentley
803 - 21st Avenue
Salem, MA 01924-3214

**Document 21-4**

Mr. Lee Lopez
402 North 62nd Street
Detroit, MI 48205-4422

Related to Document 21-4

Mr. Lee Lopez
402 North 62nd Street
Detroit, MI 48205-4422

## Lesson 22

Document 22-1

Ms. Maxine Graves
1802 Tenth Avenue
Trenton, NJ 08622-1234

Related to Document 22-1

Mrs. Olga Jones
Eastern Sales Company
900 Elm Park Drive
Columbia, SC 29216-2341

Document 22-2

Micro Supply Company
4200 Central Expressway
Dallas, TX 75205-3342

Related to Document 22-2

Miss Lydia Jenkins
820 First Avenue
Dayton, OH 45355-4182

Document 22-3

Mrs. Carla Hastings
231 Kent Road
Lincoln, NE 68117-4323

Related to Document 22-3

Miss Evelyn Warren
800 - 35th Street
Birmingham, AL 36355-1233

Document 22-4

Mr. N. L. Maxwell
Western Jewelry Corporation
102 Main Street
Seattle, WA 98105-2251

Related to Document 22-4

Mr. Paul D. Henry
Ohio Jewelry Company
3300 Beltway Drive
Cleveland, OH 45266-2233

## Lesson 23

Document 23-1

Dr. A. B. Ellis
809 State Boulevard
Portland, OR 97256-1255

Related to Document 23-1

Dr. A. B. Ellis
809 State Boulevard
Portland, OR 97256-1255

Document 23-2

Ms. Olivia Joyce
Bennington Industries
2828 Wellington Drive
Carson, WV 26005-1233

Related to Document 23-2

Mr. Robert D. Anderson
Anderson and Associates
898 Blair Avenue
Carson, WV 26005-1244

Document 23-3

Ms. Martha Strong
Cranford City Council
400 Main Street
Cranford, MO 66123-4213

Related to Document 23-3

Mrs. Virginia Stern
Stern Clothing Shop
82 Broad Street
Cranford, MO 66123-4122

Document 23-4

Central Airlines
826 Central Expressway
Dallas, TX 75226-1255

Related to Document 23-4

Mr. Warren Davidson
809 Third Avenue
Garland, TX 75222-3422

## Lesson 24

Document 24-1

Mrs. Madeline Melton
Melton and Associates
9700 Lake Drive
Chicago, IL 62973-4532

Related to Document 24-1

Mrs. Madeline Melton
Melton and Associates
9700 Lake Drive
Chicago, IL 62973-4532

Document 24-2

Mr. Harold Moore
Electronic Publishers, Inc.
5700 Ocean Parkway
Orlando, FL 32822-1254

Related to Document 24-2

Mr. Milton Jenkins
Southern Sales Corporation
2100 South Main
Alexandria, LA 71446-1234

Document 24-3

Mr. James R. Potter
Attorney at Law
200 North Bell Avenue
Wheeling, WV 26303-4321

Related to Document 24-3

Ms. Elizabeth Randall
330 Ridge Drive
Covington, KY 41007-2323

Document 24-4

Miss Rita Jones
583 Central Avenue
Bangor, ME 04422-1277

Related to Document 24-4

Mr. Dwight Green
908 Oak Street
Bangor, ME 04423-1233

## Lesson 25

Document 25-1

Mr. Lawrence Leith
1402 Steadman Drive
Tulsa, OK 74202-1124

Related to Document 25-1

Mr. Lawrence Leith
1402 Steadman Drive
Tulsa, OK 74202-1124

Document 25-2

Mrs. Dorothy Ray
1809 Capitol Drive
St. Paul, MN 55123-4223

Related to Document 25-2

Mrs. Melanie Mason
24 Butler Avenue
Newton, MN 54335-1123

Document 25-3

Principal
Central High School
Carson, CO 82331-1232

Related to Document 25-3

Principal
Central High School
Carson, CO 82331-1232

Document 25-4

Ms. Yoko Nozaki
Nozaki Furniture Company
889 Division Street
Little Rock, AR 72330-1432

Related to Document 25-4

Miss Amelia Warren
2399 Brentwood Boulevard
Little Rock, AR 73220-1234

## Lesson 26

Document 26-1

Mr. Milton Morgan
Seabrook High School
100 Ocean Drive
Seabrook, FL 32344-1255

Related to Document 26-1

Dr. M. L. Pratt
Central College
4242 Southern Parkway
Lakeland, FL 34523-1234

Document 26-2

East Coast Sales Company
590 Second Street
Memphis, TN 38013-1998

Related to Document 26-2

Ms. Ann North
560 Madison Street
Memphis, TN 38010-1022

Document 26-3

Mrs. Marie Tuttle
41 Baylor Road
Hartford, CT 06124-1442

Related to Document 26-3

Mrs. Marie Tuttle
41 Baylor Road
Hartford, CT 06124-1442


Document 26-4

Miss Natalie Nelson
79 Mercer Road
Princeton, NJ 08622-1431


Related to Document 26-4

Miss Natalie Nelson
79 Mercer Road
Princeton, NJ 08622-1431


## Lesson 27

Document 27-1

Mr. John J. Edwards
C. W. Burns Company
5000 Plymouth Way
Chester, MA 01870-1124


Related to Document 27-1

Miss Elizabeth Doyle
East Coast Associates
8001 Bradenton Parkway
Chester, MA 01877-1220


Document 27-2

Ms. Maria Sanchez
Sanchez Enterprises
5050 West 27th Street
Seattle, WA 98202-1144

Related to Document 27-2

Dr. Cynthia Morse
Professor of Business
Western State College
100 Pacific Boulevard
Seattle, WA 98100-1445


Document 27-3

Mr. Kenneth Samuels
The R. J. Jennings Company
234 Broadway
Providence, RI 02887-2114


Related to Document 27-3

Mr. Benjamin Stern, President
Mason Sales Company
Jackson, MS 38802-2131


Document 27-4

Miss Alice Murphy
3200 Commerce Street
Nashville, TN 39133-2121


Related to Document 27-4

Mr. Michael Tyler
400 Main Street
Nashville, TN 39122-1223


## Lesson 28

Document 28-1

Mr. Wallace Brice
The Wells Organization
679 Third Avenue
Scranton, PA 18605-2312

Related to Document 28-1

Mr. George Casey, President
Casey and Company
800 Beaumont Street
Scranton, PA 18605-1213

Document 28-2

Miss Natalie Mason
General Manager
Starr Enterprises
200 Elm Street
Los Angeles, CA 90030-2448

Related to Document 28-2

Miss Clara Bennett
Western Sales Corporation
3389 Carter Street
Los Angeles, CA 90330-1289

Document 28-3

Mr. Charles Clark
1093 West Franklin Avenue
Trenton, NJ 08664-1244

Related to Document 28-3

Mr. Charles Clark
1093 West Franklin Avenue
Trenton, NJ 08664-1244

Document 28-4

Dr. Mary Alice Norton
Central Medical Plaza
889 Fifth Avenue
Racine, WI 53340-3349

Related to Document 28-4

Miss Alexandria Pace
Central Medical College
225 Michigan Avenue
Chicago, IL 60680-1234

## Lesson 29

Document 29-1

Attention Miss Sandra Taylor
International Publishers
45 Lexington Avenue
Milwaukee, WI 53822-2131

Related to Document 29-1

Attention Mr. James Benson
Western Publishing Company
3397 Lakeside Drive
Spokane, WA 98223-3223

Document 29-2

Dr. Darlene Taylor
Pacific Management Consultants
77 Haven Boulevard
Honolulu, HI 96778-3332

Related to Document 29-2

Attention Dr. Art Hale
Madison College
6600 Shore Drive
Miami, FL 33802-3321

Document 29-3

Attention Mr. C. T. Courtland
Legal Associates
777 Taylor Street
Cedar Rapids, IA 52767-2288

Related to Document 29-3

Attention Mr. Martin Simms
National Insurance Company
339 - 42nd Street
Harrisburg, PA 17669-8778

Document 29-4

Attention Miss Susan Marsh
General Insurance Company
55007 North Keystone Drive
Detroit, MI 48277-3322

Related to Document 29-4

Attention Miss Susan March
General Insurance Company
55007 North Keystone Drive
Detroit, MI 48277-3322

## Lesson 30

Document 30-1

Mr. Oliver Van
210 North Beltline Avenue
Baltimore, MD 21103-3322

Related to Document 30-1

Mr. Oliver Van
210 North Beltline Avenue
Baltimore, MD 21103-3322

Document 30-2

Ms. Martha Fuentes
Personnel Consultants, Inc.
505 Trinity Avenue
San Antonio, TX 78790-2211

Related to Document 30-2

Mrs. Stephanie Abbott
Personnel Manager
Southern Industries
1611 Highland Street
San Antonio, TX 78789-1021

Document 30-3

Ms. Janet Gross, Manager
Verybest Industries
887 Southern State Parkway
Knoxville, TN 38212-1243

Related to Document 30-3

Ms. Edyth Moon
Capital Industries
300 Mountain View Road
Santa Fe, NM 87552-1128

Document 30-4

Mr. Sumio Saga
9200 Park Avenue
New York, NY 10092-2231

Related to Document 30-4

Mr. Sumio Saga
9200 Park Avenue
New York, NY 10092-2231

## Lesson 31

Document 31-1

To: Mr. Elvin Grider,
        Marketing Department
From: Maria Sanchez,
        Finance Department

Related to Document 31-1

To: Miss Maria Sanchez,
    Finance Department
From: Elvin Grider,
    Marketing Department

Document 31-2

To: Mr. Tom Granger,
    Legal Department
From: Alice Simms,
    Finance Department

Related to Document 31-2

To: Mrs. Alice Simms,
    Finance Department
From: Tom Granger,
    Legal Department

Document 31-3

To: Ms. Grace Stern
From: Paul Moore

Related to Document 31-3

To: Mr. Paul Moore
From: Grace Stern

Document 31-4

To: Mrs. May Edwards
From: Rosa Lopez

Related to Document 31-4

To: Mr. Gary Kent
From: May Edwards

## Lesson 32

Document 32-1

Attention Ms. Christine Doran
Organization of Retired Executives
4920 West 42nd Street
Las Vegas, NV 89337-2289

Related to Document 32-1

Mr. George Flynn
345 Main Street
Las Vegas, NV 89336-1212

Document 32-2

To: All Employees
From: Joan Morrison,
    Employee Benefits

Related to Document 32-2

To: Mrs. Joan Morrison,
    Employee Benefits
From: Mildred Carson, Marketing

Document 32-3

Mr. J. T. Ball
239 Macon Court
Clarke, MS 39224-4345

Related to Document 32-3

Attention Mr. C. M. Green
Major Auto Service Center
400 North Main Street
Clarke, MS 39228-2311

Document 32-4

To: Mr. Max Bloom
From: Lila Blake

Related to Document 32-4

To: Miss Lila Blake
From: Max Bloom

## Lesson 33

Document 33-1

To: All Employees
From: Amanda Cole,
        Personnel Department

Related to Document 33-1

To: Miss Amanda Cole,
        Personnel Department
From: Mark Green,
        Advertising Department

Document 33-2

To: All Company Employees
From: Harold Cox, President

Related to Document 33-2

To: Mr. William Curtis,
        Personnel Department
From: Mary Bentley,
        Shipping Department

Document 33-3

Attention Mr. Kenneth Taylor
Jenson, Taylor, and Cline
341 Central Avenue
Boise, ID 83707-1234

Related to Document 33-3

Miss Hilda Swenson
890 Mountain View Drive
Missoula, MT 59231-3322

Document 33-4

To: Mr. Carl Lindsey
From: Ann Murphy

Related to Document 33-4

To: Ms. Ann Murphy
From: Carl Lindsey

## Lesson 34

Document 34-1

Mr. Wayne Paul
Southern Employment Agency
500 South Main Boulevard
Houston, TX 77000-9988

Related to Document 34-1

To: All Employees
From: Betty Henderson

Document 34-2

To: Mr. Max Peters
From: Jackie Stevens

Related to Document 34-2

To: All Employees
From: Max Peters

Document 34-3

Mr. Louis Mattingly
4992 Bennett Road
Cleveland, OH 44582-8901

Related to Document 34-3

Ms. Maxine Morton
341 Tatum Avenue
Cleveland, OH 44533-1255

Document 34-4

Mr. A. B. Peterson
1400 Riverside Drive
Chicago, IL 63772-8004

Related to Document 34-4

Mr. Clement Johnson
Johnson Tax Services
4309 State Street
Chicago, IL 63889-8991

## Lesson 35

Document 35-1

Mrs. Beverley Medlin
3976 Lone Star Drive
Arlington, TX 75799-2321

Related to Document 35-1

To: Mr. Roberto Rodriguez
From: Ethyl Glynn

Document 35-2

To: Ms. Maureen McGee
From: Nathan Cain

Related to Document 35-2

To: Mr. Nathan Cain
From: Maureen McGee

Document 35-3

To: Mrs. Nadine Short
From: Sam Wolfson

Related to Document 35-3

To: Mr. Sam Wolfson
From: Nadine Short

Document 35-4

To: Mr. Mark Peters
From: J. D. Jones

Related to Document 35-4

To: Mr. Nathan Doyle
From: Mark Peters

# SPELLING WORDS

Numbers refer to Lesson numbers.

**Lesson 22**
associates
attempt
catalog
clients
excellent
inheritance
liquidate
microcomputer
probate
received

**Lesson 23**
assured
atmosphere
banquet
buffet
disrepair
interruption
occasionally
peace
postponed
separate

**Lesson 24**
appeared
attorney
bulletin
congratulations
easement
equipment
library
piece
replacement
retract

**Lesson 25**
accept
accumulate
assigned
deposit

embarrassing
explanation
financial
percentage
restaurant
specified

**Lesson 26**
access
assistance
assistants
calendar
copyright
deductible
registration
software
sponsored
useful

**Lesson 27**
affirmative
campaign
community
definitely
expertise
integrity
occupancy
prospective
reception
soliciting

**Lesson 28**
analyzing
appropriate
imperative
liability
management
mandatory
mentioned
retention
retirement
sensible

## Lesson 29
break
copywriter
exceeding
invaluable
precede
principal
resumé
sustained
touch
vehicle

## Lesson 30
arrangements
discourteous
evaluation
former
insolvent
oversight
personnel
simulator
techniques
viable

## Lesson 31
bankruptcy
candidate
confidence
exemplary
financier
foreclose
oversee
recourse
unforeseen
vacated

## Lesson 32
advisory
completing
coupon
entrepreneurs
informal
innovative

lubrication
questionnaire
rotated
tune-up

## Lesson 33
beneficiary
contingent
impatient
maximum
perturbed
projections
rejection
resolved
revision
tender

## Lesson 34
although
excessive
exciting
hinder
incurring
lengthy
manual
professional
profitable
recommended

## Lesson 35
absence
accommodate
acquiring
compound interest
deliberation
employees
expedite
impede
repeatedly
transferred

**Lesson 36**
dispensed
eligible
generic
maintenance
pharmacy
physician
portfolio
reimbursed
spouse
underwritten

**Lesson 37**
abandon
already
choose
function key
initiate
opening menu
prompt
screen
scrolling
stacks

**Lesson 38**
charities
eventuality
indefinitely
intestate
jurisdiction

levied
livelihood
nonprofit
possessions
priority

**Lesson 39**
burden
duration
expedient
impractical
incumbent
queue
rectify
severity
time-consuming
tremendously

**Lesson 40**
adequate
adjacent
amenable
conform
integral
plain
preclude
site
transmitted
zoning

# VOCABULARY WORDS

Numbers refer to Lesson numbers.

## Vocabulary Words by Lesson

**Lesson 26**
access
deductible
pre-existing
prior
public domain

**Lesson 27**
expertise
integrity
peers
seminar
soliciting

**Lesson 28**
formal
imperative
liability insurance
mandatory
retention

**Lesson 29**
exceeding
precede
principal
resumé
sustained

**Lesson 30**
former
insolvent
personnel
simulator
viable

**Lesson 31**
bankruptcy
exemplary
financier
foreclose
vacated

**Lesson 32**
associate's degree
entrepreneurs
informal
innovative
rotated

**Lesson 33**
beneficiary
contingent
perturbed
resolved
tender

**Lesson 34**
excessive
fiscal
incurring
profit margin
tax audit

**Lesson 35**
certificate of deposit
compound interest
deliberation
expedite
impede

**Lesson 36**
dispensed
generic
reimbursed
spouse
underwritten

**Lesson 37**
function key
initiate
opening menu
prompt
stacks

**Lesson 38**
eventuality
inheritance tax
intestate
jurisdiction
levied

**Lesson 39**
duration
expedient
incumbent

queue
rectify

**Lesson 40**
adjacent
amenable
flood plain
integral
preclude

# ABBREVIATIONS

## STATE, DISTRICT, AND TERRITORY ABBREVIATIONS

| | | | |
|---|---|---|---|
| Alabama | *AL* | Indiana | *IN* |
| Alaska | *AK* | Iowa | *IA* |
| Arizona | *AZ* | Kansas | *KS* |
| Arkansas | *AR* | Kentucky | *KY* |
| California | *CA* | Louisiana | *LA* |
| Colorado | *CO* | Maine | *ME* |
| Connecticut | *CT* | Maryland | *MD* |
| Delaware | *DE* | Massachusetts | *MA* |
| District of Columbia | *DC* | Michigan | *MI* |
| Florida | *FL* | Minnesota | *MN* |
| Georgia | *GA* | Mississippi | *MS* |
| Guam | *GU* | Missouri | *MO* |
| Hawaii | *HI* | Montana | *MT* |
| Idaho | *ID* | Nebraska | *NE* |
| Illinois | *IL* | Nevada | *NV* |

| State | | State | |
|---|---|---|---|
| New Hampshire | *NH* | South Carolina | *SC* |
| New Jersey | *NJ* | South Dakota | *SD* |
| New Mexico | *NM* | Tennessee | *TN* |
| New York | *NY* | Texas | *TX* |
| North Carolina | *NC* | Utah | *UT* |
| North Dakota | *ND* | Vermont | *VT* |
| Ohio | *OH* | Virgin Islands | *VI* |
| Oklahoma | *OK* | Virginia | *VA* |
| Oregon | *OR* | Washington | *WA* |
| Pennsylvania | *PA* | West Virginia | *WV* |
| Puerto Rico | *PR* | Wisconsin | *WI* |
| Rhode Island | *RI* | Wyoming | *WY* |

# SuperWrite ABBREVIATIONS BY LESSON

## Lesson 1

| | |
|---|---|
| you, your | *u* |
| will | *l* |
| as, is | *s* |

## Lesson 2

| | |
|---|---|
| are, or, our | *r* |
| can | *c* |
| for | *f* |

## Lesson 3

| | |
|---|---|
| at, it, to | *t* |
| has, have | *h* |
| very | *v* |
| do | *d* |

## Lesson 4

| | |
|---|---|
| we | *e* |
| which | *C* |
| soon | *sn* |

## Lesson 5

| | |
|---|---|
| the | *t* |
| and, in | *n* |

## Lesson 6

| | |
|---|---|
| am, more | *m* |
| be, been, by | *b* |
| month | *mo* |

## Lesson 7

| | |
|---|---|
| from | *fm* |
| of | *o* |
| year | *yr* |
| let | *le* |

## Lesson 8

| | |
|---|---|
| after | *afl* |
| business | *bus* |
| company | *co* |
| responsible | *rsp* |

## Lesson 9

| | |
|---|---|
| was, were, with | *w* |
| importance, important | *imp* |
| department | *depl* |
| week, work | *wk* |
| employ | *mpl* |

## Lesson 10

| | |
|---|---|
| how | *hw* |
| out | *ot* |
| require | *rqr* |
| they | *ty* |

## Lesson 11

| | |
|---|---|
| appreciate | *ap* |
| please | *pl* |
| enclose | *enc* |
| thank | *tk* |
| provide | *pvd* |

## Lesson 12

| | |
|---|---|
| ever, every | *ev* |
| about | *abl* |
| complete | *cmp* |
| interest | *inl* |

## Lesson 13

| | |
|---|---|
| include | *incl* |
| information | *info* |
| program | *pgm* |
| consider, consideration | *cns* |

## Lesson 14

| | |
|---|---|
| any | *ny* |
| executive | *exec* |
| insurance | *ins* |
| hour | *hr* |
| present | *pr* |
| time | *lm* |

## Lesson 15

| | |
|---|---|
| suggest, suggestion | *sg* |
| manager | *mgr* |
| management | *mgt* |
| report | *rpt* |

## Lesson 16

| | |
|---|---|
| order | *od* |
| amount | *amt* |
| state, street | *st* |
| receive | *rec* |
| number | *no* |
| letter | *lr* |

## Lesson 17

| | |
|---|---|
| available | *av* |

## organization, organize — *org*

| | |
|---|---|
| paid | *pd* |
| represent, representative | *rep* |

## Lesson 18

| | |
|---|---|
| question | *q* |
| regard | *rgd* |
| cover | *cv* |

## Lesson 19

| | |
|---|---|
| avenue | *ave* |
| convenience, convenient | *cnv* |

## Lesson 20

| | |
|---|---|
| application, apply | *apl* |
| develop | *dv* |

# SuperWrite ABBREVIATIONS ALPHABETICAL LIST

Numbers refer to Lesson numbers.

| | | | |
|---|---|---|---|
| about | 12 | for | 2 |
| after | 8 | from | 7 |
| am, more | 6 | | |
| amount | 16 | has, have | 3 |
| and, in | 5 | have, has | 3 |
| any | 14 | hour | 14 |
| application, apply | 20 | how | 10 |
| apply, application | 20 | | |
| appreciate | 11 | importance, important | 9 |
| are, or, our | 2 | important, importance | 9 |
| as, is | 1 | in, and | 5 |
| at, it, to | 3 | include | 13 |
| available | 17 | information | 13 |
| avenue | 19 | insurance | 14 |
| | | interest | 12 |
| be, been, by | 6 | is, as | 1 |
| been, be, by | 6 | it, at, to | 3 |
| business | 8 | | |
| by, be, been | 6 | let | 7 |
| | | letter | 16 |
| can | 2 | | |
| company | 8 | management | 15 |
| complete | 12 | manager | 15 |
| convenience, convenient | 19 | month | 6 |
| convenient, convenience | 19 | more, am | 6 |
| consider, consideration | 13 | | |
| consideration, consider | 13 | number | 16 |
| cover | 18 | | |
| | | of | 7 |
| | | or, are, our | 2 |
| department | 9 | order | 16 |
| develop | 20 | organization, organize | 17 |
| do | 3 | organize, organization | 17 |
| | | our, are, or | 2 |
| employ | 9 | out | 10 |
| enclose | 11 | | |
| ever, every | 12 | paid | 17 |
| every, ever | 12 | please | 11 |
| executive | 14 | present | 14 |

# THEORY

## ALPHABETICAL LIST

| Principle | Lesson | Abbreviation |
|-----------|--------|--------------|
| *be-* | 6 | b |
| *-ble* | 8 | b |
| *ch* | 4 | C |
| *de-* | 6 | d |
| *em-* | 9 | m |
| *en-* | 6 | n |
| *enter-* | 12 | N |
| *-eous* | 19 | us |
| *ex-* | 14 | x |
| *for-* | 11 | f |
| *fore-* | 11 | f |
| *-ful* | 12 | f |
| *fur-* | 11 | f |
| *im-* | 9 | m |
| *in-* | 6 | n |
| *inter-* | 12 | N |
| *-ing* | 4 | disjoined g |
| *-ious* | 19 | us |
| *-ity* | 10 | disjoined t |
| *-ly* | 7 | l |
| *mem* | 19 | m |
| *-ment* | 8 | m |
| *oi* | 9 | oi |
| *ou* | 7 | ou |
| *-ous* | 19 | us |
| *over-* | 15 | O |
| *ow* | 7 | ow |
| *oy* | 9 | oy |
| *-pal* | 17 | p |
| *-ple* | 17 | p |
| *pre-* | 13 | pr |
| *pro-* | 13 | pr |

| | | |
|---|---|---|
| *qu* | 10 | q |
| *re-* | 6 | r |
| *-s* | 4 | s |
| *sh* | 4 | S |
| *t* | 2 | uncrossed t |
| *th* | 5 | crossed t |
| *-tion* | 7 | S |
| *trans-* | 15 | T |
| *un-* | 13 | u |
| *under-* | 16 | U |
| *-us* | 19 | us |

# INDEX OF SuperWrite PRINCIPLES

Numbers refer to Lesson numbers

# TRANSCRIPTION INDEX

Numbers refer to Lesson numbers.

## Keyboarding Style

## Punctuation